PHARAOHS
THE

PHARAOHS THE

JOYCE TYLDESLEY

Quercus

CONTENTS

*Previous page: Pharaoh Ptolemy VI offers
to the deities Horus and Hathor*

Step Pyramid of Djoser at Saqqara

The 'heretic' pharaoh Akhenaten

Wall painting of the deity Anubis

PROLOGUE
FINDING THE PHARAOHS

~◈~

THE PHARAOHS RULED EGYPT FOR OVER THREE THOUSAND YEARS. SOME WERE FEARLESS WARRIORS WHO battled to create the mightiest empire that the world had ever seen. Others were prodigious builders whose pyramids and stone temples still testify to their wealth and power. A few ruled at a disadvantage: they were women, or children, or foreign. One was rumoured to have prostituted his daughter. Another was classed as a heretic, his reign erased from official history. At least two were murdered by ambitious wives and sons. All, however, considered themselves semi-divine beings. And all expected to live beyond death as fully divine gods.

Ramesses II of the 19th Dynasty, seen here in the form of a colossal statue outside the Great Temple at Abu Simbel, Nubia.

Why did the Egyptians stick so stubbornly to their monarchy, refusing to experiment with other forms of government? The answer is simple. The pharaoh, or king (the two words are interchangeable), fulfilled a unique and vital role. He, and he alone, could communicate with the fickle deities who controlled Egypt's destiny. The priests might assist him in his duties, but the ultimate responsibility for pleasing the gods was his. Without a pharaoh on the throne the gods could not receive the regular offerings of food, drink, incense and prayer that they craved. This would be dangerous. Deprived of their offerings the gods might grow dissatisfied; they might even be tempted to abandon Egypt, allowing chaos to overwhelm *maat*, or natural harmony.

The need to maintain *maat* underpinned every aspect of official Egyptian thought. Combined with a natural conservatism, a tendency to avoid unnecessary and potentially dangerous experimentation, it led to a remarkable consistency in art, architecture and theology throughout the pharaonic age. As the upholder of *maat*, the pharaoh was naturally the highest priest of every religious cult. In addition, he was the head of the army (dedicated to repelling chaos from Egypt's borders) and the head of the civil service (dedicated to repelling chaos from within Egypt). Isolated between his mortal subjects and his gods, he topped a rigid social pyramid. A long way beneath him came the immediate royal family: his consort and her children, his mother and his sisters. Next were the élite who occupied the highest priestly, bureaucratic and military positions, who occasionally married into the royal family, and who were rewarded for their loyalty with gifts of land and impressive stone tombs. Beneath the élite were the educated classes: the scribes and specialized professionals. Finally, at the lowest level, came the peasants: the vast majority of the population who laboured for the state, for the temples and for private landowners.

MAAT

The pharaoh's foremost duty was the maintenance of *maat*: a concept of 'rightness' that embraced ideas of truth, order, justice, and the status quo. The opposite of *maat* is *isfet*, or chaos. *Maat* was personified in the form of the goddess Maat, who is identified by the prominent ostrich feather of truth worn on her head.

Amenhotep, son of Hapu, has here chosen to be depicted as a scribe, whose ability to read and write made him one of Egypt's literate élite.

For all these classes the family was the basic economic unit that, in times of crisis, would provide food, protection and healthcare. Respect for family members was an integral part of daily life. Boys were urged to marry young and found a household; girls were raised to be good wives and mothers. The young and healthy were expected to care for the elderly and the weak, the rich were encouraged to provide for the poor, while the living had a duty to remember the dead.

PROBLEMS OF PRESERVATION

It is perhaps obvious that we know far more about the lives and deaths of the literate, tomb-building élite than we do about the illiterate, almost invisible peasants, and far more about those who lived towards the end of Egypt's long history than we do about the first Egyptians. We have evidence for at least 300 pharaohs ruling from *c.*3050–30 BC, but it is not until the dawn of the New Kingdom, in *c.*1550 BC, that we have enough textual and archaeological evidence to start to see these pharaohs as something resembling well-rounded human beings. Even then, our view is veiled not only by a lack of personal documents, but also by the tradition of preserving the image and memory of the perfect, rather than the actual, pharaoh.

Our knowledge of ancient Egypt is derived from two main sources: written records and archaeological excavation. There are flaws inherent in both types of evidence.

The surviving written records are just a fraction of the records that once existed. The vast majority of these were written by and for the educated élite, and they seldom deal with humdrum, day-to-day issues. Almost invariably they exaggerate the deeds of the author: autobiographies carved on tomb walls, for example, set out to impress by stressing the virtues of the deceased, while royal texts focus on the heroism and intelligence of the king. In a land entirely lacking our modern idea of accurate history, this blatant embellishment was not seen as deceitful or shameful. Writing was the gift of the gods, and it carried its own latent magic. Committing something to writing could actually make it real so a pharaoh could, quite literally, rewrite the past.

The archaeological evidence brings its own, very obvious, bias. The Egyptians built their houses, palaces and offices of mud-brick, placing them close to water sources on

The Egyptians who live in the cultivated parts of their country have, by their habit of keeping records of the past, made themselves by far the most learned of any nation that I have visited.

HERODOTUS, (*HISTORIES* II: 77)

the edge of the fertile land lining the Nile. They built their tombs of stone in the hot, dry desert, away from their houses. Over the centuries the mud-brick architecture has been lost while the tombs and graves have survived. This means that today's archaeologists, faced with a wealth of funerary architecture, grave goods and human remains, have developed a good understanding of Egyptian expectations of life after death yet have relatively little information about the routines of daily life. This is particularly true of the earliest periods that, because they lack written records, are heavily reliant on evidence from the cemeteries. This enforced focus on death naturally gives the impression that the Egyptians were preoccupied with thoughts of their own mortality. In fact the Egyptians loved life, and pitied those unfortunate enough to be born outside their fertile and beautiful land. Their greatest hope was that they might continue to enjoy a near identical, but even better, life beyond the grave.

DATING THE PHARAOHS

Egypt's priests charted the movements of the sun, moon and stars so that they might time their offerings correctly. Their observations led to the development of a calendar whose year was divided into 12 months of 30 days plus a spare five 'days above the year'. Events were dated to the reign of the current pharaoh (Year 1 of Amenhotep, Year 2 and so on) and, as every new reign was a new beginning – a recreation of the world, each pharaoh marked his accession with a new Year 1.

The pharaohs constantly sought to confirm their right to rule by stressing continuity with a past that stretched back, beyond the time of mortal kings, through a period of semi-divine and divine rule, to the very creation of the world. To do this, they had to understand their own place in royal history. 'King lists', lists of the pharaohs and their reign lengths, were recorded on papyrus and stone and stored in the state and temple archives. The best-preserved king list is found in the Abydos temple of the New Kingdom monarch Seti I. Here we can see the pharaoh and his young son offering before the names of their royal 'ancestors', ancestors here being a somewhat loose term, as Seti's father was of non-royal birth. The list is, however, incomplete, as pharaohs who had failed to conform to expectation have simply been omitted.

Almost 3000 years after Egypt became one land, Ptolemy II Philadelphos, a pharaoh of Macedonian heritage, ruled from Alexandria. Determined to understand his adopted country's long history, he commissioned the Egyptian priest Manetho of Sebennytos to consult the ancient

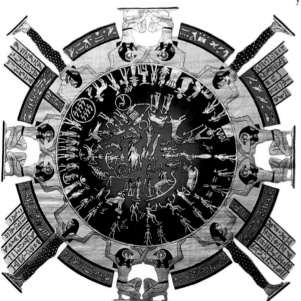

Reproduction of an Egyptian festival calendar, in the form of a circular zodiac. The original – now in the Louvre, Paris – was a sculpted bas-relief on the ceiling of the Ptolemaic Temple of Hathor at Dendera.

records and compile a definitive list of pharaohs. This Manetho did, organizing his pharaohs into dynasties: lines of kings who were connected politically, but who were not necessarily blood relatives. Manetho ended his history with the reign of Nectanebo II (Nakhthorheb), the final king of Dynasty 30 and Egypt's last native pharaoh. His list was later expanded to include Dynasty 31 (the second Persian Period), but Manetho's own age, the Ptolemaic Dynasty, was never given a number. Manetho's *History of Egypt* was lost long ago but enough has survived, embedded in the work of the writers Josephus (*c.* AD 70), Africanus (*c.* AD 220), Eusebius (*c.* AD 320) and Syncellus (also known as George the Monk; *c.* AD 800), to allow modern historians to reconstruct it with a fair degree of accuracy.

Today's Egyptologists group Manetho's dynasties into times of strong rule and cultural achievement (the Early Dynastic Period, the Old, Middle and New Kingdoms, the Late Period and the Macedonian and Ptolemaic Period) separated by times of disunity and weak rule (the three Intermediate Periods). This rather crude system certainly has its drawbacks: it is too simple, not all Egyptologists are in agreement over the allocation of the dynasties to the various periods, and there are times when dynasties overlap, while some blood-families are split not only between dynasties, but also between periods and kingdoms. But it does offer the most accurate means of referencing events within Egypt. Under this system, to take an illustrative example, Amenhotep III is classified as the ninth king of the 18th Dynasty, which itself belongs to the New Kingdom. Historians are not certain of Amenhotep's precise calendar dates (on current evidence it is likely that he ruled *c.*1390–1352 BC) and so cannot give a precise date for the wild bull hunt that is known to have occurred early in his lengthy reign. It is, however, possible to give an exact regnal date: Amenhotep himself tells us that the exciting hunt occurred in his regnal Year 2.

NAMING THE PHARAOHS

We do not know for certain how the names of the pharaohs were pronounced, as Egypt's scribes omitted the vowels that would have been obvious to their readers. This means that the name that we render as Amenhotep (or occasionally Amenhotpe) is actually preserved as 'Imn [the name of Amen, god of Thebes]–htp'. By convention we use 'e' or occasionally 'o' to replace the missing letters. Some historians have preferred to use the Greek forms of the royal names as preserved by Manetho, so that Amenhotep occasionally appears as Amenophis.

At first gods and heroes ruled Egypt for a little less than eighteen thousand years …
Mortals have been kings of their country, they say, for a little less than five thousand
years … For most of this period native kings ruled, and Ethiopians, Persians, and
Macedonians ruled only a small part of it.

DIODORUS SICULUS, (*HISTORIES* I: 44)

THE ROYAL NAME

The first pharaohs wrote their names within a *serekh*, a ribbed, rectangle representing the gateway to the archaic royal residence, so that the name within the *serekh* symbolized the pharaoh secure within his palace. Often a falcon, emblem of the god Horus, perched on top of the *serekh*. At the end of the 3rd Dynasty the *serekh* was replaced by the cartouche: an elongated oval loop representing a double thickness of rope with the ends tied to form a straight line, signifying universal rule. All pharaohs, most queens and some gods used the cartouche.

The earliest pharaohs had one recorded name, the 'Horus name'. By the 5th Dynasty it had become customary for pharaohs to use a series of five titles, each title being followed by a name specifically chosen to reflect anticipated aspects of the reign: these were political statements or statements of allegiance to particular gods. So, sticking with our customary example, Amenhotep III was more correctly known as:

1. The Horus King: Strong bull, appearing in truth.
2. He of the Two Ladies: Who establishes laws, who pacifies the Two Lands.
3. The Golden Horus: Great of strength; smiter of the Asiatics.
4. King of Upper and Lower Egypt: Nebmaatre [the sun god Re is the lord of truth].
5. Son of Re: Amenhotep, ruler of Thebes.

The cartouche of Tuthmosis III, from an obelisk at Karnak. So powerful was this symbol that this pharaoh had himself interred in a cartouche-shaped sarcophagus within a cartouche-shaped burial chamber in the Valley of the Kings.

Thus Amenhotep's string of names emphasized his military might and his respect for law and order. The last of his names, the nomen, was the personal name given by his mother at his birth. In this case, Amenhotep III was named after his grandfather, Amenhotep II. The preceding name, the throne name or prenomen, was a more formal name used in diplomatic correspondence. The nomen and prenomen were invariably presented within the cartouche. The other names never were.

THE FIRST PHARAOHS

C.5300–2686 BC

Detail of a frieze of Horus from the pylon (gateway) of the temple of Horus at Edfu in Upper Egypt. This hawk-headed deity was the first state god of Egypt. The semi-divine kings whom the Egyptians believed had preceded their first mortal ruler were known as the 'Followers of Horus'.

A TALE OF TWO LANDS
THE VALLEY AND THE DELTA

The Predynastic Period *c.*5300 – 3050 BC

THE NILE BROUGHT WATER TO AN OTHERWISE DRY LAND, YET NO ONE KNEW WHERE THIS LONGEST OF RIVERS began. Far beyond Egypt's southern border the White Nile rose to the south of Lake Victoria (Victoria Nyanza) while the Blue Nile rose in the Ethiopian Highlands. United, the broad river continued its journey northwards, flowing through the Nubian deserts (modern Sudan) and passing over a series of rapids or cataracts to enter Egypt at the border town of Aswan. For 600 miles (960 km) the river passed through sandstone and limestone cliffs and sterile desert before splitting to form a wide, flat Delta whose seven branches all emptied into the Mediterranean Sea.

Geography dictated that Egypt would always be a land of two very different halves. The contrast between life in the Valley (Upper, or southern Egypt) and life in the Delta (Lower, or northern Egypt) was remarkable. The hot, dry Valley offered a narrow, insular and inward-looking world where the Black Land, the ribbon of fertile soil edging the river, was only a few miles wide. Beyond this lay the Red Land, the barren desert, and the mountains that protected against invasion. In contrast the Delta, wider, flatter, cooler and far greener, was both open to outside influences and vulnerable to invasion. At times of contentment and prosperity – times when *maat* was obvious in the land – Upper and Lower Egypt merged into a seamless whole ruled by one pharaoh: 'king of Upper and Lower Egypt'. But at times of stress, they parted.

THE GIFT OF THE NILE

The Nile followed a predicable pattern. In late August/early September, fuelled by melting Ethiopian snows, the river burst its banks, turning fields into red-brown lakes and depositing a thick layer of mineral-rich mud. The long weeks of the season of Inundation, a time when farming was impossible, freed vast numbers of peasants to labour on state projects. By November the waters had retreated and the peasants could sow their crops in the mud-enriched fields. The spring harvest yielded a crop of cereal (barley and emmer wheat), vegetables (beans, lentils, onions, garlic, leeks, lettuces and cucumbers), fruits (grapes, figs and dates) and flax. This season of Coming Forth was followed by the season of summer; the time when the dried and cracked ground was sterilized by the hot sun.

Egypt was blessed with abundant natural resources. The fish in the river and the fowl in the marshes were available to all. The tall papyrus plants growing beside the river could be turned into sturdy boats or fine paper, while the copious Nile mud could be converted into bricks and pottery. The deserts offered inanimate treasures: precious

The first cataract of the Nile just south of Aswan (ancient name Swenet). In the pharaonic period (from around 3050 BC onwards, when the country was unified), the first cataract marked the southern boundary of Upper Egypt.

'Despite my strong interest in science,' said Caesar to the Priest of Isis Acoreus, 'nothing would satisfy my intellectual curiosity more fully than to be told what makes the Nile rise.'

JULIUS CAESAR SPECULATES ABOUT THE NILE:
LUCAN (*PHARSALIA* X: 192-331)

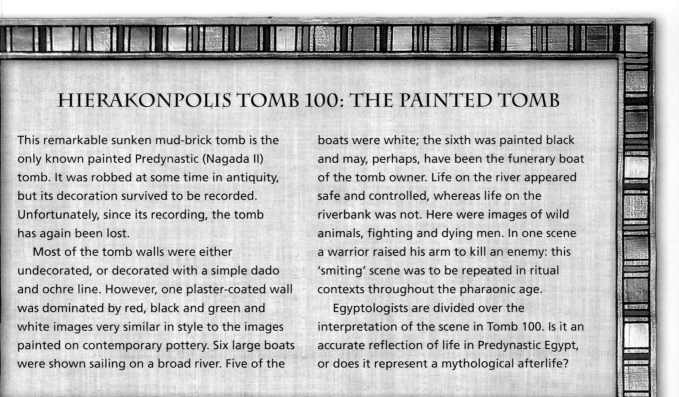

HIERAKONPOLIS TOMB 100: THE PAINTED TOMB

This remarkable sunken mud-brick tomb is the only known painted Predynastic (Nagada II) tomb. It was robbed at some time in antiquity, but its decoration survived to be recorded. Unfortunately, since its recording, the tomb has again been lost.

Most of the tomb walls were either undecorated, or decorated with a simple dado and ochre line. However, one plaster-coated wall was dominated by red, black and green and white images very similar in style to the images painted on contemporary pottery. Six large boats were shown sailing on a broad river. Five of the boats were white; the sixth was painted black and may, perhaps, have been the funerary boat of the tomb owner. Life on the river appeared safe and controlled, whereas life on the riverbank was not. Here were images of wild animals, fighting and dying men. In one scene a warrior raised his arm to kill an enemy: this 'smiting' scene was to be repeated in ritual contexts throughout the pharaonic age.

Egyptologists are divided over the interpretation of the scene in Tomb 100. Is it an accurate reflection of life in Predynastic Egypt, or does it represent a mythological afterlife?

metals (gold, copper, silver) and stone that could be used for purposes both practical (limestone, sandstone, granite, flint) and decorative (alabaster, turquoise, jasper). The Nile allowed easy communication and the transport of heavy goods, from one end of the country to the other: to travel by boat from Aswan to the Delta would take approximately three weeks. But large freight barges required good quality timber, and Egypt had no tall trees. Throughout the pharaonic age, Egypt had to import wood from the Levant (the eastern Mediterranean coast).

PREDYNASTIC EGYPT

The early Stone Age Egyptians were hunter-gatherers who roamed the grasslands at a time when the land was part savannah with occasional woodlands. The advent of agriculture (the Neolithic or New Stone Age) led to permanent settlement and the development of villages, cemeteries and craft specialization. The earliest evidence for farming in Egypt comes from the Faiyum (a natural depression in the Western Desert, centred on Lake Moeris, also known as Birket Qarun) and the western Delta where, by 4800 BC, hunter-gatherers were planting crops and herding animals.

The first evidence for farming in the Nile Valley comes from the region of el-Badari (near modern Sohag). This site has given its name to the Badarian cultural phase which flourished from around 4400 to 4000 BC, and which may have existed at least half a century earlier. The Badarian peoples lived in small villages on the edge of the Black Land. They still hunted and fished, but they also planted grain and lentils and kept livestock. Their dead were buried in simple pit graves in desert cemeteries, where they lay curled on their left sides, facing west. It is dangerous to base any assessment of a society purely on its graves, but the inclusion of goods (pottery, stone palettes, tools, figurines and jewellery) in some of the Badarian burials suggests that their society was stratified into richer and poorer members.

The next major cultural phase was identified at Nagada (near modern Quft). Focusing primarily on the pottery recovered from the cemeteries, Egyptologist Flinders Petrie divided the Nagada phase into three consecutive periods (Nagada I, Nagada II and Nagada III). The Nagada peoples lived in mud-brick villages, and in fortified towns protected by mud-brick walls. Their cemeteries show increasing social stratification, and there is a marked difference between the simple graves dug for the poor and the rectangular, brick-lined tombs provided for the élite. The richest of these élite tombs housed linen-wrapped and coffined bodies and a wide range of grave goods including stone cosmetic palettes carved in the shape of animals, human figurines, stone vessels, painted pottery, and increasing quantities of copper, silver and gold.

The Nagada culture spread through the Valley and the Delta, smothering all other cultures, until the final Nagada phase saw Egypt occupied by a series of wealthy independent city-states and their satellite farming communities.

THE CREATION OF THE WORLD

The regular flooding of the Nile, and the re-emergence of the fertile land from the receding waters, influenced the creation myth told by the priests of the sun god Re at the ancient religious centre of Heliopolis (near modern Cairo). The association of mounds with fertility and birth or rebirth was strong and enduring. Graves, regarded as places of rebirth, were often topped by an earth mound, and temple floors sloped upwards from the door to the inner sanctuary:

> *At the very beginning of time an egg floated in the waters of chaos. Inside the egg there was a spark of life, desperate to escape. Suddenly the egg cracked open, and a fertile mound burst from the waters. Seated on the mound was the creator god Atum. From the fluids of his body emerged twin children, Shu the god of the dry air and his sister-wife Tefnut, goddess of moisture. And Atum and Shu and Tefnut lived safe on their island-mound in the midst of the sea of chaos.*
>
> *One terrible day the twins fell into the waters. Blinded by tears, Atum summoned his Eye to search for his lost children. The Eye of Atum found the twins in the dark depths of the waters. With his children restored, Atum's tears of despair turned to tears of joy and, as they fell to the ground, they became men and women.*
>
> *Now gods and mortals lived in harmony on the mound.*

THE PREDYNASTIC PERIOD

*c.*5300 BC Well-developed settlements in the Western Desert.

*c.*4400 BC Badarian cultural phase produces elegant thin-walled pottery decorated with a red polish and a black rim.

*c.*4000 BC Nagada I cultural phase produces red polished pots with a white painted decoration.

*c.*3500 BC Nagada II cultural phase produces buff painted pottery with wavy handles.

*c.*3200 BC Nagada III cultural phase, a time of well-developed city-states and socially stratified cemeteries.

*c.*3050 BC Dynasty 0 (Late Nagada III), Egypt becomes one land.

THE HORUS KINGS
MENES AND NARMER

Nagada III/Dynasty 0 c.3050–3000 BC

THE EGYPTIANS BELIEVED THAT THEIR LAND HAD BEEN UNIFIED BY AN AMBITIOUS SOUTHERN WARRIOR-KING – Menes, or Men – who had raised an army and battled north from Thebes (modern Luxor) to Memphis (near modern Cairo). Here he was crowned pharaoh of a united land. The Palermo Stone, a 5th Dynasty basalt stela inscribed on both faces with details of Egypt's earliest history, lists the semi-mythological rulers who preceded Menes, and this tale is repeated in most of the king lists and in the Turin Canon, a New Kingdom papyrus chronology. Here we learn that Menes succeeded the semi-divine kings known as the 'Followers of Horus', who were in turn preceded by a line of god-kings. The Ptolemaic historian Manetho also accepted Menes as Egypt's first king, telling us that after a 62-year reign the pharaoh was seized by a hippopotamus. However, there is no archaeological evidence for a war of unification at the end of the Nagada cultural phase.

The Predynastic inhabitants of the southern town of This (modern Girga) buried their dead in the Umm el-Qa'ab cemetery at nearby Abydos. Initially used by rich and poor alike, the Umm el-Qa'ab soon evolved into Egypt's most exclusive graveyard. The most impressive of its Nagada period tombs is a 12-roomed structure, Tomb U-j.

THE SCORPION KING

Although robbed in antiquity, U-j has yielded bone and ivory artefacts, a surprisingly large quantity of Egyptian and Palestinian pottery, and 150 tantalizingly brief labels torn off the stolen grave goods: these represent the first known instances of hieroglyphic writing. It is obvious that the owner of U-j was a wealthy individual, possibly a regional king. The scorpion motif scrawled on several pots hints at his name.

'Scorpion' reappears on a large, damaged, late-Nagada macehead discovered in the dynastic temple of Horus at the southern site of Hierakonpolis (modern Kom el-Ahmar; Egyptian Nekhen). The surviving face of the macehead shows a kilted pharaoh wearing the *hedjet*, the tall white crown of southern Egypt, and it is tempting to suggest, given the Egyptian love of symmetry, that the vanished face must have shown the same pharaoh wearing the *deshret*, or red crown, of northern Egypt. Pharaoh stands in a field holding a hoe. Facing him are two servants, one carrying a sheaf of corn, the other a basket, while behind him stand two fan-bearers and a row of at least four dancing women. It seems that pharaoh, too important to perform manual labour himself, is celebrating the inauguration of a civic scheme – a new canal, perhaps – by cutting the ceremonial first sod. So far this is a peaceful scene. But above pharaoh's

Detail of the ceremonial macehead, Nagada III, found in the temple of Horus at Hierakonpolis. The two symbols next to the head of the central figure may denote his title ('King') and name ('Scorpion').

head a row of lapwings hangs by the neck from military standards, symbolizing his defeated enemies. Two small images by pharaoh's head, a rosette and a scorpion, name him. The same name, written in a *serekh* without a falcon, has been found on Predynastic pottery recovered as far north as the eastern Delta. Clearly, Scorpion was known throughout Egypt, but we cannot be certain that he ruled the entire land.

DYNASTY 0

Three more royal names, written within *serekhs*, have been discovered in late Nagada III contexts. Pharaohs Iri-Hor, Ka and Narmer have been allocated to 'Dynasty 0'; the nebulous period at the very end of the Nagada III cultural phase, immediately preceding the First Dynasty. All three built double-chambered tombs in Cemetery B on the Umm el-Qa'ab, to the south of the cemetery used by the late Nagada élite. The three tombs (B1/2, Iri-Hor; B7/9, Ka; B17/18, Narmer) have a similar plan; they are large, brick-lined, rectangular pits. The tomb superstructures have vanished, but it appears that the pits were lined and roofed with wooden planks, then covered with a rectangular mound held in place by inward sloping mud-brick walls. Little more is known about Iri-Hor and Ka, but Narmer is relatively well recorded.

MASTABA TOMBS

While the vast majority of Egyptians were buried in simple pit-graves, the First Dynasty élite cut their burial chambers deep into the rock underlying the desert sands. The ground-level wooden ceilings were covered with a low mound, which was protected by a layer of mud-bricks and surrounded by a rectangular mud-brick building known as a mastaba (Arabic *mastaba*: literally 'low bench').

The earliest mastabas had multiple storage rooms for the increasing numbers of grave goods, but this made the tomb vulnerable to robbers. By the end of the First Dynasty the number of rooms in the superstructure had been reduced and there were extensive underground storage chambers reached by a stairway. The mastaba-style tomb remained popular throughout the Old Kingdom.

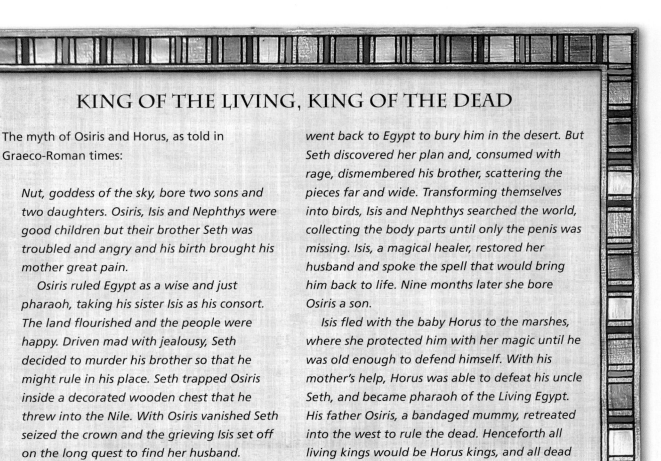

KING OF THE LIVING, KING OF THE DEAD

The myth of Osiris and Horus, as told in Graeco-Roman times:

Nut, goddess of the sky, bore two sons and two daughters. Osiris, Isis and Nephthys were good children but their brother Seth was troubled and angry and his birth brought his mother great pain.

Osiris ruled Egypt as a wise and just pharaoh, taking his sister Isis as his consort. The land flourished and the people were happy. Driven mad with jealousy, Seth decided to murder his brother so that he might rule in his place. Seth trapped Osiris inside a decorated wooden chest that he threw into the Nile. With Osiris vanished Seth seized the crown and the grieving Isis set off on the long quest to find her husband.

Isis found the dead Osiris in Byblos and went back to Egypt to bury him in the desert. But Seth discovered her plan and, consumed with rage, dismembered his brother, scattering the pieces far and wide. Transforming themselves into birds, Isis and Nephthys searched the world, collecting the body parts until only the penis was missing. Isis, a magical healer, restored her husband and spoke the spell that would bring him back to life. Nine months later she bore Osiris a son.

Isis fled with the baby Horus to the marshes, where she protected him with her magic until he was old enough to defend himself. With his mother's help, Horus was able to defeat his uncle Seth, and became pharaoh of the Living Egypt. His father Osiris, a bandaged mummy, retreated into the west to rule the dead. Henceforth all living kings would be Horus kings, and all dead kings would become one with Osiris.

The Narmer Palette was discovered in the Hierakonpolis temple precinct lying slightly apart from the Scorpion Macehead. It is one of a number of Nagada III votive palettes carved with scenes of military conflict. Narmer, his name given in a *serekh*, wears the white crown. His arm is raised to smite the enemy – a northerner from the Delta – who cringes at his feet. Behind Narmer stands a small sandal-bearer. Immediately above the prisoner, the falcon god Horus holds a captive who is restrained by a rope passing through his nose. Below, on a separate register, we see more defeated enemies. The opposite face of the palette shows Narmer wearing the red crown of northern Egypt. He is marching with a troop of soldiers whose standards represent the symbols of the Egyptian provinces, and his scribe marches before him to record his victories. Ahead of the procession lie ten decapitated victims of war, their heads tucked

The priest said that Menes was the first king of Egypt, and that it was he who raised the dyke which protects Memphis from the inundations of the Nile …

HERODOTUS (*HISTORIES* II: 99)

The Narmer Palette. This votive palette. made from greywacke, depicts Narmer performing a typical royal smiting ritual.

between their legs. Below, in a separate scene, we see two fabulous beasts; the part-snake, part-cat serpopards have their long necks twisted together, just as southern and northern Egypt are now inextricably entwined. On the bottom register Narmer takes the form of a bull to gore an enemy outside a fortified town.

RULER OF A UNITED LAND

As Narmer wears both the white and the red crown it seems reasonable to assume that he rules a united land. But is he the first king to do this? Egyptologists initially interpreted the palette as a celebration of Narmer's triumphs over the city-states of the north. However, it looks as if Narmer's enemies are desert invaders rather than Egyptians, and it may be that the palette actually celebrates Narmer's defence of an already united land against a western foe. By late Nagada/ Dynasty 0 times Egypt was experiencing the aridity which would turn her grasslands into desert. The savannah pastoralists were under increasing strain, and settlement in the fertile Delta must have seemed a tempting proposition. The need to unite Egypt's independent cities against outside invasion may have provided a strong incentive for political unification. Whoever the enemy, Narmer is clearly promoting himself as a pharaoh who establishes *maat* by subduing foreigners. It seems likely that Narmer inspired the legend of King Menes. It may even be that Narmer, whose full name is unknown, was Menes.

A third ceremonial piece from the Hierakonpolis temple allows us another glimpse of this king. The Narmer Macehead shows the pharaoh wrapped in a ceremonial cloak and wearing the red crown. He sits on a raised and canopied throne to preside over a ritual that involves prisoners, animals soldiers and an unnamed, veiled person who is brought before him on a carrying chair. Some Egyptologists have interpreted the scene as Narmer's marriage to his consort Neithhotep. Since Neithhotep's name, 'Neith is Satisfied', incorporates that of the Delta goddess Neith, it has been suggested that Narmer consolidated his position by marrying the daughter of a defeated northern enemy. However, the argument that only a northern woman would be named after a northern goddess does not stand up to scrutiny and, as weddings – even royal weddings – were considered private matters, it seems more likely the shrouded figure is a god attending the celebration of Narmer's anniversary or jubilee.

THE TOMB OF OSIRIS

By the Middle Kingdom the Umm el-Qa'ab had been identified as the burial place of Osiris, and the tomb of Djer (see pages 22–25) had been converted into a cenotaph for the dead god. Abydos rapidly became one of Egypt's leading cult centres, and pilgrims flocked to the cemetery, leaving behind the millions of pottery offerings. These have given the site its modern name Umm el-Qa'ab, or 'mother of pots'.

THE EVIDENCE FROM ABYDOS

EGYPT'S FIRST ROYAL CEMETERY

1st to 2nd Dynasties c.3000–2686 BC

AHA, OR HOR-AHA, SON AND SUCCESSOR OF NARMER, IS CLASSED AS THE FIRST PHARAOH OF DYNASTY 1. Evidence suggests that he succeeded to the throne as a young boy, and was guided in the early years by his mother Neithhotep. As he is known to have used the name Menes, it may be that he, rather than his father, inspired the myth of Menes the unifier. Aha moved the centre of government north, establishing the city of White Walls (Egyptian Ineb-hedj) at the junction of the Valley and the Delta, near modern Abusir. The capital would gradually shift south as the Nile changed its course, eventually becoming known as Mennefer – or, in Greek, Memphis – from Mennefer Pepi ('The Splendour of Pepi is Enduring': an allusion to the Sakkara pyramid built by Pepi I).

The stela of Djet from Tomb Z at Abydos. His name is represented by the rearing cobra hieroglyph within the serekh, *which is a depiction of the king's palace.*

Within the new city, the bureaucracy grew rapidly in size and capability. Aha defined the duties that would be expected of a conventional pharaoh. Labels recovered from 1st Dynasty tombs show that the subduing of rebels and foreigners was an important aspect of his reign, and there is evidence for military campaigns in Libya and Nubia, and trade with Syrio-Palestine. Religion, too, was important, and Aha played an active role in establishing the cults of the Apis Bull at Memphis, and of the crocodile-god Sobek in the Faiyum.

While the élite bureaucrats of Memphis were interred in the Western Desert at north Sakkara, their kings preferred to be buried at Abydos. Aha built his mud-brick tomb in Cemetery B (B 15). His complex, five times larger than his father's, included several separate chambers and a series of large wooden shrines, and was topped by a low mound or solid mastaba. Entirely separate from the tomb, a rectangular funerary enclosure surrounded a plastered mud-brick wall and a circle of subsidiary graves.

DJER, DJET AND DEN

Aha's successors were buried to the south of Cemetery B. Their tombs are grouped together and share a similar, gradually evolving plan. Two stelae, erected to the east of the tomb, recorded pharaoh's name. The subterranean burial chambers were lined with imported cedar wood,

TOMB LABELS

The Early Dynastic élite were buried with large quantities of grave goods. Packed into chests and boxes, these were labelled with inscribed and decorated wooden or ivory tags. Today, while most grave goods have vanished, the labels survive, providing details of the vanished goods and snippets of contemporary history.

24

Ivory statuette of an unidentified 1st Dynasty king, found by Flinders Petrie in the royal cemetery at Abydos in 1901. The figure sports the crown of Upper Egypt and the elaborate robe worn for the heb sed *jubilee marking 30 years' rule.*

roofed by planks and covered by a low, brick-covered mound that was itself incorporated in a larger mound. A short distance from their tombs, the pharaohs built large mortuary enclosures surrounded by substantial walls. Excavation of the enclosure built by the 2nd Dynasty pharaoh Khasekhemwy (the Shunet es-Zebib), suggests that these enclosures would have included an offering chapel, open spaces, mud-brick and wattle or reed buildings, and, perhaps, a mound protected by a mud-brick casing.

The Abydos tombs were looted in antiquity, and then badly excavated during the 19th century when much valuable information was lost. But in 1900, against all odds, a mummified arm was discovered in the tomb of Djer (Tomb O). The arm had been hidden behind the tomb stairway by a robber who never returned to collect his prize.

Beneath the linen bandages lay four gold bracelets of turquoise, amethyst, lapis lazuli and gold beads. Whether the arm belonged to the king himself, or to a female relation, is not obvious. An ivory tomb label recovered from Abydos shows Djer visiting the Delta; a wooden label recovered from Sakkara shows him participating in a religious ritual that may have included human sacrifice. A rock inscription at Wadi Halfa confirms that Djer's army campaigned successfully in Nubia. From Manetho we learn that the second monarch of the 1st Dynasty, 'Athothis', was a respected physician who wrote books on human anatomy. However, we cannot be certain that this Athothis is Djer.

> ## FOUND AND LOST AGAIN
>
> *... the arm of the queen of Zer (Djer) was found, hidden in a hole in the wall, with the gold bracelets in place. The lads who found it saw the gold, but left it untouched and brought the arm to me. I cut the wrappings apart and so bared the bracelets all intact ...*
>
> *When Quibell came over on behalf of the [Cairo] Museum I sent up the bracelets by him. The arm – the oldest mummified piece known – and its marvellously fine tissue of linen were also delivered at the Museum. Brugsch [Emile Brugsch, curator of the Cairo Museum] only cared for display; so from one bracelet he cut away the half that was of plaited gold wires, and he also threw away the arm and linen. A museum is a dangerous place.*
>
> Flinders Petrie finds an arm in the tomb of Djer (From *Seventy Years in Archaeology*, London 1931, p.175).

Djet, successor and probable son of Djer, built a large tomb at Abydos (Tomb Z), but is otherwise largely unknown. His successor, and putative son, Den was the first pharaoh to use stone elements in his mud-brick tomb (Tomb T). His burial chamber was paved with red and black Aswan granite and his tomb included a stairway leading to the burial chamber, a logical development that allowed the superstructure to be completed before pharaoh's burial. Den's is a long and well-documented reign. The extensive Sakkara tomb of the 'vizier of the king of upper and lower Egypt' Hemaka confirms the existence of an effective state bureaucracy at this time.

A series of labels and inscribed vessels testifies to Den's achievements. In a scene reminiscent of the Narmer Palette, a label torn from a pair of sandals shows Den with his right arm raised to smite the Asiatic (a generalized easterner) who cringes at his feet. The caption reads 'the first occasion of smiting the easterners'. At a more spiritual level, a wooden label shows Den celebrating his *heb sed* or 30-year jubilee; he runs a ritual race, then sits on a raised throne. Den, who succeeded to the throne as a child, celebrated two such jubilees; Manetho tells us that his king Usaphaidos (Udimu, or Den) ruled for 20 years but archaeology suggests that he reigned for at least half a century.

THE FIRST FEMALE PHARAOH

Just one of the Umm el-Qa'ab royal tomb complexes was built for a woman. Meritneith's large tomb (Tomb Y) was indistinguishable from the other tombs, although her stelae presented her name without the *serekh*. Clearly Meritneith was an important and influential woman, but who was she? Seal impressions and inscribed bowls link her with Djer, Djet and Den. Just one sealing, recovered from the Sakkara

1ST DYNASTY RULERS
*c.*3000–2890 BC
(precise dates unknown)

Aha
Djer
Djet
Den
Meritneith (female pharaoh)
Anedjib
Semerkhet
Qa'a

The broken stela known as the Palermo Stone, dating from the 5th Dynasty, is inscribed with royal annals. The upper half of this fragment lists the Predynastic rulers of Egypt, while below are the kings of the 1st Dynasty.

cemetery (tomb 3503), presents her name in a *serekh*. She is excluded from the king lists but included on a broken section of the Palermo Stone where she is described as a 'king's mother'. The simplest explanation is that Meritneith, daughter of Djer, was married to Djet. Following his early death she ruled on behalf of her young son Den. In recognition of his mother's role as temporary ruler of Egypt, Den then allowed her the honour of burial among her fellow rulers. This sets an important precedent. The ideal succession would always be the passing of the crown directly from dead father (Osiris) to living son (Horus), but the queen was permitted to assist the young Horus at the beginning of his reign.

THE END OF THE LINE

The Sakkara king list preserved in the tomb of the Ramesside scribe Tjenroy starts with the reign of Anedjib of This, suggesting that the earlier 1st Dynasty kings were less important in the north than their propaganda would have us believe. Manetho, who refers to Anedjib as Miebidos, tells us that he ruled for 26 years; textual evidence indicates that Anedjib was the first king to use the title 'lord of the Two Lands'. However, Anedjib's Abydos tomb (Tomb X) was small, poorly constructed, and lacking any stone elements and this, combined with the fact that Anedjib's successor erased his name from many of his inscribed vessels after his death, suggests that the king did not have total control over his country. His reign may have ended with a change of ruling family.

The next king, Semerkhet, is omitted from the Sakkara king list but is included on the Palermo Stone (nine years) and in Manetho (18 years). Semerkhet's Abydos tomb (Tomb U) was far larger and better built than that of his predecessor, but Manetho tells us that his reign was a time of disasters.

Qa'a, or Qa'a-hedjet, reigned for up to 26 years, long enough for his Abydos tomb (Tomb Q) to undergo several construction phases. A fine stela, almost certainly recovered from Abydos, shows Horus embracing Qa'a,

QUEEN OF EGYPT

In ancient Egypt all royal titles stressed the relationship of the individual to the pharaoh. The queen's title *hemet-nesu* literally meant 'king's wife': a queen was therefore any woman who was, or had been, married to a king. As Egypt's kings were polygamous, this simple definition embraced a wide range of women of different status, stretching from the high-born consort who was expected to bear the king's heir to the lowliest of the harem wives.

Queens regnant – those women who ruled Egypt in their own right – did not classify themselves as *hemet-nesu*. They considered themselves to be female pharaohs, and used the full king's titulary.

who wears the white crown. The Palermo Stone tells us that the end of the 1st Dynasty was a time of low Nile flood levels; such times were notorious for sparking civil unrest, and may explain why Manetho inserts a change of dynasty after Qa'a.

A TIME OF UPHEAVAL?

It is not clear how many pharaohs ruled during the 2nd Dynasty. While Manetho tells us that nine kings reigned for a total of 302 years, and the king lists detail 11 kings, archaeology suggests just seven kings ruling for approximately two centuries. Little is known about the first five pharaohs and their tombs have never been located. However, extensive underground galleries and storerooms in the Sakkara necropolis have yielded seal impressions belonging to kings Hetepsekhemwy, Raneb and Nynetjer, suggesting that the galleries represent tombs whose superstructures have now vanished. Despite Manetho's assertion that the 2nd Dynasty pharaohs hailed from This, the change of cemetery from Abydos to Sakkara suggests a change of ruling family from a southern line to a northern one. The fact that Hetepsekhemwy, 'The Peaceful One of the Two Powers [Horus and Seth?]', buried his predecessor at Abydos, leaving his own seal impressions in Qa'a's tomb, need not negate this. It was accepted that a new pharaoh should hold a funeral service for the old king in order to justify his own claim to the throne.

SETH AND HORUS: PERIBSEN AND KHASEKHEMWY

Peribsen, penultimate pharaoh of the 2nd Dynasty, returned to the Umm el-Qa'ab to build a modest tomb and an extensive mortuary enclosure. He may have had little choice. The fact that his name is not found outside Upper Egypt until after his death suggests that his authority was confined to southern Egypt. This would explain why the king, early in his reign, changed his name from Hor-Sekhemib to Set-Peribsen, becoming the only pharaoh to boast a Seth-name: a Seth animal (a curious, long-eared mythological beast) rather than a Horus falcon guards his *serekh*. Much later, the Egyptians would start to regard Seth as a mischievous god, the sworn enemy of Horus. But there is no evidence that he was regarded in this way during the Early Dynastic period, when he appears to have been just one of many local deities. Indeed, it may be that this early association with rebellion, or chaotic behaviour, influenced the way that later Egyptians thought about their god.

Peribsen's successor reverted back to the traditional Horus-name, but his Horus invariably wore the southern white crown, never the northern red crown. Pharaoh's

A WASTEFUL PRACTICE

The 1st Dynasty royal tomb complexes included subsidiary graves: long, narrow trenches divided into individual chambers. Most of these subsidiary graves shared a common roof, suggesting that they covered a mass burial. The occupants of the graves were wrapped in natron-coated cloth, then buried in squat wooden coffins with assorted grave goods. Their names were recorded on small limestone stelae. Djer's complex, the largest, included 338 of these subsidiary graves, some of which were never occupied, and these have yielded 76 stelae carved for women and 11 for men. These are not queens, princesses or high-ranking officials. They are pharaoh's personal retinue, his servants, minor officials and favourite young women. It is not now possible to determine how they died, but it is hard to escape the conclusion that they were either killed or persuaded to commit suicide at the time of pharaoh's death.

2ND DYNASTY RULERS
*c.*2890–2686 BC
(precise dates unknown)

Hetepsekhemwy

Raneb

Nynetjer

Weneg

Sened

Peribsen

Khasekhemwy

original name, Khasekhem or 'The Power [i.e. Horus] Rises', is recorded on vessels discovered in the Hierakonpolis temple and dated to 'the year of fighting the northern enemy within the city of Nekheb'. Later Khasekhem revised his Horus-name to Khasekhemwy, 'The Two Powers [Horus and Seth?] Rise', and topped his *serekh* with both Horus and Seth. This new name is accompanied by the phrase 'the Two Lords are at peace in him'. It seems that after a bloody struggle in which over 40,000 northerners died, Khasekhem, pharaoh of southern Egypt, was able to reunite his land. Two inscribed statues of Khasekhemwy, recovered from Hierakonpolis, confirm his victory, and show the seated king wearing the white crown and the *sed* cloak. Around the statue bases are images of his dying enemies.

Khasekhemwy stamped his authority on Nubia with a small campaign early in his reign. The Palermo Stone tells us that he ordered fleets of ships and, in Year 15, commissioned a copper statue named 'High is Khasekhemwy': a stone fragment recovered from Byblos (Lebanon) shows us that his name was recognized outside Egypt's borders. A prolific builder, Khasekhemwy worked extensively at Hierakonpolis and endowed a series of temples in Egypt's major cities. At Abydos he constructed a large mud-brick tomb with a limestone burial chamber on the Umm el-Qa'ab (Tomb V), and the extensive Shunet es-Zebib mortuary enclosure on the desert edge. His tomb was robbed in antiquity, but excavators have recovered stone, metal and pottery vessels, copper and flint tools, semi-precious beads, inlays from vanished wooden furniture, a broken sceptre and some human remains.

… this is their procedure for the most perfect style of embalming. First of all they draw out the brain through the nostrils using an iron hook. When they have extracted all that they can, they wash out the remnants with an infusion of drugs. Then, using a sharp obsidian stone, they make a cut along the flank. Through this they extract the whole contents of the abdomen. The abdomen is then cleaned, rinsed with palm wine and rinsed again with powdered spices but not frankincense, and stitched up. And when they have done this they heap the body with natron for seventy days, but no longer, and so the mummy is made. After the seventy days are over they wash the body and wrap it from head to toe in the finest linen bandages coated with resin ….

HERODOTUS (*HISTORIES* II: 86)

MUMMIFICATION

For many centuries Egypt's dead were interred in pits dug into the hot desert sands. The sterile sand drained the fluids away from the bodies, allowing the deceased to dry quickly and naturally, producing desiccated but lifelike bodies. Realizing that their corpses could cheat decomposition, the Egyptians soon decided that a preserved body was essential for the rebirth of the soul. Anyone who wished to enjoy an afterlife now had to ensure that his or her body survived in a recognizable form.

But the élite were not content with simple graves. They wanted coffins – rectangular boxes suitable for holding contracted burials – and brick- or plaster-lined tombs, and these separated the bodies from the preserving sand. As their corpses began to rot, their chances of an afterlife faded.

This was an intolerable situation. The obvious answer was to abandon the coffins and tombs.

A mummy in a wooden coffin, from Gebelein in Upper Egypt. From a Persian word meaning 'bitumen', mummies were so called because their blackened skin was wrongly thought to have been preserved in tar.

Instead, the Egyptians decided to find an artificial means of preserving the body. The first attempts at artificial mummification concentrated on preserving shape at the expense of tissue. Layers of well-padded, plaster-soaked bandages allowed the undertakers to mould limbs and features into an acceptable shape. By the end of the 3rd Dynasty evisceration followed by chemical drying in natron salt was becoming routine and the hollow bodies, no longer contracted, were being bandaged and buried in full-length coffins. Centuries of experimentation led to the perfection of the technique.

PHARAOHS AND PYRAMIDS

C.2686–2181 BC

The first step pyramid was built by pharaoh Netjerikhet Djoser at Sakkara. During the 3rd Dynasty Djoser employed the architect Imhotep, whom Manetho praised as 'the inventor of the art of building with hewn stone'.

STAIRWAYS TO THE STARS
THE STEP PYRAMIDS

3rd Dynasty *c*.2686–2613 BC

Tᴇ ᴇxᴀᴄᴛ sᴇǫᴜᴇɴᴄᴇ ᴏꜰ ᴛʜᴇ 3ʀᴅ Dʏɴᴀsᴛʏ ᴘʜᴀʀᴀᴏʜs ʜᴀs ʏᴇᴛ ᴛᴏ ʙᴇ ᴅᴇᴛᴇʀᴍɪɴᴇᴅ. Tʜᴇ ꜰɪʀsᴛ ᴘʜᴀʀᴀᴏʜ, Nebka (or Sanakht), is a shadowy figure, a possible descendant of Khasekhemwy. Although his 18-year rule is recorded by Manetho, there is some evidence to suggest that he may have been the fourth rather than the first pharaoh of his dynasty. His reign saw the first serious exploitation of the copper and turquoise resources of the Sinai Peninsula and, almost certainly, the foundation of an unfinished stone structure at north Sakkara known today as the Gisr el-Mudir, but is otherwise ill recorded. Nebka has no known tomb and is attested only in posthumous references.

3RD DYNASTY RULERS

c.2686 BC Nebka/ Sanakht?

c.2667 BC Netjerikhet Djoser

c.2648 BC Sekhemkhet

c.2640 BC Khaba
Nebka/Sanakht?

c.2637 BC Huni

The Step Pyramid of Djoser at Sakkara. The original limestone casing was removed by ancient thieves, allowing archaeologists to see how the pyramid was built.

Egypt's next pharaoh, Netjerikhet Djoser, was the son of Khasekhemwy and Nimaathap. The Turin Canon, recording his name in the red ink reserved for significant events, tells us that he enjoyed 19 years of prosperous rule, while Manetho allows him a more generous 30 years. Djoser's ability to build an extensive stone pyramid complex proves that he was a competent and secure pharaoh who ruled over a prosperous and united land; it is therefore disappointing that we know little about his reign. We do, however, have evidence of further profitable expeditions to Sinai, while the inscribed fragments of a broken shrine recovered from Heliopolis show a large scale Djoser sitting on a throne with three miniature women standing by his leg: two of these are named as the King's Daughter Intkaes and 'She who sees Horus and Seth' Hetephernebty.

A STONE PALACE FOR A DEAD KING

Djoser built his funerary complex on the high ground of the north Sakkara cemetery, near his palace at White Walls. Above ground his complex resembled Khasekhemwy's Abydos funerary enclosure: underground, the maze of galleries recalled the Sakkara gallery systems of Hetepsekhemwy, Raneb and Nynetjer. But Djoser's complex was innovative in one major respect: it was the world's first substantial stone building. The Egyptians would continue to build their domestic architecture from mud-brick, but from this time onwards the élite would build stone tombs. By the New Kingdom many large state temples, too, would be stone-built.

Mud-brick architecture had been both simple and cheap. Stone architecture offered a welcome permanence, but was far more expensive and required a complete control over resources. Quarrying, transporting and laying stone blocks demanded skilled manpower, and the workforce not only needed effective tools, they needed accommodation, food, healthcare and efficient management. The scribes and accountants who co-ordinated the labours of thousands of workers were as essential to the project

NETJERIKHET DJOSER

Dynasty: 3rd

Father: Khasekhemwy

Mother: Nimaathap

Consort: Hetephernebty

Burial place: Sakkara Step Pyramid

Successor: Sekhemkhet

as the architects and the artisans who were summoned to work on a temporary basis from the villages of the Valley and Delta.

Djoser's pyramid complex was designed by the multi-talented Imhotep, 'Treasurer of the king of Lower Egypt, the first after the king of Upper Egypt, administrator of the great palace, hereditary lord, high priest of Heliopolis, Imhotep the builder …' The ancient thieves who stripped the Step Pyramid of its outer covering of polished Tura limestone, revealed that Imhotep's masterpiece had been built in stages. It had started life as a square mastaba topping a subterranean burial shaft. This was extended on all four sides to form a two-stepped mastaba, then extended again on the eastern side to make a rectangular mastaba. This mastaba then became the bottom step of a four-step pyramid. Finally the base was extended to form a six-step pyramid standing 60 metres (197 ft) high. The subterranean burial chamber, now inaccessible, lies at the centre of a maze of corridors and store-rooms. Here the 'king's apartment' is decorated with thousands of green faience tiles. One wall includes three limestone false door stelae bearing scenes of the *sed* festival ceremonies; in two of the doors Djoser runs a hard race, carrying the scroll which documents his entitlement to rule Egypt. In the third he stands vindicated before the gods.

The Step Pyramid was surrounded by a 'fossilized palace' of courts and stone buildings, and protected by a massive stone enclosure wall. Each building was designed to meet a particular practical and/or theological requirement: together, they created a potent magic that would help the dead pharaoh to live again. Several of the buildings

RE OF HELIOPOLIS

The Old Kingdom saw the northern sun god Re of Heliopolis rise to become Egypt's foremost deity. Re, who may be equated with the creator god Atum, is represented either as a falcon or as a winged sun disk. He rules over the heavens just as Osiris rules the dead and Horus rules the living. He recreates himself and is reborn every day. At dawn he is represented as Khepri, the scarab beetle who pushes his ball of dung (the sun) tirelessly before him. At noon Re is strong and powerful. At dusk he has become a tired old man and is represented as Atum, the most ancient of the creator gods.

Sun temples had open ceilings that admitted sunlight. There were solar temples throughout Egypt, but Re's main temple was situated at Heliopolis (ancient Iunu; Biblical On; archaeological Tell Hisn). Here the *benben* stone, the sacred ray of the sun in solid form, stood in place of a cult statue of Re. There is no surviving illustration of the original *benben*, but Egyptologists assume that it was a naturally shaped round-topped or conical stone, possibly even a meteorite.

REMEMBERING THE BUILDERS

Djoser's prodigious achievement would never be forgotten. Twenty-five centuries after his death, during the reign of Ptolemy V, the 'Famine Stela' was carved on the Island of Sehel (Aswan). The stela, inscribed with an entirely fake 3rd Dynasty text, celebrates Djoser as a wise and revered ruler.

Imhotep, too, would be remembered. During the Late Period he was deified and worshipped as Imouthes, son of Ptah, a popular patron deity of architecture and healing linked with the Greek god of medicine Asclepius.

were functional spaces designed to allow the living to perform the death rites and service the cult of the deceased king. Other spaces were provided for the dead pharaoh's personal use; they were replicas of Egypt's most important shrines and stone versions of the mud-brick timber and reed buildings used in the rituals of living kingship. The stone doors of these symbolic buildings neither opened nor shut. They did not need to: Djoser's spirit could pass freely through the stone to celebrate his rituals for all eternity.

FAILED PYRAMIDS AND FORGOTTEN KINGS

The history of the late 3rd Dynasty is essentially a list of ill-remembered names and ill-preserved funerary architecture. Manetho gives six kings reigning for a total of 157 years; archaeology suggests that there were no more than four pharaohs ruling for approximately 35 years.

Sekhemkhet, son and successor of Djoser, ruled for no more than seven years. A relief in the Wadi Maghara, Sinai, shows him wearing both the red and white crowns as he triumphs over Egypt's eastern enemies. A mason's scribbled inscription suggests that, like his father before him, Sekhemkhet employed Imhotep to design his Sakkara

A copper-alloy figurine of the architect and physician Imhotep.

In the Djoser pyramid complex, it often feels as if we are in Sleeping Beauty's palace.

Everything is dead, and everything is made for death.

FRENCH EGYPTOLOGIST JACQUES VANDIER (1904–73)

Then the majesty of king Huni died and the majesty of king Snefru was raised up as beneficent king in this whole land. Then Kagemni was made mayor of the city and vizier.

THE MEMORY OF HUNI IS PRESERVED IN *PAPYRUS PRISSE*: AN OLD KINGDOM INSTRUCTION TEXT ADDRESSED TO KAGEMNI. THE BEGINNING OF THE PAPYRUS IS LOST

pyramid complex. But his complex was never completed and the pyramid, which would have been both taller and one step higher than Djoser's, was only about 7 metres (23 ft) high when it was abandoned. The complex had completely vanished when, in 1951, Zakaria Goneim, Chief Inspector of Sakkara, re-examined a large, rectangular 'natural terrace' to the southwest of the Step Pyramid. The terrace proved to be the base of Sekhemkhet's enclosure wall. Goneim next discovered the sloping trench leading to the entrance to the burial chamber. The substructure yielded animal remains, a set of 26th Dynasty papyri, some 700 stone vessels, and a 3rd Dynasty collection of golden objects, and clay sealings bearing Sekhemkhet's name. Unfortunately, although apparently sealed, the king's alabaster sarcophagus was empty.

Khaba is probably the owner of the unfinished and ruined 'Layer Pyramid' built at Zawiyet el-Aryan, a part of the Memphite cemetery approximately 4 miles (6.4 km) to the north of Sakkara. His name has been found on sealings at Hierakonpolis, and on stone vessels at Dahshur and Zawiyet el-Aryan, but little is known of his six-year reign.

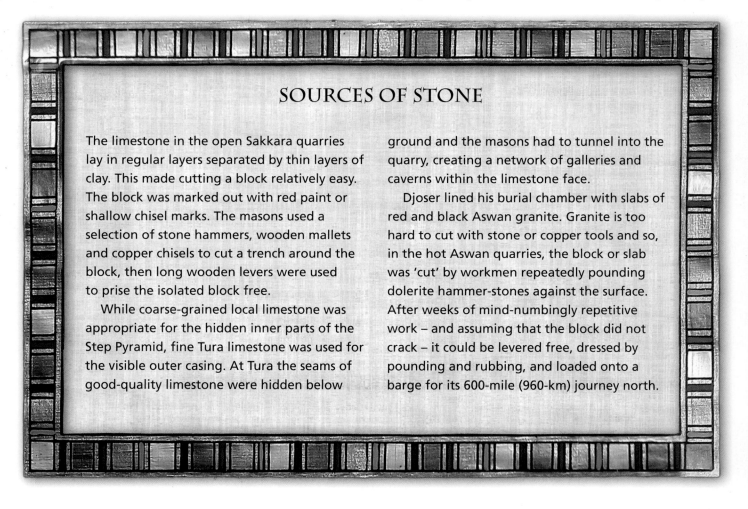

SOURCES OF STONE

The limestone in the open Sakkara quarries lay in regular layers separated by thin layers of clay. This made cutting a block relatively easy. The block was marked out with red paint or shallow chisel marks. The masons used a selection of stone hammers, wooden mallets and copper chisels to cut a trench around the block, then long wooden levers were used to prise the isolated block free.

While coarse-grained local limestone was appropriate for the hidden inner parts of the Step Pyramid, fine Tura limestone was used for the visible outer casing. At Tura the seams of good-quality limestone were hidden below ground and the masons had to tunnel into the quarry, creating a network of galleries and caverns within the limestone face.

Djoser lined his burial chamber with slabs of red and black Aswan granite. Granite is too hard to cut with stone or copper tools and so, in the hot Aswan quarries, the block or slab was 'cut' by workmen repeatedly pounding dolerite hammer-stones against the surface. After weeks of mind-numbingly repetitive work – and assuming that the block did not crack – it could be levered free, dressed by pounding and rubbing, and loaded onto a barge for its 600-mile (960-km) journey north.

Sanakht – who may, perhaps, be the 'Nebka' recorded by Manetho at the start of the 3rd Dynasty – possibly succeeded Khaba. Although he is the first pharaoh known to have to written his name in a cartouche, his fleeting reign has left little trace in the archaeological record. The Turin Canon accords him a reign of 24 years.

Huni was an ambitious builder who probably founded the Elephantine fortress at Egypt's southern border, and who definitely raised a chain of small three- and four-stepped pyramids throughout Egypt. Six of these have survived at Zawiyet el-Meitin (near Minya), Sinki (south Abydos), Tukh (near Nagada), el-Kula (near Hierakonpolis), south Edfu and Elephantine West Isle. A seventh example, at Seila (Faiyum), probably belongs on the list. Huni's mortuary complex has yet to be confirmed.

Few artefacts survive from the reign of the late 3rd Dynasty pharaoh Sanakht. This relief fragment shows him wearing the red crown of Lower Egypt and smiting an enemy with a mace.

THE GREAT BUILDERS
SNEFRU AND HIS FAMILY

4th Dynasty c.2613–2494 BC

THE 4TH DYNASTY WAS THE AGE OF THE GREAT PYRAMIDS; A TIME WHEN ARTS, ARCHITECTURE AND SCIENCES flourished in the bright light shining from the powerful sun god Re. The god-like pharaohs of the 4th Dynasty were each descended from Snefru, Egypt's most prolific pyramid builder. They ruled a centralized state with absolute power. Snefru's greatest achievement was an absolute control of resources that allowed the building of Egypt's first three true pyramids. His combined monuments are estimated to hold more than 3.5 million cubic metres (124 million cu ft) of stone. In recognition of his great achievements, and despite the fact that he is likely to have been the son of the 3rd Dynasty pharaoh Huni, Manetho chose Snefru as the first king of the 4th Dynasty.

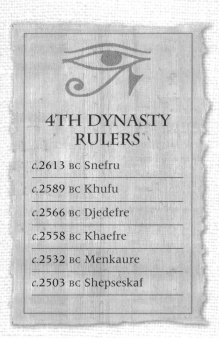

4TH DYNASTY RULERS

c.2613 BC Snefru

c.2589 BC Khufu

c.2566 BC Djedefre

c.2558 BC Khaefre

c.2532 BC Menkaure

c.2503 BC Shepseskaf

The pyramid of Menkaure at Giza (foreground, with subsidiary queens' pyramids in front), with the pyramid of his predecessor Khaefre in the background.

THREE PYRAMIDS BUT NO BURIAL

Like Djoser before him, Snefru would be remembered as a kind and wise pharaoh – a judgement that may have been unduly influenced by his name, which incorporates the element *nefer*, meaning 'good' or 'beautiful'. Snefru enjoyed a long, active and enviably prosperous reign: 24 years recorded by the Turin Canon; 29 years by Manetho; 40–50 years suggested by graffiti at Meidum and Dahshur. The Palermo Stone confirms that he developed the diorite quarries at Abu Simbel and imported timber to build boats and a magnificent wooden palace. A competent military leader, he pushed back Egypt's southern frontier to establish a trading settlement at Buhen (Nubia), returning home with 7000 prisoners and 20,000 cattle. Meanwhile, campaigns in the Sinai kept the Bedouin under control and protected the turquoise and copper mines.

Meidum, 30 miles (48 km) south of Memphis, had probably been Huni's chosen pyramid site but after Huni's death Snefru took over. The pyramid, which had initially been designed as a seven-stepped pyramid, was extended to a more impressive eight steps. Then, after 15 years of work, the pyramid was abandoned as Snefru began to build at Dahshur. Towards the end of his reign workmen returned to convert the step-pyramid into a true pyramid by extending the sides and filling in the steps with a packing of local stone. The pyramid was

SNEFRU	
Dynasty:	4th
Father:	Huni?
Mother:	Meresankh I
Consort:	Hetepheres I
Burial place:	Dahshur?
Successor:	Khufu

The scribe Ankhkheperresenb, son of Amenmesu ... came here to see the beautiful temple of the Horus King Snefru ... He found it like heaven within when the sun god is rising in it ...

NEW KINGDOM GRAFFITO SCRAWLED IN THE MEIDUM MORTUARY TEMPLE

then re-covered in Tura limestone and once again abandoned. Unfortunately, lack of proper bonding eventually caused the heavy outer layers of the pyramid to slide downwards, leaving a tower-like core standing in a collapsed heap of sand and rubble.

Snefru's first Dahshur pyramid was designed from the outset to be a true pyramid, but his architects miscalculated; the initial angle of 60° was far too steep for safety and soon had to be adjusted to 54° by extending the pyramid base. As the pyramid continued to demonstrate a worrying instability, the angle was readjusted to 43° 21' some 45 metres (148 ft) above ground. Stability was restored and the flatter angle lowered the finished height, reducing the amount of stone needed. But the pyramid, known today as the 'Bent Pyramid', was far from perfect and so, during his 30th regnal year, Snefru started work on a second Dahshur pyramid. Finally he achieved success. His North or Red Pyramid is a stable, gently sloping true pyramid with a square base. The pyramid burial chamber has yielded human remains belonging to a man in late middle age. If these are Snefru's remains – and this is by no means certain – he must have acceded to the throne as a very young boy.

KHUFU AND HIS GREAT PYRAMID

Khufu, son of Snefru, survived at least three older brothers to become pharaoh at approximately 40 years of age. He enjoyed a lengthy but ill-recorded reign of somewhere between 23 years (Turin Canon) and 63 years (Manetho, who knew the

---

SNEFRU AND THE MAGICIAN

Pharaoh was bored! He summoned the high priest, Djadjaemankh, and asked his advice. Djadjaemankh knew his king well, and devised a wonderful entertainment. Snefru was to sit on his golden throne, beside the palace lake. Twenty of Egypt's most beautiful maidens would take to the waters and row on the palace lake.

Snefru watched entranced as the maidens rowed up and down wearing dresses made from fishing nets. Suddenly, everything stopped. The leading maiden was in tears. A precious turquoise ornament had fallen from her hair and was lost

in the water. Snefru offered to replace the trinket, but the maiden was too distressed to continue.

Again Snefru summoned Djadjaemankh. The high priest spoke a magic word and the waters of the lake became solid. Carefully folding the lake in half, the priest bent down to retrieve the ornament. A second word then restored the lake to its usual form. The maidens cheered, and Snefru was mightily impressed.

From the *Papyrus Westcar* (see p.47)

king as 'Suphis'). There is evidence of trading missions outside Egypt: to Byblos to acquire wood, to Aswan to quarry granite, to Nubia to obtain ivory and gold, and to Sinai to control the Bedouin and exploit the turquoise and copper reserves, and it is probably during Khufu's reign that the Sadd el-Kafara – Egypt's first dam – was built. The Palermo Stone, which records just four years of Khufu's reign, mentions the carving of statues. However, today Khufu's statuary is all lost and our only view of the king is provided by a small ivory figurine of uncertain date which shows Khufu seated on a throne and wearing the red crown.

Khufu built his funerary complex on the Giza Plateau, close by White Walls. His Great Pyramid, the last surviving wonder of the ancient world, stands 146.59 metres (480.9 ft) high, with a slope of 51°50'. Its sides are orientated almost exactly towards true north and its base is almost completely level. The pyramid holds three chambers linked by passageways. From the entrance on

THE CLASSIC PYRAMID COMPLEX

Meidum was far from an architectural triumph. But it served as a blueprint for all subsequent pyramid complexes.

The complex was now a linear one. The true pyramid stood in the desert, orientated to face the rising sun. The royal tomb was contained within or beneath the pyramid, and a small-scale satellite pyramid was sited to the south of the main pyramid. The mortuary chapel, built against the eastern face of the pyramid, was the focus for offerings to the deceased. It was linked by a long causeway to the valley temple, which lay on the edge of the cultivation. The valley temple, which was joined by a canal to the Nile, served as the gateway to the funerary complex and may have been used during the mummification rituals.

Egypt's earliest true pyramid, at Meidum. Structural deficiencies caused the base of the four outer buttress walls to give way, and the walls to slip down, leaving the central 'tower' core we see today.

KHUFU
(KHNUM-KHUEF-
WI; CHEOPS)

Dynasty: 4th

Father: Snefru

Mother: Hetepheres I

Consorts: Meritetes,
Henutsen

Burial place: Giza,
Great Pyramid

Successor: Djedkare

the northern face, a passageway drops through the pyramid masonry and the underlying bedrock to enter the unfinished 'Subterranean Chamber'. Part way along the descending passageway is the entrance to the equally steep ascending passageway. This opens into the 'Grand Gallery', a tall corridor whose walls are made from seven layers of overlapping limestone blocks. The lower west wall of the Gallery includes the entrance to the 'well', a vent which drops to meet the descending passageway, and a horizontal passageway leads into the 'Queen's Chamber' (an unfortunate name given by early explorers: there is no evidence that a queen was ever buried in the pyramid). The Gallery continues upwards to an antechamber that gives access to the 'King's Chamber', Khufu's red granite burial chamber. The masonry directly above the burial chamber carries the only inscriptions in the pyramid, scribbles left by the workforce that confirm that Khufu is the pyramid owner.

Khufu's complex included three small queens' pyramids. All three were looted in antiquity but part of the burial equipment of his mother, Hetepheres I, survived under curious circumstances. In February 1925 an American survey team working to the east of the Great Pyramid discovered a blocked shaft hidden under a thick layer of plaster. The shaft was 27 metres (89 ft) long, and completely filled with limestone blocks and rubbish. A doorway led to a simple chamber at the base of the shaft. Here they found Hetepheres' burial equipment, including such personal items as gold razors and knives, alabaster perfume pots and jewellery stored in a wooden box covered with gold leaf. There were thousands of fragments of pottery and a remarkable collection of wooden furniture, including a bed, two chairs and a carrying chair.

THE 'AIR-SHAFTS'

In the Great Pyramid of Khufu, long, square, narrow passageways lead from the 'King's Chamber' and 'Queen's Chamber' (see above), pointing towards the northern pole star and the constellation of Orion. Although these passageways are generally known as 'air-shafts', it is unlikely that they had any sort of practical purpose. They certainly would have had no effect on the quality or quantity of air circulating within the pyramid.

The shafts leading from the 'Queen's Chamber' extend only a short distance into the pyramid masonry. A pounding stone, a small wooden board and a forked copper tool were discovered in the northern shaft. In 1993 a team from the German Archaeological Institute in Cairo sent a small robotic video camera along the southern shaft, but the robot found its way blocked by a stone plug fitted with two copper pins.

The shafts leading from the King's Chamber run through the body of the pyramid and, perhaps, originally pierced the now-vanished outer casing. As yet these shafts remain unexplored.

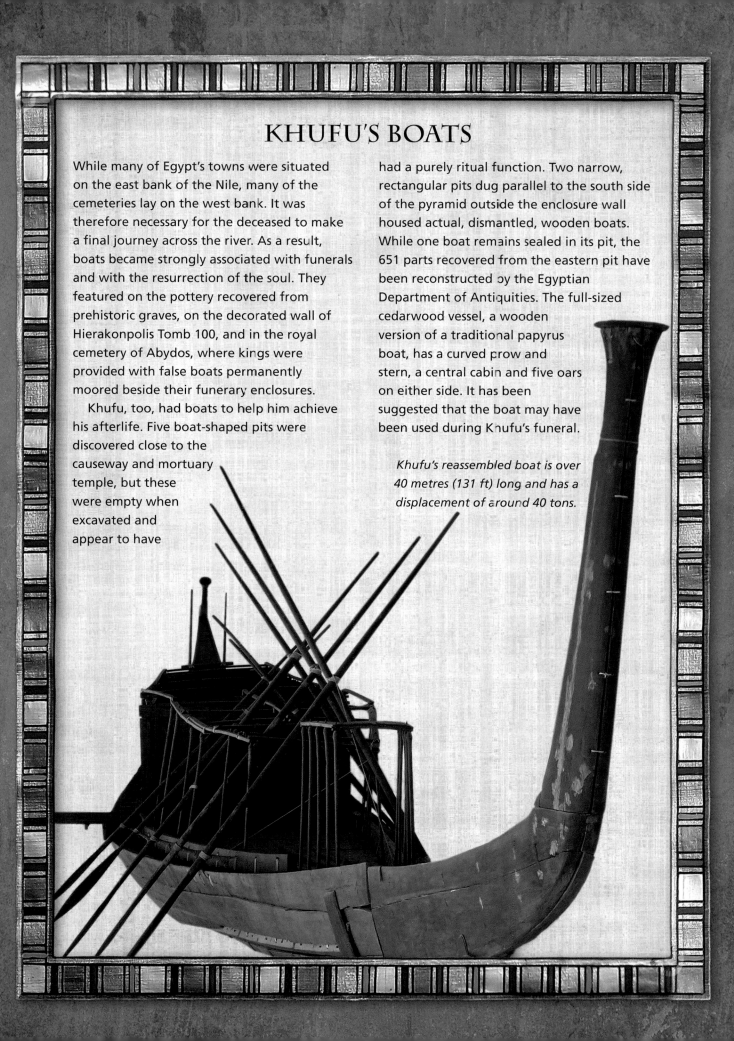

KHUFU'S BOATS

While many of Egypt's towns were situated on the east bank of the Nile, many of the cemeteries lay on the west bank. It was therefore necessary for the deceased to make a final journey across the river. As a result, boats became strongly associated with funerals and with the resurrection of the soul. They featured on the pottery recovered from prehistoric graves, on the decorated wall of Hierakonpolis Tomb 100, and in the royal cemetery of Abydos, where kings were provided with false boats permanently moored beside their funerary enclosures.

Khufu, too, had boats to help him achieve his afterlife. Five boat-shaped pits were discovered close to the causeway and mortuary temple, but these were empty when excavated and appear to have

had a purely ritual function. Two narrow, rectangular pits dug parallel to the south side of the pyramid outside the enclosure wall housed actual, dismantled, wooden boats. While one boat remains sealed in its pit, the 651 parts recovered from the eastern pit have been reconstructed by the Egyptian Department of Antiquities. The full-sized cedarwood vessel, a wooden version of a traditional papyrus boat, has a curved prow and stern, a central cabin and five oars on either side. It has been suggested that the boat may have been used during Khufu's funeral.

Khufu's reassembled boat is over 40 metres (131 ft) long and has a displacement of around 40 tons.

DJEDEFRE

Dynasty: 4th

Father: Khufu

Mother: Meritetes?

Consorts: Khentetka,
  Hetepheres II?

Burial place: Abu
  Roash

Successor: Khaefre

It took almost two years for the archaeologists to empty the 'tomb'; only then did it become apparent that, although the alabaster canopic chest found in a niche in the western wall still held the queen's linen-wrapped internal organs, the alabaster sarcophagus was empty.

A BRIEF REIGN

Djedefre buried his father, leaving his own cartouche sealed within Khufu's boat pit, and took the title 'Son of Re'. He was included in the Turin Canon and the Abydos and Sakkara king lists, but the Greek historians ignored his reign while early Egyptologists believed, wrongly, that Djedefre had murdered his older half-brother Kawab, only to be murdered in turn by a third brother.

Djedefre built his pyramid complex in an ancient cemetery on the edge of the Delta near the modern town of Abu Roash. He simplified the pyramid's internal structure and reduced its size; the emphasis was now to be on the complex as a complete entity rather than just on the pyramid. But Djedefre's reign – eight years in the Turin Canon, at least ten years suggested by an inscription at Giza, between 11 and 22 years suggested by the annual/biennial cattle count – was too short. At his death his red granite temples were unfinished and, while his sub-structure had been cut and roofed, his pyramid remained an indistinct mound.

MODEL FOR THE SPHINX?

Khaefre, another son of Khufu, demonstrated his allegiance to his father by building his mortuary complex to the south of the Great Pyramid. The second Giza pyramid was smaller than its predecessor but was built on higher ground and this, together with its slightly steeper angle, makes it appear the larger.

While Khufu remains a veiled figure, Khaefre lived in an age of stone statues. His mortuary temple displayed sculptures of the king, the king and his queen, and the king in his unique role of a living god while his valley temple yielded the fragments of over 50 hard-stone statues. But the most famous representation of Khaefre is the Great Sphinx that lounges beside his valley temple. The Sphinx is a composite animal: Khaefre's head (or, just maybe, Djedefre's head if the Sphinx was started in an earlier reign), tops a disproportionately large lion's body. The head wears a head cloth rather than a mane and is apparently clean-shaven, a circumstance that has led to the popular misconception that it is female. In 1817, however, fragments of a long, plaited, curved

Beginning of the instructions made by the hereditary prince, the king's son, Hardjedef for his son, his nursling … When you prosper found your house. Choose a hearty wife and a son will be born to you. It is for the son you build a house …

PRINCE HARDJEDEF WAS REVERED, AFTER HIS DEATH, AS A WISE MAN. THE INSTRUCTIONS OF HARDJEDEF WAS ATTRIBUTED TO HIM, BUT WAS PROBABLY WRITTEN DURING THE 5TH DYNASTY

This seated statue of Khaefre was found by French archaeologist Auguste Mariette in 1860 in the ruler's valley temple at Giza. It is carved from greywacke.

beard were discovered in the sand between the sphinx's paws. Whether this is an original 4th Dynasty beard, a New Kingdom 'restoration', or an original Old Kingdom beard remodelled during the New Kingdom is not now obvious.

Khaefre died after a reign of somewhere between 66 years (Manetho) and 24 years (Turin Canon). The period immediately following his death is a confusing one. The Turin Canon tells us that Nebka, who is otherwise invisible, succeeded to the throne; it may be that Nebka is the owner of the unclaimed Unfinished Pyramid at Zawiyet el-Aryan. A Middle Kingdom list of cartouches carved on a rock face in the Wadi Hammamat gives the succession Khufu, Djedefre, Khaefre, Hardjedef, Baufre. Hardjedef and Baufre are also mentioned in Papyrus Westcar. Hardjedef is Khufu's second son; we know that he was buried in a large mastaba at Giza. His brother Baufre has no tomb, suggesting that his name may be a corruption or the throne name of Khufu's other sons. Eventually the throne passed to a third brother, Menkaure, Khaefre's son born to Khamerernebty I.

A BAD PRESS

The classical historians, hailing from lands where slavery was commonplace, equated large pyramids with tyranny. The fifth-century BC Greek historian Herodotus, for example, happily perpetuated the myth that Khufu and Khaefre ruthlessly exploited Egypt and its people for their own ends. Among Khufu's crimes Herodotus lists closing the state temples, banning animal sacrifices and enslaving the people. This is not supported by any archaeological or textual evidence; on the contrary, there is clear evidence that the Giza pyramid workers were well looked after.

KHAEFRE (CHEPHREN)

Dynasty: 4th

Father: Khufu

Mother: Henutsen?

Consort:
Khamerernebty I,
Persenet,
Hekenuhedjet,
Meresankh III

Burial place: Giza,
second pyramid

Successor: Menkaure

Likewise, as the builder of a relatively small pyramid, Menkaure was remembered as a good man: a pharaoh who freed his people from bondage, reopened the temples, and once again allowed offerings to the gods. In fact Menkaure's small pyramid had far less to do with 'goodness' than with a lack of resources following the completion of his predecessors' monuments. Originally intended to be entirely covered in granite, it was completed by his successor Shepseskaf with just 16 granite courses.

For some reason that is now no longer clear; Menkaure's reign became the stuff of legends. Herodotus, for example, preserves the story of Menkaure's beloved only daughter who, having died young, was entombed in a gold-plated wooden cow. Herodotus was apparently able to inspect this very cow, and its ranks of colossal wooden female attendants, in a room in the royal palace at Sais. A second, less romantic version of this tale sees Menkaure raping his daughter who, humiliated, hangs herself. The queen, believing her daughter to have been betrayed by her serving maids, cuts off their hands. Herodotus points out that this would explain why the Sais statues have no hands, before sensibly adding:

MENKAURE (MYCERINUS)	
Dynasty:	4th
Father:	Khaefre
Mother:	Khamerernebty I
Consort:	Khamerernebty II
Burial place:	Giza, third pyramid
Successor:	Shepseskaf

Personally I think that this story is nonsense; especially as an explanation for the statues' missing hands – I could see with my own eyes that they had simply fallen off due to old age. They are still there, visible to all, lying on the ground near the statues' feet.

AN ANCIENT CINDERELLA

Herodotus reports, but quickly dismisses, rumours that Menkaure's Giza pyramid was built by Rhodophis, a courtesan of outstanding beauty. The Greek geographer Strabo based a Cinderella-like tale on this legend.

Strabo tells how Rhodophis's sandal was stolen by an eagle that flew to White Walls and dropped it into pharaoh's lap. He, entranced by the shoe's perfume, ordered an immediate search for its owner. Rhodophis was found, brought to White Walls, and married pharaoh, who built her a pyramid as a token of his undying love.

It is not clear what Herodotus was shown at Sais: but it is extremely unlikely to have been a 2000-year-old cow-coffin.

While the Turin Canon claims that Menkaure ruled for 18 years, it seems that he may have reigned for far longer. With the heir to the throne, Khuenre, dead, Menkaure was succeeded by Shepseskaf, possibly a son born to a secondary wife.

BREAKING WITH TRADITION

Shepseskaf 's innovative 5–6 year reign saw a break with tradition as, abandoning the pyramid form, he moved to the Sakkara south necropolis to build a relatively small stone mastaba known today as Mastabat Faraoun ('Pharaoh's Bench'). Whether this change in tomb-style indicates a change in religious belief, or a decline in royal power, or simply a lack of time and resources, is not now clear. Shepseskaf was worshipped

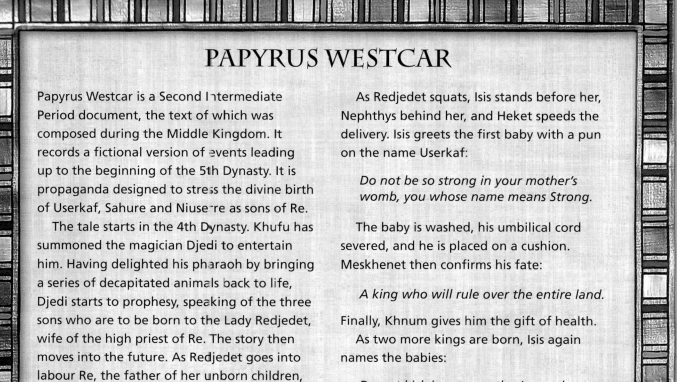

PAPYRUS WESTCAR

Papyrus Westcar is a Second Intermediate Period document, the text of which was composed during the Middle Kingdom. It records a fictional version of events leading up to the beginning of the 5th Dynasty. It is propaganda designed to stress the divine birth of Userkaf, Sahure and Niuserre as sons of Re.

The tale starts in the 4th Dynasty. Khufu has summoned the magician Djedi to entertain him. Having delighted his pharaoh by bringing a series of decapitated animals back to life, Djedi starts to prophesy, speaking of the three sons who are to be born to the Lady Redjedet, wife of the high priest of Re. The story then moves into the future. As Redjedet goes into labour Re, the father of her unborn children, sends the goddesses Isis, Nephthys, Meskhenet and Heket to help her. Escorted by the creator god Khnum they arrive at her house disguised as travelling dancers.

As Redjedet squats, Isis stands before her, Nephthys behind her, and Heket speeds the delivery. Isis greets the first baby with a pun on the name Userkaf:

Do not be so strong in your mother's womb, you whose name means Strong.

The baby is washed, his umbilical cord severed, and he is placed on a cushion. Meskhenet then confirms his fate:

A king who will rule over the entire land.

Finally, Khnum gives him the gift of health.

As two more kings are born, Isis again names the babies:

Do not kick in your mother's womb, you whose name means Kicker (Sahure) and *Do not be dark in your mother's womb, you whose name means Dark* (Neferirkare-Kakai).

---

at the Mastabat Faraoun during the Middle Kingdom, and his tomb was restored by the Ramesside prince-turned-archaeologist Khaemwaset.

Shepseskaf's mastaba served as the model for a curious tomb – a limestone mastaba-style superstructure topping a natural rock base – built to the south of Khaefre's pyramid. A granite doorway names the tomb's owner as Queen Khentkawes, lists her titles and then adds a phrase which could, with equal validity, be translated either as 'King of Upper and Lower Egypt and Mother of the King of Upper and Lower Egypt' or as 'Mother of the Two Kings of Upper and Lower Egypt'. Initially it was thought that Khentkawes was the daughter of Menkaure and mother of Sahure and Neferirkare, the second and third pharaohs of the 5th Dynasty. However, while Khentkawes's name is not written in a cartouche, her doorway shows her seated on a throne, wearing the false beard and uraeus (the rearing cobra symbolizing royal authority) and carrying the pharaoh's sceptre. This strongly suggests that Khentkawes ruled Egypt as regent on behalf of an infant pharaoh. Her reward for this loyal service was a tomb alongside the dead pharaohs.

SHEPSESKAF

Dynasty: 5th

Father: Menkaure?

Mother: unknown

Consort: Bunefer?

Burial place: Sakkara, Mastabat Faraoun

Successor: Userkaf

THE CHILDREN OF RE
FROM USERKAF TO UNAS

5th Dynasty c.2494 – 2345 BC

THE ECONOMIC BENEFITS OF LARGE-SCALE PYRAMID BUILDING HAD BEEN FELT THROUGHOUT EGYPT. THE unyielding urge to build, provision and maintain the royal cemeteries was felt throughout the land, with large numbers of workers either summoned from their villages to labour on the building sites, or employed indirectly in the numerous support industries (as scribes, farmers, sailors, rope makers, carpenters, tool makers and masons to name just a few) that made the pyramids possible. The whole, highly centralized operation was controlled from Memphis, home of the court, the élite, the more influential cults and the civil service, and a vast economic and cultural gulf separated the capital from the provinces. An even wider gulf separated the semi-divine and enormously wealthy pharaoh from his people.

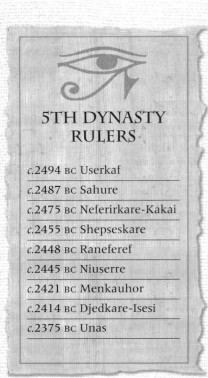

5TH DYNASTY RULERS

c.2494 BC	Userkaf
c.2487 BC	Sahure
c.2475 BC	Neferirkare-Kakai
c.2455 BC	Shepseskare
c.2448 BC	Raneferef
c.2445 BC	Niuserre
c.2421 BC	Menkauhor
c.2414 BC	Djedkare-Isesi
c.2375 BC	Unas

Things were, however, slowly starting to change. Although, in theory, pharaoh owned the land of Egypt and everything in it, successive kings had sacrificed part of their wealth – vast estates yielding high incomes – to finance the mortuary priests who would ensure that their pyramid cults were serviced in perpetuity. At the same time the élite, who had for many decades been rewarded with private estates, owned a growing percentage of the remainder of Egypt's land. Literacy was spreading and a new administrative class was emerging. As the civil service expanded to meet the demands of an increasing population, pharaoh could no longer rely on his immediate family to administer his land. Meanwhile, the moist climate was slowly but surely vanishing. The desert was spreading, the oases were drying up and the people who had once occupied the marginal zones were being drawn inwards, towards the river and the Delta.

PYRAMIDS AND SUN TEMPLES
It is likely that the next pharaoh, Userkaf, was a member of the extended royal family, possibly a son of Menkaure, yet he was considered different enough from his predecessor for historians to class him as the founder of the 5th Dynasty. Following the model set by the 4th Dynasty pharaohs, Userkaf campaigned in Nubia, and endowed a new temple at the southern Egyptian city of Tod and, perhaps, new chapels at Heliopolis and Buto. Trade flourished, and a stone vessel inscribed with his name has been recovered on the Aegean island of Kythera.

Userkaf reinstated the pyramid as the royal tomb, but the age of massive pyramid construction was over and his was a scaled-down version that allowed him the

resources to build an open-air sun temple complex. Pyramids and sun temples were physically separate buildings – Userkaf's sun temple complex was built at Abu Gurob to the north of Abusir while his pyramid complex was at Sakkara – but they shared a similar architecture (with a squat, brick-built obelisk replacing the pyramid in the sun temple complex) and both were connected with solar worship and the rituals of the dead pharaoh. The tradition of the diminished pyramid and the prominent sun temple would be followed by six of the nine 5th Dynasty kings, although to date only two sun temples have been discovered.

Userkaf died after seven years on the throne. His successors – his son or half-brother Sahure, a second son Neferirkare, his grandson Raneferef,

The remains of the Abu Gurob sun temple of Niuserre, with the altar in the foreground and the ruined obelisk in the background.

SAHURE

Dynasty: 5th

Father: Userkaf ?

Mother: Khentkawes I

Consort:
 Neferethanebty

Burial place: Abusir

Successor:
 Neferirkare-Kakai

**NEFERIRKARE-
KAKAI**

Dynasty: 5th

Father: Userkaf ?

Mother:
 Khentkawes I ?

Consort:
 Khentkawes II

Burial place: Abusir

Successor:
 Shepseskare ?

**RANEFEREF
(NEFEREFRE)**

Dynasty: 5th

Father: Neferirkare

Mother:
 Khentkawes II ?

Consort: unknown

Burial place: Abusir

Successor: Niuserre

NIUSERRE

Dynasty: 5th

Father: Neferirkare

Mother:
 Khentkawes II ?

Consort: Reptynub

Burial place: Abusir

Successor: Menkauhor

a second grandson Niuserre – built their pyramids at Abusir, about 1 mile (1.6 km) to the south of Userkaf's sun temple. From the start of Sahure's rule to the end of Niuserre's was no more than 75 years, with Niuserre ruling for some 25 to 30 of those years. Sahure's own reign lasted for 14 years.

Sahure's mortuary temple preserves pictorial evidence of Mediterranean trade; the fleet, crewed by a mixture of Egyptians and Asiatics, returns from Byblos with much-needed wood. This emphasis on trade is confirmed by finds of Sahure's cartouche on seals at Buhen, and by the discovery of his name on an inscribed artifact in the Turkish 'Dorak Treasure'. Other scenes show a victory over Libyan nomads, while the Palermo Stone mentions expeditions to the copper mines of Sinai, the diorite quarries of Abu Simbel and the remote trading post of Punt, situated somewhere on Africa's eastern coast.

Neferirkare-Kakai was the first pharaoh to use the double cartouche. Unfortunately, the records preserved on the broken Palermo Stone end during his reign and we know little more about him. His funerary complex was raised on the highest part of the Abusir cemetery, where his pyramid began as a step pyramid before being converted into a true pyramid. As Neferirkare died before his complex could be completed, a wood and mud-brick mortuary temple was provided by his heirs. This temple has yielded a collection of late 5th–6th Dynasty papyri, the 'First Abusir Archives', which provide the earliest known examples of hieratic writing on papyrus.

GROWTH OF THE OSIRIS CULT

Neferirkare-Kakai was probably succeeded by Shepseskare, an ill-recorded king whose pyramid was barely started at his death and whose position in the succession had been questioned, as some Egyptologists would place him after Egypt's next pharaoh, Raneferef. Raneferef, the son of Neferirkare and Khentkawes II, started to build a mortuary complex to the southwest of his father's pyramid. As he died when his pyramid was nowhere near finished, it was converted into a mastaba so that the king could be buried in the original burial chamber in a granite sarcophagus equipped with a set of alabaster canopic jars. Human remains recovered from this chamber suggest that the pharaoh – if the remains are indeed his – died in his early twenties. This contradicts Manetho's assertion that Raneferef ruled for 20 years, and most archaeologists agree that he is likely to have ruled for no more than two.

Although Egypt's next pharaoh, Niuserre, enjoyed a lengthy and relatively successful reign – he is known to have celebrated a *sed*-jubilee, and his funeral complex shows him active in Palestine, in Libya and Sinai, while his cartouche has been recovered from Byblos and Buhen – his relatively unambitious mortuary complex suggests that he may have struggled to find the finances to complete both his own pyramid and the pyramids of his relatively short-lived predecessors. He was succeeded by Menkauhor, whose pyramid has vanished – although some Egyptologists believe that it may be the so-called 'Headless Pyramid' at Sakkara – and whose reign is more or less a blank. A *sed*-festival statue is

Painted limestone low-relief from the pyramid complex of Sahure at Abusir, showing a procession of gods. The reliefs in Sahure's pyramid complex are renowned for their high degree of technical accomplishment.

unlikely to be a commemoration of a genuine 30-year anniversary as other authorities inform us that Menkauhor ruled for either eight (Turin Canon) or nine (Manetho) years.

The next pharaoh, Djedkare-Isesi, did enjoy a lengthy reign: 28 years according to the Turin Canon, 44 years given by Manetho, evidence for the celebration of a 30-year *sed*-festival. There were successful military campaigns to the east – the Deshasha tomb of Inti shows troops using ladders to scale the town walls and desperate foreign women fighting in the streets – and trade missions that culminated in a successful expedition to Punt.

While the cult of Re remained highly influential and the pyramid remained the royal tomb of choice, the cult of Osiris was gaining in importance and the afterlife was slowly becoming available to all. Djedkare did not feel the need to build a sun temple and confined himself to a mortuary complex raised at south Sakkara.

HIERATIC, DEMOTIC AND COPTIC

Hieroglyphs were beautiful to look at, but time-consuming to produce. For over 2000 years Egypt's scribes routinely used hieratic, a speedy cursive script written from right to left with a brush and ink, for their secular and informal writings. Hieratic could be written on papyrus or leather scrolls, on wooden and ivory labels, or on limestone flakes or broken pot sherds (*ostraca*).

In c.700 BC a third script, demotic, became the standard means of communication. In around AD 500 this was in turn replaced by the Coptic script, which used mainly Greek letters.

THE PYRAMIDS SPEAK

For many centuries Egypt's highly centralized government had been focused on Memphis. Some local rulers had been allowed to control their own regions but only after a period of training (or indoctrination) in the north. In most cases northern administrators had been charged with controlling southern affairs. Now a dedicated administrative department was created for southern Egypt with a bureaucratic capital based at Abydos, parallel to that at Memphis, headed by an 'overseer of Upper Egypt' who was answerable directly to pharaoh. For the first time the élite who governed the provinces actually lived in the provinces and, as their positions quickly became hereditary, a provincial aristocracy developed. Local, rather than national loyalties mattered now, and the cultural and economic differences between Memphis and the provinces dwindled.

This new shifting of authority to the regions extended to the afterlife as the increasingly influential god Osiris started to offer the possibility of survival for all. The 4th Dynasty pharaohs had known that they, and they alone, had a spirit strong enough to break free of the tomb. Their subjects could live beyond death, but they were essentially confined to the grave. The pharaohs had designed and built mastaba tombs for their most loyal courtiers, placing them around their own pyramids, where the élite dead might benefit from proximity to their dead king. Now the provincial cemeteries grew rich as individuals started to take responsibility for their own tombs. The new, privately built mastabas show a relaxing of the uniformity and restraint that characterized the earlier élite cemeteries. They have multiple chambers whose stone walls preserve both scenes of daily life and detailed, highly stylized autobiographies. These autobiographies served two purposes. Designed to justify admittance to eternal life, they were also intended to impress literate passers by, in the hope that they might be inspired to leave an offering.

RULING IN UNCERTAIN TIMES

Unas, a man of unknown parentage, became the last pharaoh of the 5th Dynasty and ruled for between 30 and 33 years. These were difficult times. Egypt was growing drier year by year causing the habitable land to contract, and there were problems over the southern trade networks that saw pharaoh travelling to Elephantine to liaise with Nubian chiefs. Unas's

KHENTKAWES II

Khentkawes II, consort of Neferirkare-Kakai, owned an impressive pyramid complex close by her husband's tomb. Inscriptions scrawled on the masonry show that her complex was initially considered a part of Neferirkare's own complex. When the king died, work on the queen's complex was abandoned. Later, the builders returned to complete her complex as an independent monument for Khentkawes in her role as queen mother, built by her son Niuserre.

Khentkawes's mortuary temple stood to the east of her pyramid. Contemporary papyri tell us that it included at least 16 statues of the queen, although these are now lost. Included amongst the images on the temple walls is one remarkable scene that shows Khentkawes sitting on a throne holding a sceptre and wearing the uraeus, although she does not wear a false beard. Her title is the intriguing 'Mother of Two Kings of Upper and Lower Egypt' or 'King of Upper and Lower Egypt and Mother of the King of Upper and Lower Egypt'. For many years this shared title led to the misidentification of the Abusir Khentkawes II with the Giza Khentkawes I. However it is now generally accepted that these are two separate queens, who shared both a name and a role as regent for a young king.

THE PYRAMID TEXTS

The Pyramid Texts are a collection of more than 700 spells designed to help the mummified king or queen to be reborn into the royal afterlife. The spells name the pharaoh and, as they are carved into the very fabric of his pyramid, will ensure that he is protected for ever, even if his cult fails and his mummy is destroyed. The spells tell the story of the deceased, his burial, his life within the tomb and his daily journey across the sky in the sun boat of Re.

Utterance 217:

> Re-Atum, this Unas comes to you,
> An indestructible spirit who lays claim to
>   the place of the four pillars.
> Your son comes to you. Unas comes to you.
> May you cross the sky together in the dark
> May you rise in the land of light, the place
>   where you shine.
> Horus – proclaim to the powers of the east,
>   and to their spirits:
> 'Unas comes; an indestructible spirit.
> Whom he wishes to live will live, whom he
>   wishes to die will die.'

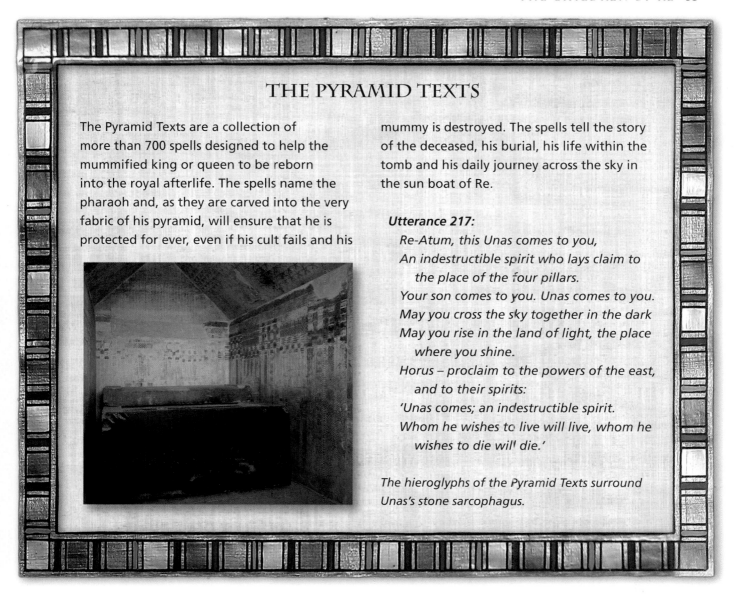

The hieroglyphs of the Pyramid Texts surround Unas's stone sarcophagus.

surprisingly small pyramid complex was raised at Sakkara between Djoser's and Sekhemkhet's tombs. Uniquely, his decorated causeway carries scenes of starving men. These are not Egyptians but desert-dwellers who are apparently suffering the effects of increasing desertification. Food shortages were always a matter of concern: the Egyptians monitored the annual Nile flood levels anxiously, and temple and palace warehouses held a grain reserve against times of need. However, this concern had never before been expressed in such an obvious way.

Unas's burial chamber has yielded a greywacke sarcophagus, a pit designed to hold a canopic chest and fragmentary human remains. Around the sarcophagus the walls had been carved and painted to allow Unas to gaze into a blue sky filled with golden stars. The remaining walls, together with those of the antechamber and part of the passageway, were covered in spells or utterances known today as the Pyramid Texts (see feature box above). These Pyramid Texts would appear in all subsequent Old Kingdom kings', and some queens', pyramids.

UNAS

Dynasty:	5th
Parents:	unknown
Mother:	unknown
Consorts:	Nebet, Khenut
Burial place:	Sakkara
Successor:	Teti

DECENTRALIZATION AND DROUGHT

THE END OF THE OLD KINGDOM

6th Dynasty c.2345–2181 BC

The first pharaoh of the 6th Dynasty, Teti, was either the son or son-in-law (or both) of Unas, while his vizier, Kagemni, had already served under both Unas and Djedkare. There was therefore no obvious break between the 5th and 6th Dynasties, yet both Manetho and the Turin Canon separate the two. Teti himself suggests a reason with his chosen Horus name 'He Who Reconciles Both Lands', a name redolent of resolved civil unrest, but there is no archaeological or textual evidence of conflict at this time. It therefore may be that the moving of the capital city to Memphis was enough to trigger Manetho's division. From Teti's reign until the end of the Old Kingdom, Memphis would remain the capital city and Sakkara the royal burial ground.

Missions continued to depart for Sinai, returning laden with copper and turquoise. Ships set sail for Byblos and, although the permanent Egyptian trading post at Buhen was long gone, traders still trekked across the desert to the oases and into Nubia. Large amounts of stone were transported from Hatnub and the Wadi Hammamat and there were new building projects at Bubastis and Heliopolis, where Teti became the first pharaoh to raise an obelisk cut from a single block of stone. While the obelisks incorporated in 5th Dynasty sun temples had been squat, brick-built towers, Teti's was a tapered monolith representing a solid ray of sunlight and, perhaps, serving as a phallic symbol. To cut, transport and erect an obelisk was a magnificent technical achievement and an unmistakable mark of powerful kingship. Unfortunately, Teti's obelisk was shattered in antiquity, and his only substantial surviving monument is his ruined pyramid.

TROUBLE IN THE HAREM

The Palermo Stone indicates that Teti presided over six biennial cattle counts; this suggests a reign of no more than 13 years. Manetho, in contrast, believed that Teti, whom he knew as Othoes, enjoyed a reign of some 30–33 years before being assassinated by his bodyguard. We have no contemporary evidence to confirm that the

6TH DYNASTY RULERS

c.2345 BC Teti

c.2323 BC Userkare?

c.2321 BC Pepi I

c.2287 BC Merenre

c.2278 BC Pepi II

c.2184 BC Merenre II ?

c.2184 BC Nitocris ? (possibly a fictitious pharaoh)

The pyramid of Teti, founder of the 6th Dynasty, is the northernmost royal pyramid in the Sakkara complex.

Rise up O Teti,

Take your head,

Collect your bones,

Gather your bones and shake the earth

from your flesh!

FROM THE PYRAMID TEXTS OF TETI

TETI

Dynasty: 6th
Father: Unas?
Consorts: Iput, Khuit
Burial place: Sakkara
Successor: Pepi I

PEPI I

Dynasty: 6th
Father: Teti
Mother: Iput
Consorts:
  'Weret-Yamtes',
  Ankhnes-Merire I,
  Ankhnes-Merire II
Burial place: Sakkara
Successor: Merenre I

MERENRE I

Dynasty: 6th
Father: Pepi I
Mother: Ankhnes-
  Merire I
Burial place: Sakkara
Successor: Pepi II

king was murdered but this does not mean that he was not. There was always a worry that committing a thought to writing might reinforce the thought or even cause it to happen. Egypt's scribes therefore showed an understandable reluctance to record anything that might suggest an absence of *maat*. This, combined with the fact that pharaohs, like modern politicians, were keen to expunge from the record anything that might suggest weakness, means that official writings invariably presented a sanitized version of events.

Teti may have been succeeded by Userkare, a king (and king killer?) of unknown origin whose 2–6-year reign has had little impact on the archaeological record. Pepi I, successor either to Userkare or Teti, inherited his throne as a child ruling under the guidance of his mother, Iput. As an adult, Pepi authorized successful expeditions to Sinai, Wadi Hammamat, Nubia, Palestine and Punt, and there were punitive expeditions to subdue the 'Sand Dwellers' in Palestine: the military aspect of his reign was reflected in his pyramid complex, which has yielded multiple statuettes of kneeling prisoners of war. But, much closer to home Pepi, like Teti before him, had problems. A cryptic section in the autobiography of the courtier Weni suggests that there may have been trouble in Pepi's harem. Unfortunately, Weni was too circumspect to give more details of what may, perhaps, have been an attempted coup, and we learn neither the outcome of the investigations nor the fate of the queen.

THE AUTOBIOGRAPHY OF WENI

When the courtier Weni built his simple tomb-chapel at Abydos he dedicated an entire wall to his autobiography. Here we can read how, having commenced his service under Teti, he became one of Pepi's most trusted officials:

> *When there was a secret charge in the royal harem brought against Queen Great-of-Sceptre* [a made up name: we do not know the queen's real name], *his majesty made me hear it alone. No chief judge and vizier, no official was there, only me... Never before had someone like me heard a secret of pharaoh's harem; but his majesty made me hear it, because I was worthy in his majesty's heart more than any other of his officials ...*

When Pepi I was succeeded by Merenre, Weni became 'overseer of Upper Egypt', the first non-élite person to hold this important position. He took to his new role with enthusiasm, taxing the people, digging canals and quarrying the stone that would be used for Merenre's sarcophagus.

The problems of decentralization that were becoming apparent towards the end of the 5th Dynasty continued into the 6th and are made clear in the growing number of autobiographical inscriptions in private tombs. As the provinces became increasingly independent Pepi showed his support for prominent local cults, and his name has been associated with Hathor of Dendera, Horus of Hierakonpolis, Min of Koptos, Osiris of Abydos and Bast of Bubastis. At the same time, perhaps in response to the growing local autonomy, he built a series of royal *ka*-chapels to emphasize the spiritual presence of the king throughout long, thin Egypt.

Towards the end of his 53-year reign (Manetho) Pepi embarked on a series of diplomatic marriages in a transparent attempt to strengthen the links between the waning royal family and the vigorous regional aristocracy. His pyramid complex includes an unprecedented six queen's pyramids and, given that pyramids were only built for the most prominent royal ladies, we must conclude that Pepi was surrounded by even more influential women. The most important of his marriages were with the two daughters of Khui of Abydos. Confusingly, both sisters were named Ankhnes-Merire or its variant, Ankhnes-Pepi ('She lives for King Merire', 'She lives for King Pepi'); it seems likely that they acquired their highly apposite names when they were married. Each sister bore a son and so, although it seems almost inconceivable that the much-married Pepi did not have older sons, he was succeeded by the young Merenre, born to Ankhnes-Merire I. A remarkable copper statue recovered from the temple of Hierakonpolis shows Pepi I and Prince Merenre together.

A FAMILY IN DECLINE

As Merenre took his throne his uncle Djau took up the position of vizier. Egypt was now effectively controlled by the family from Abydos. Merenre ruled Egypt for between seven and 11 years. We can learn something about his ill-documented reign from the autobiography carved by the courtier Harkhuf in his Aswan tomb (see page 58). Like Weni, Harkhuf served as overseer of Upper Egypt, first under Merenre and then under Pepi II, and he completed at least four prestigious trade missions; three during the reign of Merenre and one during the reign of Pepi II.

Alabaster statue of Pepi I. Perched behind the seated king is the falcon god Horus. In his hands the king holds the crossed flail and crook, which symbolize Egyptian kingship.

Merenre had planned to erect a pyramid to the southwest of his father's complex, but this was never finished so that we are again faced with an indistinct mound above a relatively complete substructure. A mummy was recovered from Merenre's black basalt sarcophagus, but this probably represents an intrusive New Kingdom burial.

The Turin Canon tells us that Pepi II reigned for 94 years; Manetho adds that he was six years old when he inherited his throne, so that he died a centurion. It is difficult to be specific about life expectancy amongst the Old Kingdom male élite, but even by modern standards this would be an exceptionally long life. It therefore seems likely that either the regnal length is wrong (possibly the scribe has confused the writing of the numbers 64 and 94) or that it is a deliberate exaggeration and, as

PEPI II

Dynasty: 6th

Father: Pepi I

Mother: Ankhnes-Merire II

Consorts: Neith, Iput, Wedjebten, Ankhnes-Merire III

Burial place: South Sakkara

Successor: Merenre II

Merenre apparently ruled for at least seven years following the death of Pepi I, it is possible that Pepi II initially served as nominal co-regent alongside Merenre. As an outside possibility, it has been suggested that Pepi may have been Merenre's son rather than his half-brother. It is interesting that Pepi's last recorded date is the year after the 31st (presumed) biennial cattle count; we therefore have no dates for the final three decades of his reign.

Pepi's early years were heavily influenced by Ankhnes-Merire II and her family. The queen mother was clearly a person of considerable importance. An alabaster statue of unknown provenance shows her wearing the vulture crown and a (now vanished) uraeus with the young pharaoh, a miniature man, sitting across her knee. This piece is highly unusual in showing a reigning pharaoh at a smaller scale than one of his subjects, and it is likely that it is intended to remind the observer of the goddess Isis and her young son Horus.

Harkhuf's autobiography includes the touching story of the pharaoh and the pygmy. Pygmies were prized as sacred dancers, and they featured in the Pyramid Texts, where their dance formed part of the mortuary ritual. Harkhuf managed to acquire a pygmy on one of his adventures, and the young Pepi could hardly control his impatience as he waited for Harkhuf to escort the pygmy to the palace. Harkhuf in turn was so delighted to receive a letter from his king that he quoted it in its entirety in his tomb.

SWANSONG OF THE OLD KINGDOM

Pepi II produced multiple children, grandchildren and great-grandchildren. But, by outliving not only his own generation but his children's generation as well, he caused

FROM THE AUTOBIOGRAPHY OF HARKHUF

His Majesty King Merenre sent me on my first mission to Yam, to explore and open up the trade route to that faraway country. And he sent my father, the Sole Companion and Lector Priest Iri, with me. I accomplished my mission in seven months. I brought all kinds of beautiful and exotic goods back from Yam, and I earned the admiration and praise of my lord for my work.

The next time, His Majesty trusted me enough to send me on a mission alone. I travelled southwards out of Egypt along the Ivory Road, and I returned northwards via Mekher, Terers and Irtjetj. I accomplished this mission in eight months, and I returned home bearing great quantities of precious things. Everyone was astonished, for no

explorer had brought so many valuable goods back to Egypt before. On my way back I travelled through the region controlled by the chiefs of Setju and Irtjet, and explored those lands. No other envoy to Yam had managed to explore these faraway places as I did.

Then His Majesty sent me on a third mission to Yam. I travelled out from the province of This along the Oasis Road. I discovered that the ruler of Yam had set off for Tjemeh-land, with the intention of smiting the Tjemeh and driving them to the western corner of the sky. I followed the ruler of Yam to Tjemeh-land, and I pacified him and made him content so that he gave praise to all the gods for the King of Egypt.

a dynastic confusion that contributed to the ending of his line. His south Sakkara pyramid was to be the last great monument of the Old Kingdom. Egypt's next pharaoh was the ephemeral Merenre II (Pepi's son?), who was in turn followed by 'Queen Nitocris' who ruled Egypt as a female pharaoh. Female rulers were not ideal but they could be tolerated if there was no acceptable male alternative. Thus Manetho is happy to praise Nitocris as 'Braver than all the men, the most noble and lovely woman of her time, fair skinned with red cheeks', while Herodotus tells how she avenged her murdered brother (Merenre II? Or perhaps the assassinated Teti?) then committed suicide by throwing herself into a chamber full of ashes 'that she might escape the vengeance whereto she would otherwise have been exposed'. However, Nitocris has left no monuments and no tomb and, although the Turin Canon does allow 'Neitaqerti' a reign of two years one month and one day (Manetho gives 12 years) it is entirely possible that this is actually a misreading of a male name.

This mastaba tomb of the governor Ima-Pepi was built during the reign of Pepi II at Balat, in the Dakhla Oasis in the Western Desert.

A LETTER FROM KING NEFERKARE PEPI II TO HARKHUF

Day 15 of the third month of inundation, Year 2.

The king writes to the sole companion, lector priest, and chief of scouts, Harkhuf. The dispatch that you sent to the palace, informing me that you and your army have returned in safety from Yam, has been received. In that dispatch you mention that you have brought with you many precious gifts. You specifically state that you have obtained a pygmy, one of the god's dancers, from the land of the horizon-dwellers...

You really know how to please your Lord. Truly, I think that you must spend all your waking hours working out how best to serve me. I will reward you and your family for many generations for this good deed... Make your way northwards to the palace, at once. Hurry, and bring with you the remarkable pygmy from the land of horizon-dwellers, so that he might perform the dances of the god and delight my heart. When he is on board the ship, make sure that he is well supervised lest he fall into the water and drown. When he is in bed at night, have your loyal men care for him in his tent. Check on him at least ten times each and every night! For I long to see this remarkable pygmy more than I covet all the precious gifts of Sinai and Punt.

PHARAOHS REINVENTED

C.2181–1550 BC

This sphinx of the 12th Dynasty pharaoh Amenemhat II
was discovered at Tanis. It is also inscribed with the
names of later Egyptian kings.

LOCAL RULE
THE FIRST INTERMEDIATE PERIOD

7th–early 11th Dynasties c.2181–2055 BC

THE FIRST INTERMEDIATE PERIOD SUFFERED FROM THE DECENTRALIZED CONTROL THAT HAD ALREADY TROUBLED the 5th and 6th Dynasties. As the monarchy grew increasingly feeble the hereditary provincial rulers, known today by the Greek term *nomarch*, grew correspondingly strong until they were able to assume many of pharaoh's traditional duties. Egypt came to be ruled by two independent dynasties, one based in the north, at Herakleopolis and one, which emerged later, at Thebes. The shortage of First Intermediate Period royal monuments and writings means that little is known of the pharaohs of this time beyond their names; in compensation, the busy provincial cemeteries and informal writings allow us to understand more of the lives of the ordinary Egyptians.

The Middle Kingdom scribe Ipuwer, looking back from a comfortable time of peace, prosperity and central government, depicted the First Intermediate Period as an un-natural age of violence and starvation; a time when certainties were cast aside as the poor turned against the rich and the defenceless dead were targeted by the desperate living. He was not alone. Ipuwer's work belongs to a genre of 'pessimistic literature' which deliberately exaggerates the horrors of a *maat*-less, uncontrolled age in order to vaunt the benefits of unity and central control. Earlier Egyptologists, seduced by these writings, classified the First Intermediate Period as a dark age of little interest to anyone.

MERELY A TRANSITIONAL PHASE?

That the Egyptians themselves regarded this as a different, or transitional, period is clear from the Sakkara king list, which omits the First Intermediate Period altogether. Yet although increasingly aridity and bureaucratic failures undoubtedly disrupted the highly centralized food distribution network, causing occasional shortages and doubtless some hunger, archaeology confirms that it would be wrong to take Ipuwer's account at face value. Food shortages were far from unusual even during the time of strong rule and, far from being a time of grinding poverty, the First Intermediate Period actually saw life improve for many. While the royal cemeteries show an abrupt decline in large-scale funerary monuments the provincial cemeteries show a trend towards social levelling and, with popular culture flourishing, there are interesting developments in pottery forms, artistic styles and grave goods, including the provision of cartonage mummy masks and wooden servant models who will work for the deceased in the afterlife. It is at this time that the exclusively royal Pyramid Texts are abandoned and replaced by the Coffin Texts: spells painted on the wooden coffins of the élite.

7TH–10TH DYNASTY RULERS

c. 2181–2160 BC Dynasties 7 and 8: A series of ephemeral pharaohs, many named Neferkare.

c. 2160–2025 BC Dynasties 9 and 10: A series of 19 pharaohs from Herakleopolis, including:

Khety (Meryibre)

Khety (Nebkaure)

Khety (Wahkare)

Merikare

THE COFFIN TEXTS

Like the earlier Pyramid Texts, the Coffin Texts were a collection of spells designed to help the deceased to live again after death. However, whereas the Pyramid Texts were restricted to the royal family, the Coffin Texts were available to everyone. At the end of the Old Kingdom the once exclusively royal kingdom of Osiris – the land of the dead – opened its gates wide, and anyone who could afford the correct funerary rituals (mummification, a tomb and a set of Coffin Text spells) could now hope to live for ever outside the confines of the tomb.

Utterance: You shine forth as the two feathers of [the god] Soped. Revered before [the god] Hapy, Nakht-Ankh, justified. Revered before [the goddess] Tefnut, Nakht-Ankh, child of Khnum-Aa. Utterance: may the donkeys come down for you.

Text from the 12th Dynasty coffin of Nakht-Ankh

The Middle Kingdom papyrus known as the Admonitions of Ipuwer *portrays Egypt during the First Intermediate Period as beset by anarchy and natural disasters. However, it is not a historical text but rather a philosophical discourse on the theme of 'order versus chaos'.*

A fig-wood statue from the 11th Dynasty, depicting the chief magician Hetepi (now in the Louvre, Paris). In his right hand the figure carries a bag containing his ritual implements.

The 7th and 8th Dynasties consist of a series of simultaneous, ephemeral local rulers, each of whom claimed, falsely, to rule the whole land. Manetho tells us that 70 7th Dynasty pharaohs ruled for 70 days; it seems likely that this is a neat exaggeration intended to convey the chaotic nature of this time. The 8th Dynasty has a more believable 17 kings, ruling for a total of 20 years from Memphis. At least one of these pharaohs, Qakara Ibi, had the resources to build a small pyramid at Sakkara.

After a century of weak rule a line of northern kings emerged at Herakleopolis (modern Ihnasiya el-Medina; close by the entrance to the Faiyum basin). Manetho split these rulers between Dynasties 9 and 10 but this seems in many ways an unnecessary division. The kings continued the tradition of pyramid burial but they lacked the resources of the Old Kingdom pharaohs and their small-scale tombs are almost entirely lost. One exception stands in the desert at Dara, Middle Egypt. What is now a shapeless heap of rubble was once an impressive mud-brick pyramid almost the size of the Step Pyramid. A second collapsed pyramid, the Sakkara 'Headless Pyramid', may also belong to this period (see also p.50). The names and deeds of the Herakleopolitan kings have largely been forgotten, although Manetho speaks of the brutal reign of the 9th Dynasty pharaoh Achthoes (Khety), who was first driven mad, then eaten by a crocodile. The more benign pharaoh Nebkaure is mentioned in the fictional Middle Kingdom Tale of the Eloquent Peasant, while the final Herakleopolitan king, Merikare, features in the Middle Kingdom wisdom text known as the Teachings Addressed to King Merikare, a treatise on kingship addressed by an anonymous old pharaoh to his young son. Merikare was to die shortly before his dynasty fell to the 11th Dynasty Theban ruler, Montuhotep II.

ANKHTIFI OF MO'ALLA

Ankhtifi was the nomarch, 'Great Overlord' and 'Overseer of Priests' of the Second and Third southern Egyptian provinces during the First Intermediate Period. His pillared rock-cut tomb, cut into a pyramid-like cliff at his home town of Mo'alla (25 miles [40 km] to the south of Thebes), includes a series of quasi-royal illustrations plus a detailed autobiography which tells how Ankhtifi was called upon to subdue a coalition of rebels from Thebes and Coptos, and to pacify Edfu.

Ankhtifi makes it obvious that he, rather than the distant and powerless pharaoh Neferkare (who is named only once) has assumed responsibility for the poor and unfortunate. He is effectively maintaining *maat* in his own land, and he takes his orders directly from the god Horus: 'all of Upper Egypt was dying of starvation and people were eating their children, but I did not allow anyone to starve to death in this nome ...'

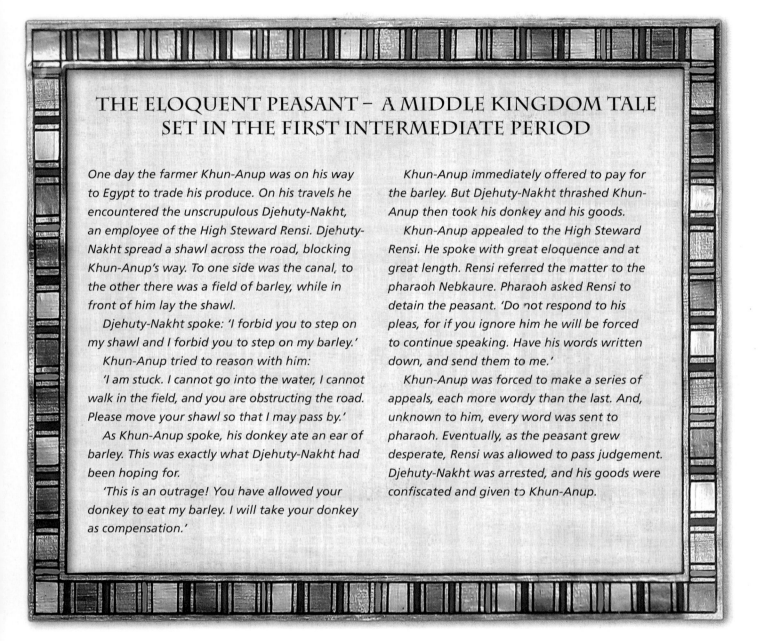

THE ELOQUENT PEASANT – A MIDDLE KINGDOM TALE SET IN THE FIRST INTERMEDIATE PERIOD

One day the farmer Khun-Anup was on his way to Egypt to trade his produce. On his travels he encountered the unscrupulous Djehuty-Nakht, an employee of the High Steward Rensi. Djehuty-Nakht spread a shawl across the road, blocking Khun-Anup's way. To one side was the canal, to the other there was a field of barley, while in front of him lay the shawl.

Djehuty-Nakht spoke: 'I forbid you to step on my shawl and I forbid you to step on my barley.'

Khun-Anup tried to reason with him:

'I am stuck. I cannot go into the water, I cannot walk in the field, and you are obstructing the road. Please move your shawl so that I may pass by.'

As Khun-Anup spoke, his donkey ate an ear of barley. This was exactly what Djehuty-Nakht had been hoping for.

'This is an outrage! You have allowed your donkey to eat my barley. I will take your donkey as compensation.'

Khun-Anup immediately offered to pay for the barley. But Djehuty-Nakht thrashed Khun-Anup then took his donkey and his goods.

Khun-Anup appealed to the High Steward Rensi. He spoke with great eloquence and at great length. Rensi referred the matter to the pharaoh Nebkaure. Pharaoh asked Rensi to detain the peasant. 'Do not respond to his pleas, for if you ignore him he will be forced to continue speaking. Have his words written down, and send them to me.'

Khun-Anup was forced to make a series of appeals, each more wordy than the last. And, unknown to him, every word was sent to pharaoh. Eventually, as the peasant grew desperate, Rensi was allowed to pass judgement. Djehuty-Nakht was arrested, and his goods were confiscated and given to Khun-Anup.

Do justice, then you will endure on Earth. Comfort the weeper; do not oppress the widow. Do not expel a man from his father's property; do not take the possessions of the nobles. Beware of punishing wrongly. Do not kill, it does not become you. Punish with beatings and with detention. Thus the land will be well-controlled.

THE TEACHINGS ADDRESSED TO KING MERIKARE

REUNITED
THE WARRIORS OF THEBES

11th Dynasty c.2125 – 1985 BC

As the Herakleopolitan pharaohs ruled the north, a line of Theban rulers emerged to control the south. These are confusing and ill-documented times, but it seems that the Theban 11th Dynasty was descended from the nomarch Intef, 'Great Overlord' and 'Overseer of Priests'. This first Intef, aware of his limitations, never claimed the title pharaoh. He was succeeded by Montuhotep I 'the ancestor', who also neglected to claim the title, but who was awarded it posthumously by his descendants. Montuhotep was followed by his two sons.

11TH DYNASTY RULERS

First Intermediate Period

? Intef

? Montuhotep I 'The Ancestor'

c.2125 BC Intef I (Sehertawy)

c.2112 BC Intef II (Wahankh)

c.2063 BC Intef III (Nakhtnebtepnefer)

Middle Kingdom

c.2055 BC Montuhotep II (Nebhepetre)

c.2004 BC Montuhotep III (Sankhkare)

c.1992 BC Montuhotep IV (Nebtawyre)

Later sources imply that Intef I did claim kingship by writing his name in a cartouche, but has left no contemporary inscriptions to confirm this. His brother, Intef II known as Intef the Great, ruled for 50 years. His reign saw a determined expansion of the Theban-held territories and the renovation of many local temples. The next pharaoh, Intef III (son of Intef I) continued the policy of aggression against the Herakleopolitans, but built little. The Turin Canon allocates him a reign of eight years.

UNIFIER OF THE TWO LANDS

Montuhotep II Nebhepetre (who is occasionally and very confusingly referenced as Montuhotep I) enjoyed 14 years of relatively peaceful local rule before resuming the push northwards. Battlefields are notoriously difficult for archaeologists to trace, but evidence for Montuhotep's campaign is provided by the Theban 'Tomb of the Warriors', a mass grave housing a group of 11th Dynasty soldiers who had been wrapped, unmummified, in linen so that their bodies were preserved through natural dehydration. By Year 39 Montuhotep 'Unifier of the Two Lands' had defeated his Herakleopolitan enemies, won the allegiance of the nomarchs, reunited Egypt, developed a full royal titulary and established a new capital at Thebes. For this magnificent achievement he is recognized as the first pharaoh of the Middle Kingdom, a decision which leaves the 11th Dynasty and, indeed, his own reign, uncomfortably split between two very different 'periods'. Later Egyptians would classify him, along with Men and the New Kingdom pharaoh Ahmose, as one of the three great unifiers of their land.

Seated statue in painted sandstone of Montuhotep II wearing the red crown of Lower Egypt. This artefact was found in the ruler's mortuary complex at Deir el-Bahri.

Montuhotep was a self-proclaimed 'son of Hathor' who wore the tall feathers of the gods Amen and Min. He campaigned in Palestine and Nubia, reorganized the Theban court so that it could better administer the state, and introduced a national programme of monumental building works as a very obvious means of stressing the restoration of *maat*. His most impressive undertaking was his temple-tomb, built in the shelter of a natural bay at Deir el-Bahri, on the west bank of the Nile at Thebes. Set in tree-planted gardens, the tomb was a tiered mastaba which may have been topped by a small pyramid.

MONTUHOTEP II
NEBHEPETRE

Dynasty: 11th
Father: Intef III
Mother: Iah
Consorts: Nefru, Tem
Burial place: Deir el-
Bahri, Thebes
Successor:
Montuhotep III

The complex included terraces, walkways, a columned hall and a sanctuary cut into the living rock of the cliff. The granite-lined burial chamber included a huge alabaster shrine which served as Montuhotep's sarcophagus.

AMENEMHAT'S ADVENTURE

After 52 years of strong rule Montuhotep died and was replaced by his son Montuhotep III. His 12-year reign saw continuing missions to the quarries and to Nubia, a trading mission to Punt, and building projects at Abydos, Armant, Thebes, Tod and Elephantine. A large-scale tomb to the south of Deir el-Bahri was once assigned to Montuhotep, but archaeology suggests that it is equally likely to have been built by the 12th Dynasty pharaoh Amenemhat I.

While Manetho places 'Ammenemes' (Amenemhat I), the first king of the 12th Dynasty, immediately after Montuhotep III, the Turin Canon allows a gap of seven years when, it seems, Egypt was ruled by Montuhotep IV. The son of the non-royal mother Imi, we know nothing of the new pharaoh's paternity and very little about his reign, although a series of inscriptions in the Wadi Hammamat tells the remarkable adventures of an expeditionary force led by his vizier Amenemhat. The intrepid vizier, intent on quarrying a stone to make his king's sarcophagus lid, witnessed two extraordinary events: first a pregnant gazelle gave birth on the very stone that had been chosen for the lid, then a spectacular rainstorm provided the thirsty adventurers with clean water. The death of Montuhotep IV marked the end of the 11th Dynasty.

THE THEBAN *SAFF* TOMBS

The rulers of the 11th Dynasty believed themselves to be Egypt's true pharaohs but, isolated from the traditional northern cemeteries and constrained by the narrow Nile Valley, they were forced to abandon the full-scale royal pyramid and develop their own funerary architecture. Intefs I, II and III were interred in rock-cut *saff* tombs in the local cemetery of el-Tarif, where their three large tombs were accompanied by the smaller tombs of the Theban élite. The impressively large tomb known today as the Saff Dawaba, which is attributed on the basis of its pottery to Intef I, is the best preserved of the three.

The *saff* tombs were constructed by driving a flat face into a sloping desert terrace until it attained the necessary height to serve as a façade. A doorway was carved directly into the face, the tomb chapel was cut into the living rock and a shaft allowed access to the burial chamber. *Saff* (literally 'row') refers to the lines of square pillars and doors that decorate the tomb façades. Some of the *saff* tombs may have had small pyramids in their courtyards, but no trace of these pyramids has survived.

THE QUEENS OF DEIR EL-BAHRI

Within his funerary complex Montuhotep II built tombs for his sister-wife Nefru, and for Tem, the mother of his successor, Montuhotep III. Separate shaft graves and chapels were provided for another six royal women: the wives Ashayt, Henhenet and Sadeh, the ladies Kemsit and Kawit, and the five-year old Mayet who is assumed to have been a royal daughter. The five adults were all priestesses of Hathor, patron goddess of the Deir el-Bahri bay, and all six had been buried at roughly the same time.

The terraced mortuary temple of Montuhotep II is situated on the west bank of the Nile opposite the city of Thebes (modern Luxor).

Henhenet's mummy reveals that she died in childbirth; her narrow pelvis had made it impossible for her to deliver a full-sized baby. Kawit's carved sarcophagus features one of several Middle Kingdom hairdressing scenes: such scenes were intended to symbolise sexual potency and rebirth.

PEACE AND PROSPERITY
AMENEMHAT AND HIS DESCENDANTS

12th Dynasty c.1985–1773 BC

THE MIDDLE KINGDOM WAS INSPIRED BY THE GLORIOUS, NEVER FORGOTTEN DAYS OF THE OLD KINGDOM. THE new pharaohs adopted the same propaganda as their predecessors; there were campaigns to quash the traditional enemies, trade missions to Lebanon and Punt and impressive pyramid complexes designed to emphasize pharaoh's hard-won authority over Egypt's resources. This appearance of continuity is, however, an illusion. The First Intermediate Period had left its mark and the pharaohs of the Middle Kingdom could never become the remote, arrogant, god-like individuals that the Old Kingdom pharaohs had been. A new realism is reflected in the royal statuary which reveals a more human, almost careworn face of kingship.

12TH DYNASTY RULERS

c.1985 BC Amenemhat I
(Sehetepibre)

c.1956 BC Senwosret I
(Kheperkare)

c.1911 BC Amenemhat II
(Nubkaure)

c.1877 BC Senwosret II
(Khakheperre)

c.1870 BC Senwosret III
(Khakaure)

c.1831 BC Amenemhat III
(Nimaatre)

c.1786 BC Amenemhat IV
(Maakherure)

c.1777 BC Sobeknofru
(Sobekkare) (female
pharaoh)

Later Egyptians, looking back to the Middle Kingdom, recognized in it a golden era of peace and prosperity. Arts, crafts and literature flourished as strong kings raised pyramids and stone temples to their gods. Today, with much of the Middle Kingdom architecture lost and the pyramids stripped to their rubble and sand cores, it can be hard to recapture this sense of an inspiring classical age.

A PHARAOH FROM THE SOUTH

Amenemhat I, 12th Dynasty pharaoh of Egypt, is almost certainly to be equated with Amenemhat, 11th Dynasty vizier, overseer of the south, and witness to two desert miracles. We do not know how Amenemhat seized his throne, but as the Wadi Hammamat inscription tells us that he had 10,000 loyal men under his command, he may not have found it too difficult. His throne name (Sehetepibre: 'He who pacifies the heart of Re') and Horus name (Sehetepibtawy: 'He who pacifies the heart of the Two Lands') certainly suggest that the new pharaoh saw himself as a unifier or restorer, and this impression is confirmed by the fictional Middle Kingdom text known as the Prophecy of Neferti, which celebrates Amenemhat as the hero who rescues Egypt from chaos. A second Horus name, Wehem-mesut ('Repeater of births' or

Pillar statue of Senwosret I (Kheperkare) as Osiris, from the Karnak temple of Amen. The king's devotion to Osiris encouraged Egypt's élite to raise stelae and shrines in honour of the god of the dead.

AMENEMHAT I

Dynasty: 12th
Father: 'God's Father' Senwosret?
Mother: Nefret
Consort: Neferitatjenen
Burial place: Lisht
Successor: Senwosret I

'Renaissance') indicates that he intended his reign to be both a new beginning and a continuation of the old ways.

Amenemhat moved his court northwards from Thebes to the purpose-built city of Amenemhat-Itj-Tawy ('Amenemhat seizer of the Two Lands'). His new capital, which is now entirely lost, lay not far from Memphis and was conveniently close to the entrance to the fertile Faiyum depression. Lisht, which we presume was near Itj-Tawy, became the royal necropolis. At this burial place Amenemhat raised the last royal pyramid to be built entirely of stone blocks, some of which he thriftily recycled from the nearby Old Kingdom pyramid cemeteries.

The new pharaoh, aware of Egypt's vulnerable northeastern border, instigated a series of campaigns against the Asiatics. The 'Walls-of-the-Ruler', a fort or, perhaps, a chain of forts, now protected the eastern frontier and it seems likely that the eastern Delta was similarly protected against the Libyan nomads. Regnal Year 29 saw a successful mission in Lower Nubia, while Year 30 saw a brief campaign to subdue the Libyans. There were building works at many of Egypt's major temples (including Tod, Armant, Karnak, Koptos, Dendera, Memphis and Bubastis), and at least one quarrying expedition to the Wadi Hammamat. As Egypt grew wealthy the bureaucracy expanded and an efficient taxation system developed.

PIONEER OF JOINT RULE

Acutely conscious of the need to strengthen central authority, Amenemhat implemented a series of political reforms designed to reduce the influence of the nomarchs. Plus, in order to ensure a trouble-free succession he introduced the idea of the co-regency, nominating his son, Senwosret, as his junior partner and allowing him to take charge of Egypt's defences.

THE STORY OF SINUHE

Prince Senwosret was returning from a successful campaign against the Libyan tribes when messengers arrived from the palace. 'The king is dead!' The prince abandoned his troops and rushed to the palace to claim his inheritance.

Meanwhile the courtier Sinuhe, 'a servant of the royal harem assigned to the princess Nefru, wife of King Senwosret and daughter of Pharaoh Amenemhat', suffered a disproportionate reaction to the news of pharaoh's death: his senses were disturbed and he trembled all over. Most unaccountably – unless, perhaps, he was somehow involved in the murderous plot – Sinuhe ran away, passing the Walls-of-the-Ruler and entering the land of the Asiatics. He was to spend many years in exile, raising a family of foreign sons, before returning home to die.

The pragmatic expedient of co-regency flew in the face of the time-honoured principle of the dead Osiris father passing the throne to his living Horus son, but the royal family were prepared to overlook this inconvenient inconsistency and the co-regency would be used throughout the 12th Dynasty, and again during the New Kingdom, as a means of ensuring that the preferred successor inherited the crown. Amenemhat's early nomination of a successor, however, would have done little to endear him to his own family and this may go some way towards explaining why, after three decades of irreproachable rule, he was assassinated. The details of his death are related in the 'Instruction of King Amenemhat', which claims to be a posthumous letter addressed by the deceased king to his successor Senwosret I.

> As I began to drift into sleep, the very weapons which should have been used to protect me were turned against me while I was like a snake of the desert. I awoke with a jump, alert for the fight, and found that it was a combat with the guard. Had I been able to seize my weapon I would have beaten back the cowards single handed, but no one is strong at night. No one can fight alone and no success can be achieved without a helper...

As we have already seen at the Old Kingdom court, accounts of crimes against the pharaoh – the ultimate chaotic crime against *maat* – are few and far between. It therefore comes as little surprise that we have no official record of Amenemhat's murder and can only deduce that he was killed at night, as he slept, by his own bodyguard. However, the Middle Kingdom Story of Sinuhe, an epic and almost certainly fictional tale of travel and adventure outside the controlled safety of Egypt's borders, offers partial confirmation of the uncertain state of affairs following Amenemhat's sudden death.

SENWOSRET I

Dynasty: 12th

Father: Amenemhat I

Mother: Neferitatjenen

Consort: Nofru

Burial place: Lisht

Successor: Amenemhat II

THE GOLDEN YEARS

Senwosret I continued to strengthen Egypt's borders. Nubia was colonized as far south as the second cataract, and an enormous mud-brick fort was raised at Buhen to protect the interests of the Egyptian traders who were now engaged in a vigorous exploitation of the abundant local resources which included gold, granite, diorite and amethyst. There were further missions to the Wadi Hammamat, the development of the Coptos gold mines, and expeditions to the desert oases and to the east, where Senwosret rejoiced in the far-from-subtle title 'the throat-slitter of Asia'.

Back home there were innovative building projects at Elephantine, Coptos and Abydos where the temple of Osiris, Foremost of the Westerners, was totally rebuilt; here the king's conspicuous devotion to Osiris encouraged Egypt's élite to raise stelae and shrines in honour of the god of the dead. At Heliopolis, Senwosret marked his *sed*-festival by erecting a pair of red granite obelisks, each over 20 metres (66 ft) tall and weighing 121 tons, in the temple of Re. While Re's temple has today completely vanished, one of Senwosret's obelisks still stands.

The next year saw the building of the 'White Chapel', a beautifully carved alabaster boat shrine in the Karnak temple of Amen. The walls of the chapel were carved with the register of nomes: details of the provinces, their measurements, towns and gods.

Detail of a section of the wall inscriptions in the 'White Chapel' of Senwosret I in the Karnak temple of Amen. Comprising lists of the 'nomes' (regions) of Egypt, the inscriptions specify their size, their principal towns and the number of cattle herds in each.

Senwosret, well aware of the importance of efficient administration, ordered that the nome-boundaries be reorganized and redefined by boundary stelae, and that local governors of proven loyalty replace less reliable colleagues. The vizier now effectively ran Egypt on pharaoh's behalf. This new system of centralized control was put to the test when, in Year 25, Egypt was overwhelmed by a famine whose effects were to be felt for many years thereafter.

Senwosret raised his pyramid at Lisht just over a mile (1.6 km) to the south of his father's mortuary complex. Here, after 30 years of solo rule plus a further three years as senior co-regent with his son, he was buried by his chosen successor, Amenemhat II.

In many ways the 34-year reign of Amenemhat II was the unremarkable continuation of what had gone before. There was a successful mission to Punt, several expeditions to Sinai, and a continuous participation in the thriving Mediterranean diplomatic and trade network that led to jewellery bearing Amenemhat's cartouche being included in the royal tombs at Byblos, and Egyptian artefacts

AMENEMHAT II

Dynasty: 12th
Father: Senwosret I
Mother: Nofru
Consort: unknown
Burial place: Dahshur
Successor:
    Senwosret II

being exported to Crete. Conversely, Minoan pottery has been discovered at several Middle Kingdom domestic sites, while the 'Tod Treasure', four bronze chests discovered in the temple of Montu at Tod, yielded silver, lapis lazuli and gold objects of Minoan or Syrian origin.

EXPLOITING THE FERTILE FAIYUM

Amenemhat's reign saw the first serious economic exploitation of the Faiyum, with the development of a network of canals and dykes, and the widening of the Bar Yusuf canal linking the Faiyum to the Nile, designed to reduce the waters flowing into Lake Moeris and allow the reclamation of fertile land. This emphasis on the Faiyum may explain why Amenemhat II abandoned the Lisht cemetery, building a simplified pyramid complex to the east of the Red Pyramid at Dahshur. His pyramid was robbed in antiquity, but the associated tombs of the royal princesses yielded the 'Dahshur Treasure', a collection of jewellery including diadems and pectorals. Amenemhat II was succeeded by his co-regent, and probable son, Senwosret II.

The peaceful seven-year reign of Senwosret II saw the continued development of the Faiyum irrigation scheme. Senwosret built his pyramid complex at Lahun (also known as Illahun or Kahun), close by the opening to the Faiyum. Here he constructed a mud-brick pyramid over a natural stone core, casing the whole in fine limestone. Unusually, the entrance to his pyramid was situated not on the traditional north face but to the south, where it was hidden amongst the shaft tombs built for the king's daughters. The incorporation of this simple security measure suggests that the pyramid builders were starting to feel threatened by the tomb robbers who preyed remorselessly on all of Egypt's dead. Sadly, the misplaced entrance did not fool the ancient thieves who may, of course, have been the very workmen responsible for disguising the entrance.

SENWOSRET II

Dynasty: 12th

Father:
  Amenemhat II ?

Mother: ?

Consort:
  Khnemetneferhedjet

Burial place: Lahun

Successor:
  Senwosret III

Senwosret's complex included a queen's pyramid, a row of eight mastabas which, curiously, lacked burial shafts, and four shaft tombs. These tombs, too, were robbed in antiquity but the shaft tomb of Princess Sithathoriunet, yielded the 'Illahun Treasure': five mud-coated boxes of jewellery and toiletries which had been hidden in a recess.

Near Senwosret's pyramid, on the desert edge, was the town built to house the priests, scribes and labourers who would first build the pyramid complex and then maintain pharaoh's funerary cult in theory for all eternity (although archaeology indicates that the town was actually abandoned after a century of occupation). Today this town is known as Kahun or Lahun; the Egyptians knew it as Hetep-Senwosret, or 'Senwosret is Satisfied'.

Bounded by a thick mud-brick wall, the square town was divided by wide, straight streets with central, stone-lined drains. It offered a variety of accommodation, ranging from back-to-back terraces of three-roomed single-storied houses provided for the more humble residents to large estates complete with bathrooms, granaries and garden pools for the most important. The 'acropolis', once identified as a possible royal residence, is likely to be another large estate. It has been estimated that, in its heyday, Kahun was home to as many as 5000 residents.

Although approximately half of the town of Kahun is today lost under modern cultivation, it has yielded up an invaluable and unique assortment of artefacts used by ordinary Egyptians in their daily life, including an extensive collection of pottery, wooden and basketry work tools, religious artefacts and children's toys (see page 78). Papyri found at the site include letters, wills, medical texts and Egypt's only known veterinary papyrus.

MILITARY CAMPAIGNS

Although we have no regnal year date later than Year 19 the Turin Canon accords Senwosret III a reign of 30 years, while archaeology suggests that he may have ruled for an additional seven years.

SENWOSRET III
Dynasty: 12th
Father: Senwosret II
Mother: Khnemetneferhedjet
Consort: Khnemetneferhedjet II
Burial place: Dahsur?
Successor: Amenemhat III

Manetho tells us that the new pharaoh was unusually tall (4 cubits, 4 palms 2 fingers breadth; over 6ft 6 inches; 2 metres) and a great warrior. The latter certainly seems to be true: it was under Senwosret's early rule, starting in Year 8, that Nubia was finally subdued in a series of viciously efficient military campaigns which were followed by a phase of brutal punishments and ended with Senwosret being worshipped as a local god. There would be brief campaigns in Years 15 and 19 but to all intents and purposes Nubia was now an Egyptian province. Senwosret continued the efforts of his namesake, Senwosret I, not only to crush the Nubians but also to build fortresses to hold conquered territory. Under Senwosret III a great series of mud-brick fortresses grew from the rocky cliffs and islands of the second Nile cataract, making this the effective southern border of Egypt's Middle Kingdom empire. Economic factors played an important part in this empire, and Senwosret ordered that the old canal bypassing the first cataract at Aswan be widened and cleaned to facilitate the transport of gold and other products.

Nubia was not Senwosret's only target. There was at least one Palestinian campaign, and the Abydos autobiography of the soldier Khusobek confirms that 'his majesty proceeded northwards to overthrow the Mentiu of Asia … and then the soldiers of the army were engaged in close combat with the Asiatics …' Execration texts, lists of enemies recorded on ritually smashed

THE 'TWO BROTHERS'

The undecorated tomb of the 'Two Brothers' was cut high in the cliffs above the village of Rifeh, Middle Egypt. Discovered in 1907 by Flinders Petrie, the undisturbed 12th Dynasty tomb yielded the modest funerary equipment of two men, Khnum-Nakht and Nakht-Ankh. Their grave goods included painted wooden box-coffins, a canopic chest, wooden servant models, figurines of the deceased and two model boats which would allow them to make a symbolic pilgrimage to Abydos.

The entire tomb group was donated to the Manchester Museum where, in 1908, the mummies were unwrapped by a team of scientists led by Egyptologist Margaret Murray. More recently, the bodies have been examined by the Manchester Egyptian Mummy Research Project, headed by Professor Rosalie David. This work has revealed that the two men suffered a range of illnesses and dental problems. The precise relationship between the 'Brothers', whose skeletons suggest that they may have had a different racial heritage, has not yet been conclusively proved.

I have made my boundary further south than my fathers. I have added to what was bequeathed to me. I am a king who speaks and acts. That which my heart plans is done by my arm.

FROM THE BOUNDARY STELA OF SENWOSRET III ESTABLISHED AT SEMNA, NUBIA, IN YEAR 16

Colossal head of Senwosret III in pink granite. The pharaoh has the large ears and almond-shaped eyes which typify 12th Dynasty royal sculpture.

pottery, demonstrate a serious attempt to destroy Egypt's eastern enemies by remote, magical means.

Meanwhile political reforms back home reduced the powers of the local governors. The country was now to be divided into three administrative districts: North, South and Head of the South (Elephantine and northern Nubia) and the districts were to be governed by a council reporting directly to the vizier. This re-establishment of central authority is most obvious in the provincial cemeteries, which hold fewer élite burials and more middle-class tombs.

WAR BOOTY FUNDS BUILDING

The hard-won Nubian gold was used to renew and redecorate the temples of Armant, Tod, Herakleopolis and Hierakonpolis. Records confirm a donation of six life-sized statues of Senwosret to the Deir el-Bahri tomb of Montuhotep II, and the refurbishing of the sacred boat and chapel of Osiris at Abydos. Medamud, to the north of Thebes, received a new temple dedicated to Montu, and there was investment in the Karnak temple of Amen.

Senwosret returned to Dahshur to build a mud-brick, limestone-covered pyramid constructed around a mud-brick core whose crevices were filled with sand. Although a granite sarcophagus was discovered in the burial chamber, there is no evidence to prove that the pyramid was actually used for the pharaoh's burial. However, some of the royal women were buried within the pyramid complex, and underground galleries have yielded the looted remnants of the burials of Sithathor (daughter of Senwosret II) and Meret (wife of Senwosret III). Three separate caches of jewellery, the 'Dahshur Treasure', were recovered from the royal cemetery.

Senwosret built a second tomb at Abydos. This new tomb combined elements of the northern pyramid enclosure, the southern *saff*-tomb and the archaic Abydene complex. Against the cliff a large T-shaped enclosure allowed access to a lengthy curving passage leading to several underground chambers. A causeway led across the desert to a chapel on the edge of the cultivation. To all intents and purposes this was a cenotaph and, as at Dahshur, there is no firm evidence that it was used for Senwosret's burial. However, below ground the architects had installed a sophisticated system of anti-theft devices which suggest that this 'cenotaph' may, after all, have served a practical purpose.

A LONG AND STABLE REIGN

Amenemhat III, son, co-regent and successor to Senwosret III, ruled Egypt for 45 well-regulated years which saw further exploitation of the Faiyum, the strengthening of the southern border and many successful expeditions to the stone quarries and the Sinai mines. Amenemhat built throughout Egypt but his projects were focused on the Faiyum, where he raised two lakeside seated colossi at Biahmu and founded a small temple to the snake goddess Renenutet at Medinet Maadi as well as an extensive temple to the crocodile-headed god Sobek at Kiman Faris (Greek: Crocodilopolis).

Like his father before him, Amenemhat built two tombs. This time both were pyramids, and both were raised in the north. His Dahshur pyramid was a mud-brick, limestone-cased structure. Pharaoh's limestone-lined burial suite could be entered via both the eastern and the western faces, and a series of corridors and stairways led to rooms, storerooms, a chapel and the burial chamber. On the south face two separate entrances led to two queens' tombs within the pyramid masonry. One, belonging to Queen Aat, has yielded a sarcophagus, canopic chest, sundry burial equipment and human bone. The other has yielded the remains of a rich burial. The queens' tombs were linked via a corridor to each other and to the king's suite.

AMENEMHAT III

Dynasty: 12th
Father: Senwosret III
Mother: unknown
Consort: Aat?
Burial place: Hawara
Successor:
    Amenemhat IV

Amenemhat III, as portrayed in a copper alloy statue smaller than life-sized.

FUN AND GAMES AT KAHUN

The children of Kahun played with wooden spinning tops, and eleven short, shaped wooden sticks have been identified as the 'cats' used in an ancient version of the traditional British game 'tipcat' or 'piggy'. In the modern version of the game a hard piece of wood, the 'cat' is laid across a flat stone or brick and then hit with a stick so that it flies up into the air. The aim is to strike the airborne cat with the stick so that it travels as far as possible.

It can be difficult for archaeologists to distinguish children's dolls and toys from small votive offerings or funerary models, but a herd of small clay animals recovered from Kahun have been accepted as toys modelled for or by children. The collection includes a pig, a crocodile, a hippopotamus, an ape, a man and a boat. Kahun has also yielded a collection of dolls, and even a 'doll maker's workshop' where Flinders Petrie discovered bundles of hair waiting to be implanted into small wooden heads.

I have seen this building, and know that it is beyond my power to describe it. It must have cost more in labour and money than all the walls and public works of the Greeks put together...

HERODOTUS (*HISTORIES* II: 148) DESCRIBES THE 'LABYRINTH'; ACTUALLY THE MORTUARY TEMPLE OF AMENEMHAT III

Amenemhat's second pyramid, built at Hawara, followed a very different plan. It was smaller and flatter than the Dahshur pyramid, and had only one entrance. Internally there were more security measures including trapdoors and blocked passageways. Most secure of all, the burial chamber was hollowed from a massive block of quartzite and roofed with three large granite slabs. This ingenious, doorless room could only be entered via the ceiling, and could only be sealed after the burial, when the one raised ceiling slab, which rested temporarily on pillars supported by sand, was lowered mechanically into place by releasing the sand. Needless to say, this did not deter the robbers: they simply hacked a hole through the ceiling. The pyramid mortuary temple was of such a complicated design, with a confusing number of courtyards, halls and passageways, that the classical authors, visiting when the temple had fallen into disrepair, believed it to be the remains of the labyrinth which inspired Daedalus to build the famous labyrinth of Crete.

PTAHNOFRU AND SOBEKNOFRU

The obvious prosperity of Amenemhat's lengthy reign makes it difficult to understand how his dynasty could collapse soon after his death. The erratic behaviour of the Nile may have been a contributing factor; official records from Nubia show that, while flood levels were high at the beginning of his reign, they had fallen dramatically by Year 40. It may, however, be that the late 12th Dynasty suffered from something as simple as a lack of a suitable male successor and, given the clear

Pyramid of Amenemhat III at Hawara. The elaborate security measures that this ruler put in place to try and prevent the desecration of his burial failed to deter grave-robbers.

evidence for multiple royal wives at this time, it seems likely that the absence of one, universally acknowledged heir was made worse by a proliferation of distantly related potential male successors.

Support for this theory comes from Amenemhat's Hawara pyramid. This has yielded an alabaster table and some jars and duck-shaped vessels inscribed for the princess Ptahnofru. The burial chamber held the remains of two wooden coffins, two canopic chests and two uninscribed quartzite sarcophagi: a large, well-made sarcophagus intended for the pharaoh, and a smaller, cruder version created between the larger sarcophagus and the chamber wall, which was presumably intended for Ptahnofru. The crude sarcophagus must have been made when the king's sarcophagus was already in place, although not necessarily before his burial. A second pyramid, just over a mile (1.6 km) away, has yielded a large pink granite sarcophagus inscribed for Ptahnofru. This suggests that the princess, having died before her own tomb was complete, was temporarily interred in her father's pyramid, but was moved out of her father's burial chamber before his interment saw the lowering of the ceiling. Today Ptahnofru's own pyramid is collapsed and waterlogged, its burial chamber inaccessible.

The unusually close relationship between Amenemhat III and his daughter, and Ptahnofru's use of a cartouche in her later inscriptions, suggests she was her father's intended successor. But, with Ptahnofru already dead, Amenemhat III was succeeded, briefly and unremarkably, by Amenemhat IV, a king who is generally thought to have been either the son or grandson of Amenemhat III. His death, after a nine-year reign, saw his widow Sobeknofru, daughter of Amenemhat III, take the throne.

There is no reason to assume that Sobeknofru was a temporary regent ruling on behalf of an infant son. Indeed, there is no evidence that she had a son, and a cylinder seal confirms her personal status by presenting her name, 'The Female Hawk, beloved of Re', in a *serekh* topped with a falcon. The Turin Canon allows her a reign of three years, ten months and 24 days: her inclusion in the king lists is a sure sign that her rule was acceptable to subsequent pharaohs. And, although Sobeknofru concentrated her building activities on the Faiyum, an inscription dating to the third year of her reign, discovered at the Nubian fortress of Kumma, confirms that she ruled a united Egypt.

Centuries of tradition dictated that, whatever the real situation, pharaohs should always appear as young, fit and male, while women should be slender, pale and passive. This gave royal artists a headache. How to present a female king? An uneasy compromise was reached. While the scribes gave their new pharaoh both masculine and feminine titles, the artists gave her an unhappy combination of male and female clothing. Three headless statues of Sobeknofru have been recovered out of context at the Delta site of Avaris (modern Tell el-Daba); these almost certainly came from the Faiyum, possibly from her lost mortuary temple. The most interesting piece is a damaged red quartzite torso depicting Sobeknofru's obviously feminine body in both a female shift dress and a pharaoh's kilt. A badly damaged sphinx shows the female pharaoh in the form of a lion.

Sobeknofru's pyramid has never been discovered and the end of her reign is obscure, although there is nothing to indicate that she died an unnatural death. Her passing marked the end of her dynasty.

AMENEMHAT IV

Dynasty: 12th

Father: Amenemhat III

Mother: Hetepti

Consort: Sobeknofru

Burial place: Dahshur?

Successor: Sobeknofru

SOBEKNOFRU

Dynasty: 12th

Father: Amenemhat III

Mother: unknown

Husband: Amenemhat IV

Burial place: unknown

Successor: Amenemhat III

DECLINE
THE END OF THE MIDDLE KINGDOM

❧

13th Dynasty c.1773–1650 BC

U P TO 70 13TH DYNASTY PHARAOHS RULED FOR UP TO 150 YEARS. IT IS NOT CLEAR HOW THE CROWN PASSED from one pharaoh to the next in these unstable times, but it seems that at least two of the earlier kings may have been the sons of Amenemhat IV, while others came from Egypt's élite families and were not necessarily related to each other. The disjointed succession, combined with an abrupt decline in the size of the royal tombs, encouraged earlier Egyptologists to classify the 13th Dynasty within the Second Intermediate Period. This view has recently been revised as archaeology has demonstrated, for the greater part of the dynasty, a bureaucratic stability and a continuity of administration and royal residence far more reminiscent of the Middle Kingdom.

Initially the 13th Dynasty retained control over Nubia. There were trade missions to Byblos, and building works up and down the Nile. However, the pharaohs lacked the resources to leave significant funerary monuments. The looted burial of King Hor – a basic shaft tomb dug close by the Dahshur pyramid of Amenemhat III – shows just how low royal expectations had fallen (or, perhaps, how low the royal finances had sunk): the simple tomb has yielded various abandoned funerary items, including a life-sized wooden *ka*-statue and the king's mummy and canopic chest. Khendjer, a king with an intriguingly foreign name, did complete a pyramid at Sakkara, and another three Sakkara pyramids have been tentatively assigned to the 13th Dynasty.

Outside Egypt's borders, the eastern Mediterranean was troubled by disruption and mass migration. As always, the dispossessed and hungry were drawn towards Egypt and the Delta was becoming uneasy. Ever since the end of the Old Kingdom, economic migrants had been crossing the Sinai land bridge to make a new life in the towns and villages of the eastern Delta. The new arrivals had been accepted and had developed their own hybrid tradition combining elements of Canaanite and Egyptian culture. During the Middle Kingdom Asiatics could be found serving alongside native Egyptians as soldiers, servants and administrators and, from time to time, their numbers were swelled by prisoners-of-war brought to Egypt to work on state projects. Now, however, as the Levantine states came under pressure from eastern migrants, the trickle of immigrants became a flood. And, as the new arrivals started to outnumber the native-born Egyptians, the towns of the eastern Delta grouped together to form an informal, semi-autonomous Canaanite colony with a Near Eastern, rather than Egyptian, culture. The situation was exploited by the provincial governors, who took the opportunity to rebel against the curtailment of their inherited authority imposed

by the 12th Dynasty kings. To make matters worse, a series of abnormally high Nile levels caused floods and disruption to the food supply.

The end came with a surprising swiftness. The common-born Sobekhotep III, ruler of a united Egypt and Nubia, was able to carve inscriptions at sites stretching from Elephantine in the south to Bubastis in the Delta. His successor, Neferhotep I, lost control of the Delta, which was now ruled by local governors. During the reign of Sobekhotep IV, Nubia started to rebel against Egyptian authority. When Ay, the last effective pharaoh of the Middle Kingdom, fled south, Itj-Tawy was abandoned.

A wooden statue of the 13th Dynasty pharaoh Hor. The uplifted arms on his head represent the hieroglyphic sign 'ka', meaning 'spirit' or 'soul'.

INVASION AND EXPULSION

THE SECOND INTERMEDIATE PERIOD

❦

14th–17th Dynasties c.1650–1550 BC

THE SECOND INTERMEDIATE PERIOD SAW EGYPT RULED BY TWO RIVAL COURTS, WITH A SCATTERING OF independent city-states claiming autonomy in the Delta. In the north the so-called 'Hyksos', an ill-understood dynasty of Canaanite extraction, emerged from the fortified Delta city of Avaris to take Memphis and rule Lower Egypt. At Thebes a native Egyptian dynasty claiming descent from the 13th Dynasty ruled southern Egypt. Meanwhile, to the south of Elephantine, the Nubian kingdom of Kerma ruled Egypt's former southern territories unchallenged. The 14th Dynasty was a line of ephemeral local kings who ruled the eastern Delta for 57 years; they were contemporary with the late 13th Dynasty.

'Hyksos' is a royal title and not, as was thought for many years, an ethnic group. Manetho records the Hyksos as 'six rulers of foreign countries' while the Turin Canon lists six 'rulers of the hill-lands' who ruled Egypt for 106 years, but does not allow them cartouches or a royal titulary and mentions only one ruler, Khamudi, by name. In this context, 'foreign' is a relative term. The new pharaohs were Semites, but they cannot be classed as invaders, since they hailed from the essentially Canaanite Delta city of Avaris. Nor is there any evidence that they indulged in the indiscriminate looting described by the first-century AD Roman-Jewish historian Josephus or, indeed, that they desecrated the native temples. While the Hyksos primarily addressed their devotions to Sutekh, a mixture of the Syrian weather-god Baal Zephon, the Hittite weather-god Teshub and the Egyptian god Seth (a god who also controlled the

Invaders of obscure race marched confident of victory against our land … By main force they seized it easily, without striking a blow. And having overpowered the rulers of the land they then burned our cities ruthlessly, and razed to the ground the temples of the gods, and treated all the people with a cruel hostility …

FLAVIUS JOSEPHUS' (FACTUALLY INACCURATE) ACCOUNT OF THE HYKSOS
'CONQUEST' OF EGYPT

weather), they encouraged the state temples to maintain their traditional role as centres of learning, and it was at this time, in the reign of Apepi, 'Son of Re', that the Rhind Mathematical Papyrus, a highly complex text requiring specialist knowledge, was copied by a temple scribe.

Hyksos Hegemony

It is, however, true that the Hyksos proclaimed their dominion over the whole of Egypt. This was an exaggerated claim. During Khyan's reign the Hyksos had pushed as far south as Thebes, but this had been a short-lived achievement, and by the start of the 17th Dynasty Hyksos control extended only as far south as Cusae, some 25 miles (40 km) to the south of Hermopolis Magna (modern Ashmunein). Here a customs post marked the border between Egypt's two lands. The southern Egyptians, isolated from Memphis, Idj-Tawi and the royal pyramid fields, grumbled that those wishing to pass

Detail of a woodcut, after a drawing by the 19th-century German illustrator Hermann Vogel, depicting the 'invasion' of Egypt by the Hyksos. Vogel evidently believed the Hyksos to be of Nubian origin.

THE QUARREL OF APEPI AND SEKENENRE

This is a wonderful but sadly unreliable tale written during the 19th Dynasty, which tells of the unreasonable demands made by the Hyksos court. The story opens with Egypt suffering under foreign domination. Sekenenre Taa II rules Thebes while Apepi rules the north from Avaris. Apepi has decided to pick a quarrel with his neighbours. He claims that he is unable to sleep at night because the roaring of the hippopotami at Thebes – 500 miles (800 km) away – is keeping him awake. Sekenenre Taa II summons his councillors to discuss this obviously outrageous complaint. The stage seems set for a grand battle, but unfortunately the only surviving copy of the story breaks off at this point and the reader is left in suspense.

the border were expected to pay a heavy tax. The northern Egyptians generously allowed the Thebans to graze their cattle on the fertile Delta pastures and charged them for the privilege.

The Hyksos probably retained Memphis as their bureaucratic capital while regarding Avaris as their home. Avaris was well placed. The Pelusiac Branch of the Nile allowed unrestricted access to the international trade routes and to Memphis and the Nile Valley beyond, while the eastern border could be controlled via the 'Way of Horus', a 140-mile (225-km) long road which allowed caravans to cross the Sinai Peninsula. Desert tracks passing through the oases, and conveniently bypassing the Theban kingdom, allowed Avaris to keep in contact with Nubian Kerma and, indeed, Tell el-Yahudiya ware (the characteristic Hyksos pottery) has been recovered from the Buhen cemetery. Avaris was a cosmopolitan city defended by Palestinian-style fortifications, totally different in character from insular, traditional Thebes. Sadly, our understanding of life at Avaris is limited by a shortage of textual information and, as successive pharaohs did a good job of destroying the physical evidence for the Hyksos 'occupation', the archaeological evidence is more limited than we might have hoped.

They discovered, placed around the head of the mummy, but over the linen, a diadem composed of silver and beautiful mosaic work, its centre being formed of gold, representing an asp, the emblem of royalty. Inside the case, alongside the mummy, were deposited two bows, with six arrows.

EGYPTOLOGIST GIOVANNI D'ATHANASI DESCRIBING THE DISCOVERY IN 1836 OF THE TOMB OF INTEF VII AT DRA ABU EL-NAGA

REVILED BY HISTORY

The southern Egyptians, who have left far more writings than their northern neighbours, found it impossible to accept that foreigners could have ruled even a part of their country with any degree of success or popular support. As the eventual victors in the power struggle, they were able to preserve their own version of events, so that official Egyptian history promotes the memory of Hyksos rule as a time of horrific anarchy, in which law and order (*maat*) held no sway. In fact the Hyksos proved to be efficient rulers who were respected, if not loved, by the Egyptians under their control. Strongly Egyptianized (they used non-Egyptian clay tablets but wrote in hieroglyphs, employed traditional throne names and regalia and carved Egyptian-style statues and reliefs) the new pharaohs opened conservative Egypt up to new ideas. International diplomacy – the exchange of letters, presents and perhaps brides with fellow monarchs – was an important feature of the new regime and there was continued trade with Cyprus, Palestine and the Levant. The Hyksos introduced new weaponry (including the horse-drawn chariot and the compound bow), new pottery forms, metal working techniques and cattle, but left no royal funerary monuments. We know the names of several Hyksos pharaohs, but understand little of their reigns. The most prominent is Apepi, who ruled for at least 40 years and fought against two Theban pharaohs. His successor, Khamudi, was the last of the Hyksos kings.

THE THEBAN REVIVAL

Contemporary with, and entirely dominated by, the Hyksos, the pharaohs of the 16th Dynasty were isolated, impoverished and insignificant. All ruled southern Egypt, although it is not certain that all ruled from Thebes. Neferhotep, who definitely did rule from Thebes, raised a stela claiming various victories, but there is no evidence to indicate that he fought the Hyksos. Indeed, it seems that relations between northern and southern Egypt were relatively amicable.

Considering themselves the true rulers of Egypt, the 16th Dynasty pharaohs clung to the old traditions. With the northern royal cemeteries inaccessible, they buried their dead in the Dra Abu el-Naga cemetery on the west bank of the Nile at Thebes, opposite the east bank Karnak temple of Amen. Here they raised narrow pyramids: steep, elegant mud-brick structures capped with inscribed stone pyramidions.

ADVENT OF A NEW DYNASTY

A change of ruling family heralded the start of the 17th Dynasty. Intef VII was the first of the strong Theban kings; although his reign was a peaceful one his temple of Min at Coptos included a highly traditional scene of Nubian and Asiatic captives forced to submit to Egypt's might. Intef VII was succeeded by the ill-documented Intef VIII. The next ruler, Sobekemsaf II, sent a small quarrying expedition to the Wadi Hammamat, and was wealthy enough to be buried in some style with Queen Nubemhat beneath a small-scale pyramid filled with expensive grave goods. His pyramid attracted unwelcome attention, and the burial was robbed during the reign of Ramesses IX of the 20th Dynasty (see page 88). Details of the theft are preserved in a group of New Kingdom documents known collectively as the 'Tomb Robbery Papyri'.

THE SECOND INTERMEDIATE PERIOD

*c.*1773 BC 14th Dynasty: a line of ephemeral rulers contemporary with the 13th Dynasty.

*c.*1650 BC 15th Dynasty: the Hyksos pharaohs, including:
  Sekerher
  Khyan (Seuserenre)
  Apepi (Aauserre)
  Khamudi

*c.*1650 BC 16th Dynasty: a line of Theban rulers descended from the 13th Dynasty and contemporary with the 15th Dynasty.

*c.*1580 BC 17th Dynasty: a line of Theban pharaohs, including:
  Rahotep
  Sobekemsaf I
  Intef VI (Sekhemre)
  Intef VII (Nubkheperre)
  Intef VIII (Sekhemreherhermaat)
  Sobekemsaf II
  Siamun?
  Senakhtenre Taa I
  Sekenenre Taa II
  Kamose (Wadjkheperre)

TESTIMONY OF A TOMB ROBBER

The stonemason Amen-Panufer confesses during the late New Kingdom reign of Ramesses IX:

We discovered pharaoh's mummy lying at the back of the tomb. Then we worked out that the burial chamber of his wife, Queen Nubemhat, must be nearby ... we prised open the sarcophagi and coffins, and found pharaoh's noble mummy holding a sword. Around its neck there were lots of amulets and gold jewels, and his mummy was still wearing its gold funerary mask. Pharaoh's noble mummy was covered with gold from head to toe. His coffins were also lined with silver and gold, inside and out, and were studded with all sorts of precious stones. We tore off the gold which we found on pharaoh's mummy, took the amulets and jewellery that were around its neck and dismantled the coffin it was lying in. The queen's body was similarly adorned and we stripped it in exactly the same way. Then we set fire to their coffins ...

Head of the 17th Dynasty pharaoh Kamose, from his sarcophagus. Kamose was prominent in the struggle to expel the Hyksos rulers from the Nile Delta.

Senakhtenre Taa I was either the son or brother of Sobekemsaf II; his consort, Tetisheri, was the daughter of a couple named Tjenna and Nefru. The late 17th Dynasty pharaohs accepted that their womenfolk were capable of assuming a prominent political and religious role and were happy to acknowledge their contribution. And so, after her death, Tetisheri's grandson Ahmose established a cenotaph for her in his own cult centre at Abydos 'because he loved her more than anything'.

Sekenenre Taa II, son of Taa I and Tetisheri, dared to challenge the formidable Apepi of Avaris. He fought valiantly at the border town of Cusae, but fell in battle. The death of a pharaoh at the hands of an enemy was a gross affront to *maat* which was never going to feature prominently in Egypt's official history, and this particular death goes unrecorded. However, Taa's mummy allows us to recreate the king's final moments without venturing too far into the realm of speculation. Taa had been fatally stabbed behind the ear by a dagger. As he sank to his knees, and before he could raise his arms to defend himself, two or more assailants armed with a mace and a Hyksos-style battle-axe battered his head, shattering his skull, cheekbone and eye sockets. The king's body was hastily mummified, returned to Thebes, and buried beneath a small-scale mud-brick pyramid.

KAMOSE THE BRAVE

Taa II had taken his sister Ahhotep as his consort. She had given him four children: two daughters and two sons, both named Ahmose. Ahmose the elder had died young and it was Ahmose the younger who would eventually succeed his father. But first the throne passed to Kamose, a man with no proven link to the previous pharaoh, although his age suggests that he may have been Sekenenre's brother. Whatever his lineage, it is reasonable to assume that 'Kamose the Brave' was a warrior chosen for his ability to continue the struggle against the north. Initially,

SENAKHTENRE TAA I

Dynasty: 17th
Father: unknown
Consort: Tetisheri
Burial place: unknown
Successor: Sekenenre Taa II

SEKENENRE TAA II

Dynasty: 17th
Father: Senakhtenre Taa I
Consort: Ahhotep
Burial place: unknown
Successor: Kamose

HIS MAJESTY ADDRESSES HIS ADVISORS IN THE PALACE

How can I claim to be powerful, when there is a ruler in Avaris and another in Kush? I am no different from an Asiatic and a Nubian – each of them has his piece of Egypt too, and shares the land with me. Now that Apepi controls Hermopolis, there is no way past him to Memphis, the port of Egypt. [And even if there was], no one lands there now, because of the crippling Asiatic taxes. It is up to me to take him on and rip his belly open. The time has come to liberate Egypt and crush the Asiatics.

From the Karnak Stela of Kamose

however, Kamose looked southwards. By his regnal year 3 the Kerma Nubians had retreated southwards, Theban troops had recaptured the second cataract fortress of Buhen and Nubian gold was once again flowing north. Having built a fleet of boats, Kamose was ready to face the Hyksos. The story of his struggle is told on two now-damaged Karnak stelae and on a scholar's writing-board known today as the 'Carnarvon Tablet'.

Kamose's own account of events, hardly an unbiased history, tells us that Apepi had drafted a peace treaty which would allow the rival kingdoms access to each other's lands. Such a compromise would allow both sides to live together with honour, and Kamose's advisors thought it a good idea. Kamose, however, was not prepared to compromise. He ignored his advisors, launched a surprise attack and, after some fierce fighting, advanced as far north as Avaris, where he got close enough to the palace to be able to see the royal women peering out of the windows. Although Avaris remained intact, Kamose seized a vast amount of treasure from captured Hyksos ships. His daring raid was a huge propaganda victory and, 'every face was bright... Thebes was in festival'. The seemingly invincible Apepi was left shocked and demoralized, and things took a turn for the worse when he realized that he had lost control of the desert routes linking Avaris to Kerma. This severing of communications between his two enemies had been a vital part of Kamose's strategy, as he had reason to believe that the Hyksos king was inciting the Nubians to distract the Thebans by attacking from the south.

The young pharaoh seemed destined for a glorious military career, but after a mere three years on the throne he lay in his simple Theban tomb. It is tempting to speculate that he too died in battle. As Kamose was succeeded by Ahmose, the younger son of Sekenenre Taa II and Queen Ahhotep, Apepi died and was succeeded by Khamudi. This change in leadership led to a break in hostilities of over a decade as Ahhotep raised her son.

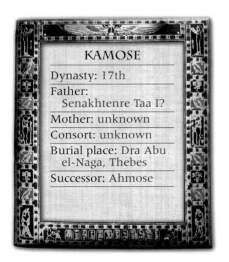

KAMOSE

Dynasty:	17th
Father:	Senakhtenre Taa I?
Mother:	unknown
Consort:	unknown
Burial place:	Dra Abu el-Naga, Thebes
Successor:	Ahmose

Double the food that your mother gave you, and support her as she supported you, for you were a heavy burden to her yet she did not abandon you. When you were born after your months she was still tied to you as her breast was in your mouth for three years. As you grew and your excrement was disgusting she was not disgusted.

ADVICE OFFERED BY THE NEW KINGDOM SCRIBE ANI

QUEEN AHHOTEP

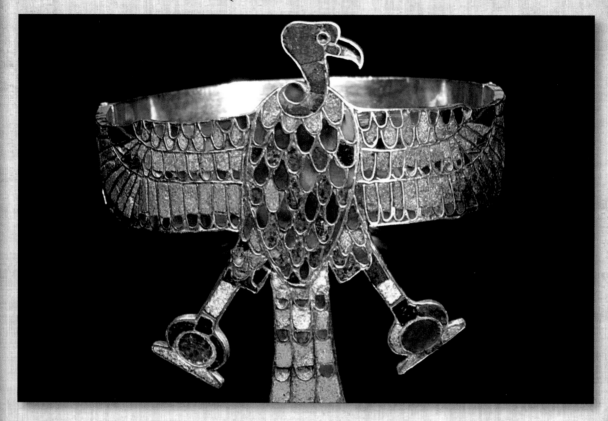

The adult Ahmose recognized the deep debt that he owed to his mother. On a stela recovered from Karnak he revered her as 'one who has accomplished the rites and taken care of Egypt … she has pacified Upper Egypt, and expelled her rebels'.

Ahhotep's burial is an Egyptological puzzle which, as yet, remains unsolved. In 1859 labourers employed by Egyptologist Auguste Mariette uncovered an intact tomb in the Dra Abu el-Naga cemetery. The coffin was labelled for the 'king's great wife Ahhotep'. As Mariette was absent, the local governor took it upon himself to open the coffin. Inside he found a mummy, which he stripped and discarded, and a collection of golden artefacts including jewellery, a ceremonial axe, a gold dagger and sheath, and three golden flies of valour: the traditional reward for Egyptian

A golden upper arm bracelet found in the coffin of Ahhotep, inlaid with lapis lazuli, carnelian and turquoise.

soldiers. Although some of the items bore the name of Kamose, more were inscribed for Ahmose, and it seems likely that he must have been responsible for the burial.

Then, in 1881, a large outer coffin belonging to the 'king's daughter, king's sister, king's great wife and king's mother Ahhotep' was discovered in a cache of royal mummies hidden in the Deir el-Bahri cliff. Initially it was assumed that the coffin belonged to a second queen, Ahhotep II, who was either the consort of Kamose or the New Kingdom pharaoh Amenhotep I. More recently it has been accepted that the two coffins probably both belonged to Ahhotep I, mother of Ahmose.

THE
FIGHTING
PHARAOHS

C.1550–1427 BC

Seated statue of a Tuthmoside ruler, with characteristic almond-shaped eyes.

EGYPT RESTORED
THE EXPULSION OF THE HYKSOS

Early 18th Dynasty c.1550–1504 BC

From the outset, the New Kingdom was an age of imperialist expansion. With almost effortless ease – or so their propaganda would have us believe – the early 18th Dynasty pharaohs annexed Nubia and much of the Near East until their territories stretched from the Sudan to Syria and their influence was felt far further afield. Fiercely militaristic, the Theban pharaohs made no secret of their devotion to Amen-Re, a fusion of the ancient northern sun god Re and Amen, the relatively young warrior deity of Thebes. Amen-Re became the wealthiest and most powerful god in the Egyptian pantheon, while his Karnak temple evolved into one of the largest religious complexes in the world. As Memphis continued to serve as the administrative capital, Thebes became the religious capital of the richest and most sophisticated land in the Mediterranean world.

The early 18th Dynasty saw important architectural, artistic, theological and technological advances. This was a time of increased foreign contact, a time when Egypt exploited her neighbours and reaped rich rewards. Fortunately for the archaeologists of the future, it was also a time of ever-increasing bureaucracy; a time when even the most trivial of matters were documented by the expanding civil service. Increasing numbers of boys were taught how to read and write in order to meet the growing demand for scribes. Soldiers, too, were needed. An efficient fighting force was essential if Egypt was to avoid a repetition of the Hyksos period, and so the informal military structure was revised to produce a professional army.

Abandoning the traditional pyramid-tomb, the New Kingdom pharaohs split their mortuary complexes in two, building hidden rock-cut tombs in the valleys of the west bank of the Nile at Thebes, and impressive and highly visible mortuary temples at the desert's edge. Here, they hoped, their cults would be celebrated for all time.

AHMOSE UNITES HIS LAND

After 11 years of uneasy co-existence, Ahmose began the long and messy struggle to expel the Hyksos. His army slowly forced its way northwards, capturing and converting towns loyal to Khamudi. Heliopolis was taken in Year 11, Sile fell later. Then, following a protracted siege, Avaris fell and the Hyksos retreated eastwards into Palestine. Three years later, after another lengthy siege, Ahmose captured the fortified Palestinian city of Sharuhen and established a buffer zone that would prevent the Hyksos from returning to the Delta. Egypt was now united from Aswan to the Mediterranean coast, but Ahmose's troubles were not over. He thwarted a threatened Nubian invasion, only

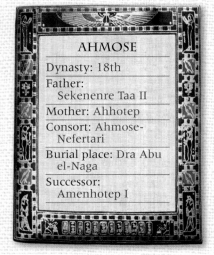

AHMOSE

Dynasty: 18th

Father:
Sekenenre Taa II

Mother: Ahhotep

Consort: Ahmose-Nefertari

Burial place: Dra Abu el-Naga

Successor:
Amenhotep I

18TH DYNASTY RULERS

c.1550 BC Ahmose (Nebhetepre)

c.1525 BC Amenhotep I (Djeserkare)

c.1504 BC Tuthmosis I (Aakheperkare)

c.1492 BC Tuthmosis II (Aakheperenre)

c.1479 BC Tuthmosis III (Menkheperre)

c.1473 BC Hatshepsut (Maatkare)

c.1427 BC Amenhotep II (Aakheperure)

c.1400 BC Tuthmosis IV (Menkheperure)

c.1390 BC Amenhotep III (Nebmaatre)

c.1352 BC Amenhotep IV/Akhenaten (Neferkheperure Waenre)

c.1338 BC Neferneferuaten (Smenkhkare)

c.1336 BC Tutankhamen (Nebkheperure)

c.1327 BC Ay (Kheperkheperure)

c.1323 BC Horemheb (Djeserkheperure)

to be faced with two further insurrections: a small and insignificant rebellion led by the foreigner Aata, and a potentially far more serious rebellion led by the Egyptian Teti-an who, we are told, 'gathered the discontented to himself'. With these rebels defeated, and their followers slaughtered, Ahmose finally became the undisputed pharaoh of a united land. For this achievement Manetho recognized him as the first pharaoh of the 18th Dynasty.

As tribute and taxes flowed into the treasury, the newly stable kingdom grew rich. Quarries and mines ran efficiently and the royal workshops, provided with plentiful supplies of raw materials, began to produce impressive works of art. As the conscripted soldiers laid down their weapons and took up their tools, building works started along

AHMOSE, SON OF IBANA

The battle for reunification was recorded on the walls of the el-Kab tomb of Ahmose, son of Ibana. Naturally, Ahmose-the-soldier highlights his own bravery in the face of danger:

> *During the siege of Avaris, pharaoh noticed me fighting bravely on foot and promoted me to his ship 'Rising in Memphis'... Then we took Avaris. I carried off four people there – a man and three women, in total four persons – and his majesty allowed me to keep them as slaves. We went on to besiege Sharuhen and his majesty sacked it after three years. I took my share of the booty there too – two women and a hand. Again, I was awarded the gold of valour and was allowed to keep the people I had captured as slaves ... Once his majesty had slaughtered the Asiatic Bedouin, he turned southward to Nubia to crush the tribes there. Pharaoh slaughtered them all in droves and I managed to carry off two live prisoners and three hands. Yet again, I was decorated with gold, and was given two female slaves. Then his majesty sailed back north, satisfied with the extent of his victories. For he had recaptured both the south and the north.*

the Nile Valley. Thebes, Memphis and Abydos all benefited from Ahmose's generosity, while Avaris was resurrected as a trading post and military headquarters.

After a quarter of a century on the throne, Ahmose was buried beneath a small pyramid in the Dra Abu el-Naga cemetery. Because his intended heir, Ahmose-Ankh, had predeceased him, a more junior son, Amenhotep I, ascended the throne under his mother's guidance.

A REDOUBTABLE MOTHER

The late 17th Dynasty had been blessed with strong queens capable of ruling in their husbands' absence. Ahmose Nefertari continued this tradition. She was already a king's daughter, king's wife and king's mother. During her son's reign she was either given, or sold, the hereditary position of 'second prophet of Amen'. She later renounced this post for an even more prestigious position, the priestly office of 'God's Wife of Amen', an honour that brought her a valuable endowment of goods and land. A third position, the office of Divine Adoratrice, brought even more independent wealth and allowed Ahmose Nefertari to make an unprecedented series of offerings throughout Egypt.

Subsequent 18th Dynasty queens would wear a wide range of crowns (preserved in statuary and illustrations; curiously, no actual king's or queen-consort's crowns have survived) and bear a range of religious and secular titles. It is perhaps no coincidence that it is now that we find king's daughters barred from marriages outside the immediate royal family. A princess would now either marry her brother or half-brother, her father (a rare occurrence) or no one, and the line of grandchildren with a claim to the throne would be naturally restricted.

With his reign untroubled by civil unrest, invasion or natural disaster, Amenhotep was able to continue the foreign policies of his father, uncle(?) and grandfather. He campaigned and built in Nubia, consolidating his father's work and installing a 'royal son of Kush' to serve as viceroy; and he probably had a nominal eastern campaign, although he made no attempt to extend his empire. Instead he used his wealth to finish his father's building projects and to start his own. This included work at Ipet-swt, or 'The most select of places', now better known as the Karnak temple complex. At the start of Amenhotep's reign the complex retained its basic 12th Dynasty form. Now, with the sandstone and limestone quarries reopened, serious building works

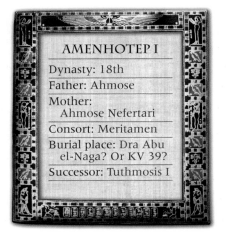

AMENHOTEP I

Dynasty: 18th

Father: Ahmose

Mother: Ahmose Nefertari

Consort: Meritamen

Burial place: Dra Abu el-Naga? Or KV 39?

Successor: Tuthmosis I

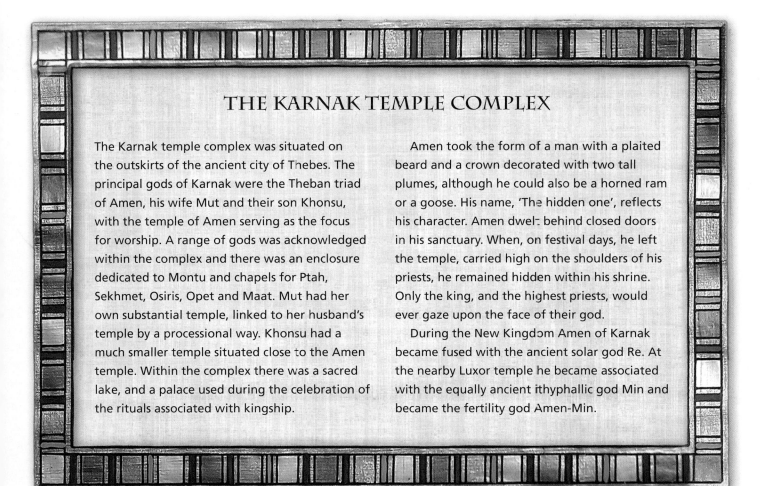

THE KARNAK TEMPLE COMPLEX

The Karnak temple complex was situated on the outskirts of the ancient city of Thebes. The principal gods of Karnak were the Theban triad of Amen, his wife Mut and their son Khonsu, with the temple of Amen serving as the focus for worship. A range of gods was acknowledged within the complex and there was an enclosure dedicated to Montu and chapels for Ptah, Sekhmet, Osiris, Opet and Maat. Mut had her own substantial temple, linked to her husband's temple by a processional way. Khonsu had a much smaller temple situated close to the Amen temple. Within the complex there was a sacred lake, and a palace used during the celebration of the rituals associated with kingship.

Amen took the form of a man with a plaited beard and a crown decorated with two tall plumes, although he could also be a horned ram or a goose. His name, 'The hidden one', reflects his character. Amen dwelt behind closed doors in his sanctuary. When, on festival days, he left the temple, carried high on the shoulders of his priests, he remained hidden within his shrine. Only the king, and the highest priests, would ever gaze upon the face of their god.

During the New Kingdom Amen of Karnak became fused with the ancient solar god Re. At the nearby Luxor temple he became associated with the equally ancient ithyphallic god Min and became the fertility god Amen-Min.

commenced. This work would never end. Successive pharaohs would provide increasingly elaborate embellishments, and the site would grow from a relatively simple collection of mud-brick chapels linked by processional ways into a vast religious complex. Amenhotep's contribution was an alabaster kiosk or boat shrine, a monumental gateway, a limestone replica of the 'White Chapel' of Senwosret I and a cluster of smaller shrines or chapels.

Amenhotep predeceased his mother. An inscription (now lost) in the tomb of the astronomer Amenemhat tells us that the deceased lived for 21 years under Amenhotep; this fits well with Manetho's reign of 20 years and 7 months assigned simply to 'Amenophis'. Although his tomb has not yet been discovered, it seems either that he was buried alongside his predecessors at Dra Abu el-Naga, or that he became the first king to be interred in the Valley of the Kings, perhaps in KV 39. In death Amenhotep became the focus of a funerary cult at the west bank village of Deir el-Medina, where he became a respected oracle worshipped variously as 'Amenhotep of the Town', 'Amenhotep Beloved of Amen', or 'Amenhotep of the Forecourt'. When she died Ahmose Nefertari, too, was deified and worshipped alongside her son as patron goddess of the Theban necropolis, 'Mistress of the Sky' and 'Lady of the West'.

Fragment of a wooden furniture fragment from Deir el-Medina depicting Amenhotep I and his formidable mother Ahmose Nefertari.

VALLEY OF THE KINGS
HOUSING THE ROYAL DEAD

THE PHARAOHS OF THE OLD AND MIDDLE KINGDOMS HAD BUILT VAST PYRAMID COMPLEXES INCORPORATING BOTH the royal tomb and the temples where the royal cult would be celebrated for all time. These vast complexes dominated the flat deserts of northern Egypt, where they were strongly associated with the cult of the sun god, Re of Heliopolis. Inevitably, the highly conspicuous pyramid cemeteries attracted the thieves who, throughout the dynastic age, plagued all of Egypt's graveyards, and the pyramids and their associated temples were robbed repeatedly.

Naturally, the pyramid builders attempted to protect their tombs. The pyramid could not be hidden but, perhaps, the route to the burial chamber could be concealed? Architects experimented with a variety of physical barriers, incorporating hidden entrances, false chambers, stone portcullises and blocked passages in their designs. But, as the robbers were likely to be the very men who had built the pyramids, nothing worked. By the end of the pyramid age the bodies of the pharaohs had been stripped of their bandages and abandoned by callous thieves searching for the amulets hidden within their wrappings. For a people who believed that the survival of the soul was dependent upon the survival of the corpse, this was a very serious matter.

The early New Kingdom pharaohs, natives of Thebes, were aware of this wanton desecration. The obvious answer was to abandon the expensive grave goods, replacing them with illustrations or models that would magically come alive in the afterlife, but no one wanted to take this drastic step. Instead, their strong devotion to Amen, along with an equally strong wish for security in death, led the pharaohs to devise an alternative funerary complex. Its two important parts were to be physically separated. The tomb – the eternal home of the body – would be hidden in the living rock of the Theban West Bank, opposite the temple of Amen-Re, where the peaked mountain itself would perhaps serve as a symbolic pyramid rising above the hidden grave. The mortuary temple, conspicuous and accessible, would be built on the edge of the cultivation for all to see.

The mortuary temple of Hatshepsut, sixth pharaoh of the 18th Dynasty, at Deir el-Bahri in the hills of the Theban West Bank, close to the Valley of the Kings. This monumental complex was perhaps designed and built by her vizier, Senenmut (see p.108).

THE MORTUARY TEMPLES OF THE WEST BANK

In its most basic form, the mortuary chapel or temple was the place where the living could go to make the offerings of food, drink and incense which would sustain the dead in the afterlife. A royal mortuary temple, however, served more than this basic requirement. The deceased pharaoh had a number of equally valid options: he could chose to spend eternity sailing in the solar boat with Re, relaxing in the Field of Reeds with Osiris, or twinkling as an undying star in the night sky. New Kingdom royal mortuary chapels had to reflect these different options, providing a dark shrine for the worship of Osiris and an open-air solar shrine for the worship of Re, while reflecting

... And when the burial of all the kings was made I reported Paneb's theft of the things of King Seti Merenptah... and he took away the covering of his chariot... and he took away his wines and sat on the sarcophagus of pharaoh although he was buried... and he hacked up the ground which is sealed in the place which is hidden ...

THE FOREMAN PANEB STEALS FROM THE TOMB
OF SETI II: PAPYRUS SALT 124

the growing power of Amen-Re. Amen-Re played a prominent role in the scenes that decorate the walls, and his shrine now formed the focus of the mortuary chapel so that the temples effectively became temples to Amen-Re. Strongly connected with the personal identity of the king, the temples were decorated with large-scale images of him performing his traditional duties.

A DELIBERATELY INACCESSIBLE SITE

The Biban el-Muluk, the 'Valley of the Gates of the Kings', now better known as the Valley of the Kings, was a remote *wadi* (dry river bed) far off the beaten path. Its steep sides and narrow entrance made it very easy to guard; no wonder Ineni, architect of Tuthmosis I, the first king known to have been buried in the Valley, boasted of building his master's tomb 'none seeing and none hearing'. Ineni was able to increase security by employing a reduced workforce. The pyramids had been built by thousands of conscripted labourers plus a core of permanent employees; an estimate of some 20,000–30,000 labourers working in three-month shifts for maybe 20 years seems reasonable. Now the enclosed nature of the rock-cut tomb called for a smaller and more specialized workforce. Initially transient labourers, the 'Servants in the Place of Truth' soon became full-time state employees whose loyalty was guaranteed by their generous pay and by an oath of allegiance sworn at the time of their appointment.

Entrance to and exit from the necropolis was strictly controlled, the workmen were isolated and kept under constant supervision, and there were frequent tours of inspection designed to detect even the most minor breaches of tomb security. So confident were the royal architects that the 19th and 20th Dynasty monarchs abandoned the practice of concealing the tomb doorways, choosing instead to make a feature of the entrance that now presented an imposing façade to the world.

Using a system devised by Egyptologist John Gardiner Wilkinson, the tombs in the Valley of the Kings are conventionally identified by numbers (KV i.e. King's Valley 1, 2 etc). A similar system is used to identify the tombs of the Valley of the Queens (QV), Deir el-Bahri (DB) and the wider Theban necropolis (TT). Not all the tombs in the Valley of the Kings belong to kings, and not everything identified by a KV number is a tomb.

DEIR EL-MEDINA

The tomb workers and their families lived at Deir el-Medina, a purpose-built walled village near the entrance to the Valley. Within the wall the terraced houses stretched in dark, ordered lines. Beyond the wall there were tombs, chapels and desert. With no natural water supply the villagers were entirely dependent upon the vizier's office for their rations of water, food and clothing. Every ten days the workmen left the village to walk to the Valley. There they lived for eight days and nights, camping in temporary huts, before returning home for the ninth and tenth days – the weekend.

PRESERVING THE PHARAOHS

Absolute security was impossible: everyone knew that the Valley of the Kings was home to unimaginable treasures. While Egypt remained strong, this did not matter overmuch. The narrow entrance to the steep-sided Valley could be guarded, and regular tours of inspection would ensure that attempted robberies were quickly detected. But, towards the end of the New Kingdom, Egypt started to suffer the combined effects of inflation, bureaucratic corruption and civil unrest. As the food distribution networks failed, the workers of Deir el-Medina grew hungry and Theban monuments started to come under attack. Ramesses XI was forced to abandon his almost complete tomb (KV 4), and made plans to be buried in the north. Deir el-Medina was abandoned at the end of the 20th Dynasty and its workforce resettled at Medinet Habu.

The Third Intermediate Period High Priests of Amen took it upon themselves to bring order to the plundered Valley. The royal tombs were opened and emptied and the mummies were 'restored' (i.e. stripped of all valuables and rebandaged) and placed in plain wooden coffins. The mummies were then stored in well-guarded tombs dotted around the necropolis. From time to time these collections were inspected, amalgamated and moved until there were two major royal caches, one in the tomb of the High Priest Pinodjem II (DB 320) and one in the tomb of Amenhotep II (KV 35). The mummy of Tutankhamen, sealed in a forgotten tomb, was spared this brutal treatment.

The Deir el-Bahri cache was found in the early 1870s by the Abd el-Rassul brothers, a family of experienced tomb robbers. They told no one of their discovery but started to sell its antiquities. After several years of lucrative trading two of them were arrested and their secret was revealed. The collection included the labelled mummies of at least 40 kings, queens and priests dating to the 18th, 19th, 20th and 21st Dynasties, including Sekenenre Taa II, Ahmose, Amenhotep I, Ahmose Nefertari and Tuthmosis II and III. Unfortunately the restorers had muddled the mummies, coffins and grave goods so that the coffin of Ahmose Nefertari, for example, also housed the mummy of Ramesses III.

The Amenhotep II cache was discovered in 1898 by Victor Loret, inspector of antiquities at Thebes. The rebandaged Amenhotep II lay in a wooden coffin in his original sarcophagus. A side chamber yielded three unlabelled and coffinless mummies lying side by side, each with a hole in the head and a damaged abdomen, while a walled-up side room held nine coffins belonging to, amongst others, Tuthmosis IV, Amenhotep III, Seti II, Siptah and Ramesses IV–VI.

The artisan settlement at Deir el-Medina. Its houses were all state-owned and appointment to a place in the work-gang was accompanied by the allocation of a tied home. The village was surrounded by a thick mud-brick wall that, for many years, had only one gateway; this single entrance allowed guards to question and search anyone entering or leaving the village.

DEVELOPING THE EMPIRE
THE TUTHMOSIDE KINGS

Mid-18th Dynasty c.1504 – 1427 BC

AMENHOTEP I HAD NO SON TO SUCCEED HIM. FREE TO SELECT AN HEIR, HE LOOKED BEYOND THE CHILDREN of the harem and selected a seasoned soldier and experienced politician. It seems likely that general Tuthmosis belonged to a collateral branch of the royal family, although he himself never claimed royal blood. His father goes unnamed while his mother, Senisenb, is simply described as a 'king's mother'. His wife, Ahmose, uses the title 'king's sister' but not 'king's daughter', a strong indication that she was neither the daughter nor the sister of Amenhotep I. However, she could have been the sister or half-sister of her husband, Tuthmosis I. If this is the case, we may deduce that their marriage occurred after Tuthmosis's adoption into the royal family as, before the Roman Period, commoner sibling marriages are extremely rare.

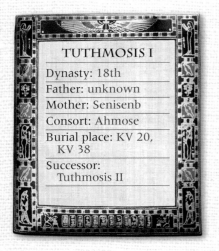

TUTHMOSIS I

Dynasty: 18th

Father: unknown

Mother: Senisenb

Consort: Ahmose

Burial place: KV 20, KV 38

Successor: Tuthmosis II

Tuthmosis and Ahmose had two well-attested daughters, Hatshepsut and Neferubity. Tuthmosis also fathered two sons, Wadjmose and Amenmose, who predeceased their father. Both appear in the tomb of the royal tutor, Paheri, at el-Kab, and the older brother, Wadjmose, plays a prominent role in a funerary chapel built by Tuthmosis on the west bank at Thebes, where a side-room serviced the cults of family members including a young man named Ramose and the lady Mutnofret whose statue wears a uraeus and whose name is written in a cartouche. Mutnofret is better known as the mother of Tuthmosis's eventual successor, Tuthmosis II. The younger brother, Amenmose, bore the title 'Great Army Commander', the role normally allocated to the crown prince. A broken stela tells us that during his father's Year 4 Amenmose hunted wild animals in the Giza desert near the Great Sphinx. But, if Amenmose was the son of Ahmose, and if his parents married only after Tuthmosis became king, Amenmose can have been barely four years old during Year 4. This strongly suggests that Amenmose and Wadjmose, and perhaps the ephemeral Ramose, were the children of an earlier wife, Mutnofret.

SECURING EGYPT'S BORDERS

Obelisks raised by Tuthmosis I and Hatshepsut within the temple of Amen at Karnak. The caps of both obelisks ('pyramidions') were once clad in electrum, a natural alloy of gold and silver.

Tuthmosis I embarked on a series of highly successful foreign campaigns. In Year 2 he sailed into Nubia where, as Ahmose son of Ibana tells us, he 'destroyed insurrection throughout the lands and repelled the intruders from the desert region', advancing past the third cataract and reaching the island of Argo. Pharaoh returned home in triumph with the body of a Nubian chieftain hanging over the bow of his ship. He left behind him a subdued land controlled by a string of colonial settlements.

Tuthmosis next looked to the east. After establishing new military headquarters at Memphis he marched eastwards into Naharin, crossing the River Euphrates and seizing the territory ruled by Egypt's most significant foe, the king of Mitanni, whose homeland was situated in what is now northern Syria, eastern Turkey and northern Iraq. A commemorative stela was set on the bank of the Euphrates. Egypt would long reap the commercial benefits of his campaigns, while remaining free from the threat of eastern invasion, for four affluent centuries.

Back home there were extensive building programmes at all the major Theban sites. At Karnak the original mud-brick Middle Kingdom temple was enclosed within a sandstone wall, the processional ways were extended, and two white stone gateways (Pylons IV and V) were installed, the area between them being roofed over to form a pillared hall. Most impressive of all, two inscribed red granite obelisks, each 19.5 metres (64 ft) tall with a golden tip, sparkled in the sunlight before the main temple entrance.

Tuthmosis had reigned for no more than 15 years before he 'rested from life'. His tomb (KV 38) was ready. Designed by Ineni, it is a relatively simple rock-cut structure consisting of a rectangular antechamber, a pillared burial chamber and small storeroom linked by a series of passages and stairways.

TUTHMOSIS II

Dynasty: 18th

Father: Tuthmosis I

Mother: Mutnodjmet

Consort: Hatshepsut

Burial place: KV ?

Successor: Tuthmosis III

AN UNEVENTFUL REIGN

The mummy of Tuthmosis II is that of a relatively young man, indicating that he may been a child pharaoh reliant on the help of the dowager queen Ahmose. His reign was both calm and uneventful. Building works continued at the Karnak complex, where the temple of Amen-Re was embellished with a new festival court, and there were at least two military campaigns, one in Nubia and one in Palestine, although it is doubtful that Tuthmosis himself ever led his troops into battle.

His sister-wife Hatshepsut bore a daughter, Neferure, but no son. And so, Tuthmosis was succeeded by the infant Tuthmosis III, born to a secondary wife, the king's mother Isis. Egypt's new pharaoh was a baby whose mother was not able, either because she was of humble birth, or simply because she was dead, to rule as his regent. Hatshepsut therefore stepped forward to rule temporarily on her stepson's behalf.

... He [Tuthmosis II] went forth to heaven in triumph, having mingled with the gods. His son stood in his place as pharaoh of the Two Lands, having become ruler upon the throne of the one who begat him. His sister the Divine Consort, Hatshepsut, managed the affairs of the Two Lands by reason of her plans. Egypt was made to labour with bowed head for her ...

FROM THE AUTOBIOGRAPHY OF INENI

DAUGHTER OF AMEN

As queen consort, Hatshepsut had born the titles 'king's daughter', 'king's sister' and 'king's great wife', although her preferred title was always 'God's Wife of Amen'. Early in her brother's reign she had started to build a rock-cut tomb hidden high up the cliff in the Wadi Sikkat Taka ez-Zeida, a remote ravine on the Theban west bank. This tomb proved almost inaccessible for its excavator, Howard Carter, who was 'obliged always to descend in a net'. When Carter finally made his way into the burial chamber he found an impressive quartzite sarcophagus. The tomb was, however, unfinished and had never been used by its intended owner.

During the first couple of years of his reign, Hatshepsut allowed the young Tuthmosis III to take precedence in all activities. It was at this time that she erected a statue at Elephantine in memory of her dead husband-brother. But already there were signs that this was not to be a conventional regency. The queen's new title, 'mistress of the Two Lands', paralleled the traditional pharaoh's title 'lord of the Two Lands', while her commissioning of a pair of obelisks to stand in front of the gateway to the temple of Amen-Re was unprecedented for a queen.

HATSHEPSUT
Dynasty: 18th
Father: Tuthmosis I
Mother: Ahmose
Husband: Tuthmosis II
Burial place: KV 20
Successor:
  Tuthmosis III

TRANSCENDING GENDER ROLES

By the end of Year 7 Hatshepsut had taken a huge and extraordinary leap. She had become a fully-fledged pharaoh. There could be no going back. A pharaoh might take a co-regent but, once crowned. he or she could never renounce that crown. The new pharaoh was immediately faced with the problem that had vexed Sobeknofru. The traditional symbols of kingship were masculine ones. After a brief period of experimentation, where she appeared as a female dressed in male clothing and regalia, Hatshepsut chose to be depicted with the body of a typical male pharaoh. This new, masculine form of Hatshepsut continued to use feminine names and titles, so for those who could read the hieroglyphic inscriptions accompanying her images, there was no confusion over the new pharaoh's gender.

A life-sized, seated statue showing Hatshepsut in female garb and with a woman's body; however, she also wears the nemes *headcloth, a royal attribute reserved for the reigning king.*

Many depictions of Hatshepsut with the body of a male pharaoh appear on the walls of the Red Chapel at Karnak. Here, Hatshepsut is seen standing on the right before the god Amen-Re. The figure on the left is the ithyphallic fertility god, Min.

Hatshepsut never explains the specific circumstances that prompted her to take this unprecedented move, but she does go to considerable lengths to justify her right to the throne. Her primary justification is that she, the daughter of Amen-Re, is predestined to rule Egypt. This, of course, necessitated a revision of her personal history. The story of Hatshepsut's divine conception is told in a series of images and descriptive passages on the walls of her Deir el-Bahri mortuary temple; this made it accessible to her priests, her gods and the pharaohs who were to come. The story starts in heaven where Amen-Re has decided to father a daughter who will enjoy a glorious reign. Thoth, god of wisdom, proclaims the name of the chosen mother-to-be: she is Ahmose, consort of Tuthmosis I, who is 'more beautiful than any woman'. Ahmose is visited by the god (who is disguised as her husband), and they sit face-to-face on her bed. Amen-Re tells Ahmose that she is to bear a daughter and passes her the ankh, or sign of life. The ram-headed god Khnum then crafts the baby and her soul, or *ka*, on his potter's wheel. Nine months later the heavily pregnant Ahmose is escorted to the birth bower. When we next see the queen she is sitting on a throne holding baby Hatshepsut in her arms. Hathor, the royal wet-nurse, presents the baby to Amen. Hatshepsut then travels north to visit the ancient shrines of the gods, accompanied by her earthly father, Tuthmosis. There is a coronation before the gods and finally an earthly coronation by Tuthmosis, who nominates his daughter as his co-regent and intended successor. This co-regency is a complete fiction: there is no evidence to show that Tuthmosis intended to pass over his son in favour of his daughter.

A slightly different tale, preserved at Karnak, suggests a date for Hatshepsut's coronation. This text is inscribed on the wall of the Red Chapel, a red quartzite sanctuary endowed by Hatshepsut to house the sacred boat 'Mighty of Prow is Amen'. It is narrated by Hatshepsut, who describes a procession associated with the festival of Amen-Re during Year 2 of an unspecified king's reign. During the ceremony, and in the presence of the anonymous pharaoh, the oracle announces that Hatshepsut is to become pharaoh. It may be the unnamed king of the tale is Tuthmosis I and that the text therefore represents Hatshepsut's recollection – presumably fictitious – of the time when the god acknowledged her as the true heir to the crown. However, it is equally possible that the king is Tuthmosis III and that the block is therefore a record of the actual date when Hatshepsut decided to make public her claim to the throne.

A TRUSTED COTERIE

Hatshepsut had inherited a cabinet of experienced advisors, many of whom had worked for her brother and her father and all of whom seem to have been happy to switch their allegiance to the new regime. Gradually, however, she started to make her

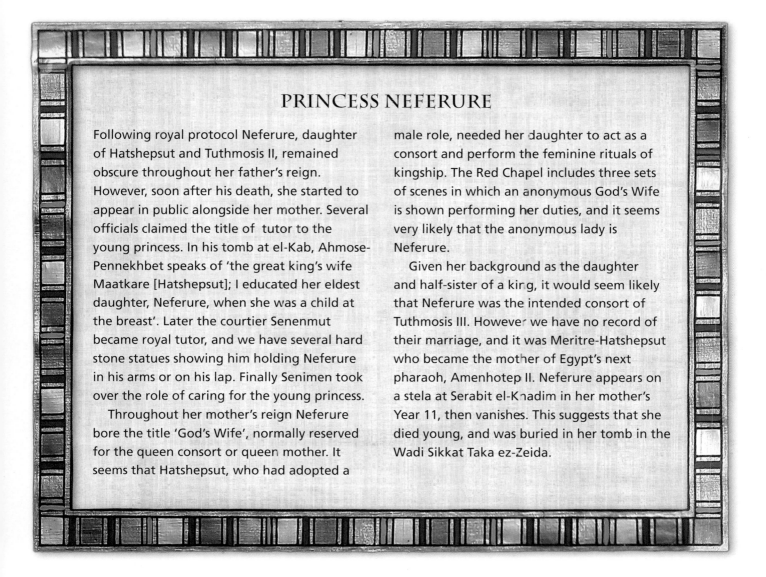

PRINCESS NEFERURE

Following royal protocol Neferure, daughter of Hatshepsut and Tuthmosis II, remained obscure throughout her father's reign. However, soon after his death, she started to appear in public alongside her mother. Several officials claimed the title of tutor to the young princess. In his tomb at el-Kab, Ahmose-Pennekhbet speaks of 'the great king's wife Maatkare [Hatshepsut]; I educated her eldest daughter, Neferure, when she was a child at the breast'. Later the courtier Senenmut became royal tutor, and we have several hard stone statues showing him holding Neferure in his arms or on his lap. Finally Senimen took over the role of caring for the young princess.

Throughout her mother's reign Neferure bore the title 'God's Wife', normally reserved for the queen consort or queen mother. It seems that Hatshepsut, who had adopted a male role, needed her daughter to act as a consort and perform the feminine rituals of kingship. The Red Chapel includes three sets of scenes in which an anonymous God's Wife is shown performing her duties, and it seems very likely that the anonymous lady is Neferure.

Given her background as the daughter and half-sister of a king, it would seem likely that Neferure was the intended consort of Tuthmosis III. However we have no record of their marriage, and it was Meritre-Hatshepsut who became the mother of Egypt's next pharaoh, Amenhotep II. Neferure appears on a stela at Serabit el-Khadim in her mother's Year 11, then vanishes. This suggests that she died young, and was buried in her tomb in the Wadi Sikkat Taka ez-Zeida.

own appointments, selecting men of relatively humble birth such as Senenmut, steward of the estates of Amen and tutor to Neferure. By selecting officials with a personal loyalty to herself, Hatshepsut was able to ensure that she was surrounded by the most devoted of courtiers; those whose careers were inextricably linked to her own. However, by no means all the new appointees were self-made men and some, like Hapuseneb, high priest of Amen and builder of the royal tomb, already had close links with the royal family. After Hatshepsut's death some of her most effective courtiers continued to work for Tuthmosis III, and there is no sign that they suffered because of their connection with the previous regime.

The Deir el-Bahri mortuary temple provides evidence of limited campaigns in Nubia (maybe as many as four, with at least one led by Hatshepsut herself) and in Palestine. But, with no rebels brave or foolish enough to challenge her authority, Hatshepsut had little need to fight. Instead she followed a vigorous policy of trade and

SENENMUT

Hatshepsut's most prominent advisor was a man of relatively humble birth. Senenmut's father, Ramose, bore the non-specific title 'the worthy', while his mother Hatnofer claimed the married woman's title 'Mistress of the House'.

Before Hatshepsut's accession Senenmut bore a clutch of prestigious titles, including 'steward of the property of Hatshepsut and Neferure', and 'tutor to the young princess'. As Hatshepsut claimed her throne he dropped his lesser posts, acquired a batch of more prestigious accolades (including 'overseer of the granaries of Amen-Re' and 'overseer of all the works of the king at Karnak'), and settled into his principal role as steward of Amen. Unofficially he seems to have acted as Hatshepsut's right-hand-man. He is often credited with building all of her monuments and, although there is no evidence that he was actually an architect, he appears to have had a hand in various construction projects in and around Thebes. His main architectural achievements must remain the overseeing of Djeser-Djeseru and the erecting of Hatshepsut's first pair of obelisks at Karnak.

At least 25 hard stone statues of Senenmut have survived. They show him in his various roles; holding Neferure in his arms, or kneeling to present a religious symbol such as a sistrum or a shrine. His close relationship to Hatshepsut, his multiple titles and his wealth have led to speculation that the two may have been lovers. However, beyond a pornographic graffito scrawled on a tomb wall, there is absolutely no evidence to support this assumption.

Senenmut built two tombs: TT 71, conspicuously sited on top of the Sheikh Abd el-Gurna hill, and TT 353, hidden beneath the precincts of Djeser-Djeseru. He vanished from public life at some point between Years 16 and 20, and was never interred in either of his tombs.

Granite sculpture of Senenmut holding Princess Neferure. The hieroglyphic inscriptions on the figure record his many titles, including 'steward of the king's daughter'.

exploration. A Year 9 expedition to Punt, clearly one of the highlights of her reign, should not be seen as an isolated event but as the climax of a series of trading missions which included visits to the Lebanon to collect wood, and the exploitation of the copper and turquoise mines in Sinai.

Back home there was an ambitious building programme, with works in Nubia, Kom Ombo, Hierakonpolis, Elkab, Armant and on the island of Elephantine. In Middle Egypt, approximately one mile (1.6 km) to the southeast of Beni Hassan, there were two new temples dedicated to Pakhet, 'She who Scratches', a fierce lion-headed goddess of the desert. The larger of these temples is today known as the Speos Artemidos. It has just two chambers: an outer pillared hall leading, via a short passage, to an inner sanctuary cut into the living rock. While scenes inside the temple stress Hatshepsut's bond with her father Amen, a long text carved across the front of the temple outlines her policy of renewal and restoration. She, Hatshepsut, is destined to restore *maat*. She even claims to have driven the Hyksos out of Egypt, although this is blatantly untrue. However, she did undertake some restoration work, concentrating on the monuments of Middle Egypt, which had suffered badly during the Second Intermediate Period. Her 'restoration' of the ancient monuments could be brutal. At Karnak, for example, she demolished a gateway built by Tuthmosis II, and remodelled her father's hall by removing its wooden roof and erecting a second pair of obelisks, commissioned to commemorate her *sed*-jubilee in Year 15, in the now-open space.

Hatshepsut was very interested in the processional rituals that saw the gods of Karnak processing both within and outside their temple complex. She improved the avenue linking the temple of Amen-Re to the temple of his consort Mut, and built a series of kiosks to provide resting places for the barque of Amen-Re. A new gateway (Pylon VIII) was built on the southern axis of the temple. This was originally decorated with images of Hatshepsut as pharaoh, but suffered at the hands of later restorers, so that Tuthmosis III and Seti I now feature on the reliefs while Tuthmosis II and Tuthmosis III appear on the doorway. Her main contribution to the temple of Amen-Re was the Red Chapel. This stood on a raised platform immediately in front of the original Middle Kingdom temple, flanked by smaller sandstone cult shrines whose decorations show Hatshepsut making offerings before a variety of gods.

I followed the good god, the King of Upper and Lower Egypt Maatkare, may she live! I saw him [Hatshepsut] overthrowing the Nubian nomads, their chiefs being brought to him as prisoners. I saw him destroying the land of Nubia …

GRAFFITO FROM THE ISLAND OF SEHEL (ASWAN), WRITTEN BY TI

A MORTUARY FIT FOR A QUEEN

Soon after Hatshepsut's accession the tomb in the Wadi Sikkat Taka el-Zeida was abandoned as work began on her two-part funerary monument: a mortuary temple close by the ruined mortuary temple of Montuhotep II at Deir el-Bahri, and a rock-cut tomb in the Valley of the Kings (KV 20). Djeser-Djeseru ('Holiest of the Holy') was a white limestone building occupying three ascending terraces set back against the Theban cliff. It was designed as a multi-functional temple: in addition to the mortuary temples of Hatshepsut and Tuthmosis I there were twin chapels dedicated to Hathor and Anubis, small shrines consecrated to the memory of Hatshepsut's ancestors, and an open-roofed solar temple dedicated to Re-Harakhty. The main shrine was devoted to the cult of Amen-Re, with whom Hatshepsut would become one after death. The temple was decorated with a series of colossal images of the queen, and its walls were carved with scenes chosen to demonstrate Hatshepsut's fitness to rule.

For many years Egyptologists assumed that Tuthmosis II had buried Tuthmosis I in KV 38. However, a recent re-examination of KV 38 has made it clear that, while this tomb was definitely built for Tuthmosis I, it is unlikely to have been started before the reign of Tuthmosis III. It therefore cannot be pharaoh's original tomb, which may still await discovery. However, it seems far more likely that he was originally buried in KV 20, and that Hatshepsut then took the unusual decision to enlarge her father's tomb, making it suitable for a father-daughter burial. This would mean that Tuthmosis I was

THE FEAST OF THE VALLEY

Djeser-Djeseru was the focus of the Amen-based 'Beautiful Festival of the Valley', an annual celebration of death and renewal held at new moon during the second month of summer (May).

Amen-Re (in the form of a statue) dwelt in splendid isolation in the sanctuary of his great temple at the heart of the Karnak complex. But on feast day he would spend the night with Hathor at Djeser-Djeseru. Hidden in a covered shrine, Amen-Re crossed the Nile and sailed along a canal to disembark at the small valley temple situated on the desert edge. He then processed along a gently sloping causeway lined with painted sphinxes. A gateway in a thick limestone wall allowed access to the temple garden. Amen-Re's route lay upwards. Passing over the lower portico he reached the flat second terrace where his path was marked out by pairs of colossal painted red granite sphinxes. A second stairway continued upwards so that Amen-Re entered the body of the temple on its upper and most important level. He passed into the cool shade and, making his way between the imposing pairs of kneeling colossal statues, he reached his own dark shrine cut deep into the rock of the Theban mountain.

That same evening Theban families would set off in procession for the west bank where they would spend the night in the private tomb-chapels of their ancestors. The hours of darkness were spent drinking and feasting as the living celebrated their reunion with the dead. After the climax of the feast, a religious rite performed at sunrise, Amen-Re sailed back to the calm of his sanctuary and the people of Thebes returned home, to bed.

actually interred twice in tomb KV 20; first during his funeral when he was placed in a traditional wooden sarcophagus (now lost) in the original burial chamber, and later, during Hatshepsut's reign, when he was provided with a quartzite sarcophagus and moved down to the new chamber. This chamber has yielded two yellow quartzite sarcophagi, Hatshepsut's matching canopic box, piles of broken pottery, smashed stone vessels, burnt wood and fragments of a large wooden statue.

A stela raised in the Armant temple of Montu records the death of the female pharaoh on the tenth day of the sixth month of Year 22 . Their joint reign now over, Tuthmosis III buried Hatshepsut alongside Tuthmosis I in KV 20, and embarked upon 30 years of solo rule. Hatshepsut's reign, falling as it did entirely within the reign of Tuthmosis III, was effectively invisible. It was excluded from the line of royal ancestors listed by Tuthmosis at Karnak, from the king lists and from the 19th and 20th Dynasty private monuments of Deir el-Medina, which recorded a host of fleeting Tuthmoside princes and princesses. However, her memory must have lingered somewhere, as Manetho was able to include a female ruler named Amense or Amensis, sister of Hebron (Tuthmosis II) and mother of Mishragmouthosis (Tuthmosis III) as the fifth ruler of the 18th Dynasty. He accorded this female ruler a reign of either 21 years 9 months (Josephus) or 22 years (Africanus).

THE 'EGYPTIAN NAPOLEON'?

Tuthmosis III spent the first 22 years of his reign as co-regent to his stepmother Hatshepsut. Many years later, exhibiting a curious insecurity over his right to the throne, he would hint that he had been associated in a co-regency with his father, Tuthmosis II; given that he was no older than six at the time of his father's death, this seems unlikely. He would also promote his non-royal mother, Iset, so that posthumously she acquired the titles of king's great wife and god's wife. And he would occasionally claim to be the son, rather than the grandson, of the great warrior pharaoh Tuthmosis I.

Initially Tuthmosis was very much the junior pharaoh in his joint reign with Hatshepsut. However, the passing years saw a gradual shift in the balance of power so that, by the time of Hatshepsut's death, Tuthmosis was commander-in-chief of the army, with full responsibility for the defence of Egypt's borders. Long after his death Egyptologists, linking pharaoh's small stature to his splendid victories, were to dub him the 'Egyptian Napoleon'. Today it is realized that, while his victories were undoubtedly splendid, Tuthmosis may not have been as short as was supposed. Anatomist G. Elliot Smith recorded the king's height at 1 metre 615 mm (5ft 3 ins), but measured the king without his feet, which had been broken off by ancient tomb robbers.

Towards the end of the co-regency, as Egypt became increasingly troubled by sporadic unrest amongst her eastern client states, Tuthmosis was forced to commit to the first of the series of military campaigns which would reimpose firm control on the Levant. The unrest intensified when Hatshepsut's death sparked revolt among a coalition of Palestinian and Syrian vassals. The coastal cities remained loyal to Egypt but to the north (in modern Turkey), the Indo-European Hittites had developed into a powerful nation who would eventually come into conflict with Egyptian interests in north Syria. Also interested in this region were the Hurrians, an ethnic group who had originated in the northern Zagros (modern Iran) and who were based in the nation-state of Mitanni, along the Upper Euphrates. Allied with the independent city-states of Kadesh and Tunip, Mitanni posed a threat to Egypt. Fortunately Nubia, repeatedly crushed by Ahmose, Amenhotep I and Tuthmosis I, was incapable of effective revolt.

Among the treasures recovered from the tomb of the three foreign (Syrian?) wives of Tuthmosis III in the Wadi Gabbanat el-Qurud was this gold headdress.

[The statue] began wandering through the colonnade... And the men leading it did not understand that it was looking everywhere for my majesty. When it reached me, it stopped ... I threw myself on my belly before him, I grovelled in the dust, I bowed down in front of him ... He opened the gates of heaven for me, he unlocked the doors of the horizon and I flew up to heaven like a divine falcon ...

THE YOUNG TUTHMOSIS III IS CHOSEN BY THE ORACLE OF AMEN-RE: FROM HIS CORONATION INSCRIPTION

THREE FOREIGN WIVES OF TUTHMOSIS III

An undecorated tomb in the Wadi Gabbanat el-Qurud ('Valley of the Cemetery of the Ape'), in western Thebes, housed the burials of three foreign women. Unfortunately the tomb was discovered by tomb robbers and, by the time of the official excavation in September 1916, the mummies had been destroyed and only the objects unwanted by the robbers remained. Archaeologists were, however, able to buy some of the looted artefacts from local dealers.

The grave goods included the names of Tuthmosis III, Hatshepsut the consort and Hatshepsut the pharaoh. The names of the three women, recorded on their canopic jars, are Manuwai, Manhata and Maruta; these names suggest that all three came from the Syro/Palestinian region. It seems likely that all three women died at roughly the same time, but as the bodies have been lost we have no means of knowing either how they died, or why they were entombed together.

Tuthmosis was to spend 17 years establishing control over his eastern vassals. His army followed a seasonal campaign trail that led them from one fortified city-state to the next. Many cities found it prudent to concede without fighting. Those who did resist soon found themselves under siege. When they ran out of supplies and surrendered – as they inevitably did – Tuthmosis would sack the city and appoint a local ruler to govern on his behalf. The male children of the local chiefs would be sent to be educated, and indoctrinated, in Egyptian schools. Their sisters would become wives in the royal harem.

In Year 22 Tuthmosis crossed the Sinai Peninsula and headed for Gaza, a city loyal to Egypt. From there he attacked and occupied Yehem, a fortified city occupied by a consortium of enemies headed by the prince of Kadesh. He then advanced eastwards across the Carmel mountain range to Megiddo (modern Israel; see p.115) where he faced another coalition of enemies again led by the prince of Kadesh. The city fell after a seven-month siege.

In Year 29 Tuthmosis captured the Tunip-controlled coastal towns of Ullaza and Ardata before, in Year 30, attacking Kadesh. Year 33 saw the Egyptian army sailing to Byblos. Here they struck camp and waited as the local carpenters built a fleet of boats which were to be loaded in pieces onto carts, and transported with the troops. After three fierce skirmishes at Aleppo, Tuthmosis stood on the west bank of the Euphrates at Carchemish, facing the Mitannian army on the east bank. Now Tuthmosis played his master-stroke. Assembling his prefabricated boats he crossed the Euphrates and advanced deep into Mitannian territory. The Mitannians, fleeing before the Egyptians, were forced to hide ignominiously in caves. Like his grandfather before him, Tuthmosis was able to erect a boundary stela on the east bank of the Euphrates. He then paused on the long journey home to enjoy a relaxing elephant hunt in Syria. His prowess as a hunter is recorded in the tomb autobiography of Amenemheb, who recounts with great admiration that his pharaoh 'hunted 120 elephants for their teeth'. This may be compared with an inscription in the Armant temple which tells how Tuthmosis III 'brought down a rhinoceros with an arrow in the southern Nubian desert'.

TUTHMOSIS III

Dynasty: 18th

Father: Tuthmosis II

Mother: Iset

Consorts: Sitiah, Meritre-Hatshepsut, Nebta

Burial Place: KV 34

Successor: Amenhotep II

Tuthmosis's celebrations proved premature. Just two years later the Egyptian army was again facing the troops of Mitanni, and this time the enemy gained the advantage. Tuthmosis campaigned in the north again in Year 42, when Tunip was captured and Kadesh attacked. This was followed, in Year 50, by a brief and unremarkable Nubian campaign.

WORKING FOR POSTERITY

Tuthmosis ruled over an empire whose borders, marked by boundary stelae, stretched from Gebel Barkal, beyond the Third Cataract in Nubia, to the banks of the Euphrates in Syria. Now he made sure that his valour would never be forgotten. The details of his campaigns had been preserved by a band of military scribes who recorded events in an official 'day book'. These were to be inscribed on the walls of two newly built halls situated behind Pylon VI in the Karnak temple of Amen-Re. Known today as *The Annals,* Tuthmosis's account is Egypt's most extensive surviving monumental inscription.

An extensive building programme was underway, benefiting all the major Egyptian towns from Elephantine to Heliopolis plus several sites in the Nile Delta and Nubia. As Amen-Re had inspired Tuthmosis it was only right that the god should benefit from his victories, and much of the booty, tribute and taxes collected from the eastern vassals was used to finance a major remodelling of the Karnak complex. This was timed to coincide with the preparations for the celebration of the *sed*-jubilee, as Tuthmosis became the first New Kingdom monarch legitimately entitled to such a celebration. The complex was embellished with two new gateways and a new temple dedicated to Ptah, while the limestone chapels built by Amenhotep I were demolished and replaced by sandstone shrines. Plans to erect a unique single standing obelisk were

The campaigns of Tuthmosis III brought the restive client states of Egypt firmly to heel. This mural, from the Theban tomb of Menkheperrasonb, shows foreigners paying homage and bringing tribute to the victorious pharaoh.

A SOLDIER'S LIFE

There was no professional Old Kingdom army. Pharaoh was protected by a company of bodyguards, and the nomarchs maintained their own private troops who could be commandeered in times of emergency. By the early New Kingdom a proper army had developed offering, for the first time, a career to young men who did not wish to follow their fathers' trade or profession. The more important military positions quickly became hereditary.

For many centuries Egypt's soldiers had carried relatively simple weapons: bows and arrows, copper axes, flint or copper-tipped spears and clubs or maces. There was no armour; soldiers fought bare-chested in a short kilt, protected by a large, rectangular, cow-hide shield. This was all very well when fighting the equally ill-equipped Nubians, but Egypt's eastern enemies were more sophisticated. The cumbersome shields were replaced by shorter, lighter versions while the simple bow was swapped for the more efficient composite bow and a new metal dagger evolved into a short sword. Body armour was made from small bronze or leather leaves sewn on to jackets. While the majority of the troops remained bare-headed, pharaoh started to wear a leather helmet known today as the blue war crown.

The horse and chariot, introduced by the Hyksos, were to play an increasingly important role in military life. Tuthmosis III fought at

Painted relief from Djeser-Djeseru, Deir el-Bahri, showing a victory parade of soldiers returning from Hatshepsut's expedition to Punt in Year 9 of her reign.

Megiddo with a large complement of foot soldiers supported by a few chariots: two centuries later Ramesses II fought at Kadesh with an army formally divided between infantry and chariotry.

DEVELOPING THE EMPIRE 115

well underway before they were shelved; the obelisk would eventually by raised by Tuthmosis's grandson, Tuthmosis IV. Meanwhile, on the Theban west bank, Medinet Habu benefited from a new temple dedicated to Amen and a new mortuary temple dedicated to the cult of Tuthmosis II. In the Deir el-Bahri bay the masons were busy creating Djeser-Akhet ('Holy of the Horizon'), Tuthmosis's mortuary temple, which was being raised between the temples of Montuhotep II and Hatshepsut. Today little more than a ruin, Djeser-Akhet was similar in plan to Djeser-Djeseru and, being built on higher ground, was designed to dominate Hatshepsut's monument.

It was at this time that Tuthmosis made a serious attempt to erase all evidence of Hatshepsut's reign by defacing her statues and inscriptions. This programme occurred throughout Egypt, but is today most obvious at Thebes, home to the majority of Hatshepsut's monuments. At Djeser-Djeseru her cartouches and images were chiselled off the walls and her statues torn down and dumped in rubbish pits, while at Karnak the Red Chapel was dismantled and her obelisks were walled up within the vestibule in front of Pylon V. Early Egyptologists, under the misapprehension that this vandalism occurred soon after Hatshepsut's death, interpreted it as evidence for a long-suppressed and entirely understandable hatred of the woman who had usurped Tuthmosis's throne. But there is no evidence of any rivalry between the two during their joint reign and, given that the campaign against Hatshepsut is now known to have been conducted after 20 years of solo rule, it seems at least equally likely that Tuthmosis was merely embarking on an impersonal cleansing of his own history. By removing every trace of Hatshepsut's reign – by relegating her to her proper place as a queen who assisted a pharaoh's rule – he could ensure that the succession ran from Tuthmosis I to Tuthmosis II and III without any female interference.

As part of his reinvention of the past, Tuthmosis III removed the body of his grandfather, Tuthmosis I, from the tomb he shared with Hatshepsut. He was reinterred in an even more magnificent tomb (KV 38) where yet another yellow quartzite sarcophagus was dedicated to Tuthmosis I and inscribed by his loving grandson: 'it was his son who caused his name to live in making excellent the monument of [his] father for all eternity'.

In Year 51 Tuthmosis appointed his son as co-regent. Two years later the 18-year-old Amenhotep II buried Egypt's greatest warrior king in tomb KV 34 in the Valley of the Kings. Tuthmosis III had ruled Egypt for 53 years, 10 months and 26 days.

THE BATTLE OF MEGIDDO

There were three possible ways of approaching Megiddo. In a council of war, Tuthmosis's generals made it clear that they preferred to travel along the wider, easier roads. But Tuthmosis, wiser and braver than his generals, disagreed. He personally led his troops on a three-day march in single file along a winding mountain pass. This daring move allowed him to creep up on the enemy camped outside the city walls.

As dawn broke over the mountains, the rising sun illuminated the high ground which, it was now obvious, was occupied by a huge Egyptian army. At the head of his troops stood Tuthmosis himself, protected by the great god Amen-Re. The battle was easily won. Then, as the defeated enemy ran back towards the city walls, the Egyptian troops defied orders and stopped to loot the abandoned camps. The city gates were slammed shut and the rulers of Megiddo and Kadesh had to be hauled to safety by their clothing. Undaunted, Tuthmosis built a thick wall around the city and waited. The outcome was inevitable.

PHARAOHS OF THE SUN

C.1427–1295 BC

*A relief from the royal tomb at Amarna (ancient Akhetaten)
shows the 18th Dynasty ruler Akhenaten and the royal
family offering to the sun disk known as the Aten.
The pharaoh and queen hold lotus flowers.*

SUNRISE

AMENHOTEP II AND TUTHMOSIS IV

Mid-18th Dynasty c.1427–1390 BC

TUTHMOSIS III WAS A VERY HARD ACT TO FOLLOW. AMENHOTEP II WAS TO ENJOY 30 YEARS OF SUCCESSFUL, prosperous rule, yet his reign is almost entirely overshadowed by his father's extraordinary achievements and Amenhotep himself remains something of an enigma. Like Tuthmosis before him, the new pharaoh was prepared to fight – and fight hard – to defend his borders. But the political climate had changed, war was slowly giving way to peace and Egypt, the acknowledged superpower of the Mediterranean world, had few enemies left to subdue.

Amenhotep enjoyed two significant, extremely bloody campaigns in the Levant, in Years 7 and 9, which ended with the corpses of his defeated enemies hanging from the temple walls. Soon after he negotiated a peace treaty with Mitanni. The rulers of Mitanni, Babylon and Hatti were now to be regarded as somewhat inferior brother kings.

Amenhotep II offers to the gods. The Sphinx Stela gives details of his accession: 'Now his Majesty appeared as king as a fine youth after he had become well developed, and had completed 18 years in his strength and bravery'.

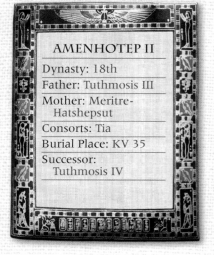

AMENHOTEP II

Dynasty: 18th

Father: Tuthmosis III

Mother: Meritre-
Hatshepsut

Consorts: Tia

Burial Place: KV 35

Successor:
Tuthmosis IV

THE SPORTING PHARAOH

With no enemies left worth fighting, Amenhotep's reign was essentially a peaceful one. There were building works at all the principal Egyptian and Nubian sites (including Heliopolis, Hermopolis, Abydos, Coptos, Esna, Elephantine, Amada and Buhen). At Karnak, where the proscription of Hatshepsut's monuments continued, he built a garden, a palace and various shrines and boat shrines. Preparations were underway for Amenhotep's *sed*-celebrations with the erection of a new festival pavilion decorated with solar images – sun disks and falcons – which would link the king with the sun god Re-Harakhty. Unfortunately Amenhotep did not live long enough to celebrate his jubilee and his pavilion was dismantled during the late 18th-Dynasty reign of Horemheb.

At Giza, Khaefre's Great Sphinx, now over 1000 years old, had become a focus for the celebration of the cult of the royal ancestors. Here Amenhotep II built a temple to the god Horemakhet ('Horus-of-the-Horizon'; a form of Re-Harakhty) who had become associated with the Sphinx, and raised a stela to commemorate his own considerable sporting achievements. He proclaimed his prowess in archery, running, rowing and riding. This was no vain boast. Victory through sport was an obvious means of demonstrating pharaoh's superiority, and every depiction of the victorious king magically reinforced his ability to succeed. Amenhotep had studied archery under the expert bowman Min of Thinis. Scenes in Min's tomb (TT 109) show a lesson in progress. The boy Amenhotep aims at a large rectangular target and his arrows stick in place; the damaged text includes some of Min's instructions: 'Stretch your bow up to your ear. Make strong …' The third Karnak pylon shows Amenhotep II standing in his

Following his return from his first victorious campaign in eastern Syria, where he had killed all his enemies and extended the borders of Egypt, Pharaoh [Amenhotep II] approached his father Amen happily, after personally smiting the seven princes who had previously ruled the land of Takhshi and hanging their corpses head-down from the prow of his flagship ... Six of these bodies he hung from the city wall at Thebes, along with their severed hands. The remaining body he transported south to Nubia to hang from the enclosure wall of Napata, so that his victories would be remembered forever throughout the land of Nubia ...

FROM THE AMADA STELA OF AMENHOTEP II

chariot to aim at an ingot-shaped target. Hunting and battle chariots normally carried both a charioteer and a huntsman or soldier, but convention dictated that pharaohs should always be shown alone, driving with the reins tied around their waists.

So confident was Amenhotep in his own physical abilities that he was prepared to risk humiliation by taking part in a genuine contest. A broken stela from Medamud tells how he first shot an arrow through a copper target three fingers deep, then offered a prize to anyone who could match his achievement. Unsurprisingly, no one could. When, in 1892, Victor Loret discovered Amenhotep lying in his sarcophagus in the Valley of the Kings (KV 35), he found the king's longbow lying by his side. The bow was stolen in 1900, and has never been recovered.

The history of the royal family grows increasingly confused towards the end of Amenhotep's reign. Unusually – since royal sons were routinely excluded from the official family groups that included their sisters – we know the names of several princes, including Amenhotep, Khaemwaset, Amenmopet, Ahmose, Webensenu and Nedjem. Despite this superfluity of sons, we know of only one queen, the shadowy consort Tia, mother of the next pharaoh, Tuthmosis IV. With no prominent consort, Amenhotep relied upon his mother, Meritre-Hatshepsut, to serve as God's Wife of Amen.

THE DREAMING PRINCE

Like his father before him, Tuthmosis IV erected a stela (the Dream Stela) between the paws of the Great Sphinx. This red granite stela tells a curious tale: Tuthmosis, a lesser son with no realistic hope of inheriting the throne, was enjoying a day's hunting in the Giza desert. Hot, thirsty and tired, he flung himself down in the shade offered by the sand-covered Sphinx and fell quickly into a deep sleep. In a vivid dream, the solar deity Horemakhet-Khepri-Re-Atum appeared before him. The god, a version of Re-Harakhty incorporating all aspects of the solar deity (Khepri the morning sun, Re the midday sun and Atum the dying evening sun), implored his 'son' to restore his neglected Sphinx. This Tuthmosis did, employing labourers to clear away a small mountain of sand and then repair a broken paw and a hole in the Sphinx's chest. The god rewarded Tuthmosis by making him pharaoh. How he did this is not made clear; we must assume that he caused the deaths of the older royal sons (natural deaths? Or deaths after a dynastic struggle?), as there is nothing to suggest that Amenhotep II ever regarded Tuthmosis as his successor. From this time on Tuthmosis acknowledged Re-Harakhty rather than Amen-Re as his own personal patron, and the solar gods started to play an increasingly important role in state religion.

Tuthmosis IV promoted his mother, Tia, to the position of God's Wife of Amen. A colossal statue recovered from Karnak shows mother and son sitting side by side, each with a protective arm around the other. This close relationship is emphasized in a series of inscriptions indicating that Tia is to be regarded as the earthly counterpart of the goddesses Hathor, Isis and Mut.

Tuthmosis travelled southwards into the eastern desert on a mission to inspect, and exert authority over, the vital gold transportation routes. He also conducted a brief, successful, 'campaign of victory' in Syria. But a treaty with the king of Mitanni, reinforced by a marriage with the king's daughter, ensured that there was little need to fight. Freed from the need to finance a large army, Tuthmosis undertook an ambitious building programme in Egypt and Nubia. The major state temples benefited from his generosity, Karnak was once again remodelled and, after a 35-year wait, the single obelisk cut by Tuthmosis III was finally raised at the eastern end of the complex and dedicated to Re-Harakhty. Unfortunately, however, time ran out and many of Tuthmosis's projects had to be finished by his son and successor, Amenhotep III. Tuthmosis's preparations for death, too, were incomplete. He had started two tombs; now the more impressive KV 22 was abandoned as KV 43 was made ready. Here, after a reign of no more than ten years, Tuthmosis was buried alongside two of his children.

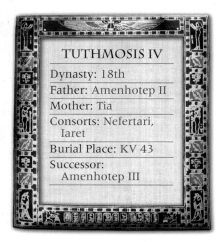

TUTHMOSIS IV

Dynasty: 18th
Father: Amenhotep II
Mother: Tia
Consorts: Nefertari, Iaret
Burial Place: KV 43
Successor: Amenhotep III

THE NEW KINGDOM HAREM

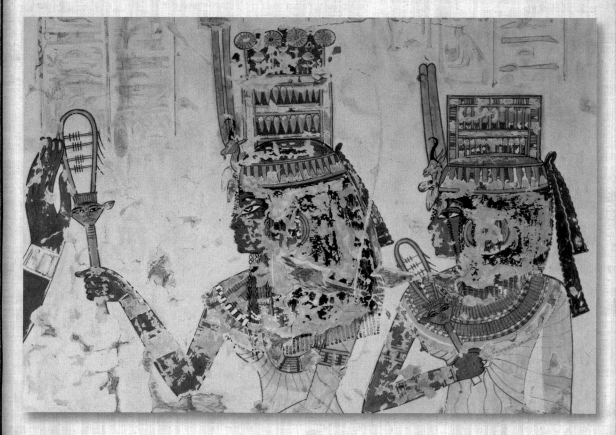

The pharaohs of the Old and Middle Kingdoms had been satisfied with one queen consort plus a harem of secondary wives about whom we know very little. But during the 13th Dynasty queen consorts started to use the title 'King's Great Wife'; a title which suggests the need to distinguish the consort from other, lesser, wives.

The New Kingdom saw a dramatic increase in the number of royal brides. By the reign of Tuthmosis IV the harem was home to a number of important foreign princesses and their retinues including a daughter of Artatama of Mitanni. These princesses travelled to Egypt with a rich dowry that was exchanged for a bride-price. Other, lesser, brides were the daughters of vassal states sent as tribute to the Egyptian king; they remained in the royal harem providing an effective

The two daughters of Menna, 'royal favourites', are shown holding the percussion instrument known as the sistrum (detail from a mural in the tomb of Menna at Thebes).

guarantee of their father's loyalty to pharaoh. The least important foreign wives were simply sent in groups to Egypt as gifts for pharaoh.

Egyptian princesses never made diplomatic foreign marriages and when the king of Babylon, whose own daughter was married to Amenhotep III, inquired about a bride for his own harem he was given short shrift: 'since the days of old, no Egyptian king's daughter has been given to anyone.' It was not until the 21st Dynasty that, so the Bible tells us, an Egyptian princess was sent as a bride to the Jewish king Solomon.

THE DAZZLING SUN DISK
AMENHOTEP III

Mid-18th Dynasty *c.*1390 – 1352 BC

THERE IS NO MENTION OF MUTEMWIA, MOTHER OF AMENHOTEP III, DURING THE REIGN OF TUTHMOSIS IV. THIS suggests that the new king's mother was a woman of humble birth whose 10-year-old son was, for some reason, selected by Tuthmosis IV as his successor. A lingering feeling of insecurity may explain why, many years later, Amenhotep had the story of his divine birth carved into the walls of the Luxor temple, a place strongly associated with celebration of the divine royal soul. His story, a blatant plagiarism of Hatshepsut's tale, tells how the beautiful, trusting Mutemwia is seduced by Amen-Re, who, cunning in his deception, has disguised himself as Tuthmosis IV.

Amenhotep III had little need to fight. He already ruled the whole world. He is therefore credited with just one or two Nubian campaigns, the best recorded of which, in Year 5, saw Amenhotep passing beyond the fifth cataract, and ended with him acquiring 740 prisoners of war and 312 hands cut from the enemy dead. This triumph was celebrated on stelae erected at Aswan and on Sai Island (Sudan), allowing Amenhotep to take his rightful place amongst the defenders of *maat*. Denied the glories of the battlefield, the new pharaoh proved his bravery by hunting big game. Amenhotep recorded his slaughter of 96 bulls on a scarab published throughout his realm in Year 2, when he is unlikely to have been more than 15 years old. A second scarab tells us that he killed an impressive 102 lions during the first decade of his reign. These scarabs formed part of a series of five large-scale commemorative scarabs, mass-produced, whose undersides were inscribed with Amenhotep's news.

> *Word reached His Majesty that wild bulls had turned up in the desert around the District of the Lake. That night pharaoh sailed north in the royal ship 'Rising in Truth'. He reached the District of the Lake safely at dawn. Then His Majesty mounted his chariot, followed by the whole of his army .... He proceeded to hunt the bulls. Out of a total of 170 bulls, His Majesty bagged 56 in a single day. For the next four days he did nothing, so that his horses could recover. Then His Majesty mounted his chariot again. This time he bagged a total of 40 bulls, making a grand total of 96 bulls.*

Detail of a statue of Amenhotep III, which came to light when a cache of royal statuary was discovered at the Luxor Temple complex in 1989.

It is from another of these scarabs that we learn of Amenhotep's marriage to Tiy: 'King of Upper and Lower Egypt, Nebmaatre, son of Re, Amenhotep ruler of Thebes, given life, and the king's great wife Tiy, may she live. The name of her father is Yuya and the name of her mother is Thuyu. She is the wife of a mighty king.'

The so-called 'marriage scarab' is tantalizingly brief, but still conveys an important message. Although Tiy is not of the royal blood she is the queen consort, and her son will inherit the throne. In fact, there seems to have been little danger that the forceful Tiy would be pushed into the background. She was consistently mentioned in official correspondence, where her reputation as the true power behind the throne endured beyond Amenhotep's death, and was even included on the scarab published to celebrate Amenhotep's marriage to Gilukhepa of Mitanni. The only prominent role that Tiy did not play was that of God's Wife of Amen.

Tiy bore six children: two sons (Tuthmosis and Amenhotep) and four daughters (Sitamen, Henut-Taneb, Isis and Nebetah). There may have been a fifth daughter. The Amarna tomb of Huya, 'Steward in the House of the King's Mother, King's Wife, Tiy' includes two scenes showing Tiy accompanied by a young girl who is simply identified as the 'King's Daughter' Beketaten. Beketaten's parents are unnamed, but it is possible that she is either a previously unknown daughter of Tiy or, perhaps, the otherwise ephemeral Nebetah under a new name.

Towards the end of her father's reign the eldest daughter, Sitamen, assumed the title 'King's Great Wife', although she never took precedence over Tiy. The obvious implication is that Sitamen must have married her father; we must ask whether this was a true marriage, or a theoretical one designed to provide the otherwise unmarriageable Sitamen with rank, a household and an income, while supplying Tiy with a deputy to assist in her many duties. If, as Egyptologists suspect, the queen's religious duties included references to her own fertility, the substitution of a daughter in some of the rituals may have made sound theological sense. Certainly pharaohs liked to be associated with three generations of royal women – their mother, wives and daughters – just as the god Re was associated with Hathor, who could be his mother, wife or daughter.

'THE LIKE OF WHICH HAD NEVER EXISTED ...'

Amenhotep's ambition was a simple one. He aimed to build monuments throughout his land, 'the like of which had never existed before'. Freed from the need to maintain a large army, and made wealthy by the taxes, tribute, Nubian gold and home-grown grain flowing into the treasury, he had the resources to achieve his goal. One of his first acts was to open new limestone quarries at Tura (near modern Cairo) and Deir el-Bersha (Middle Egypt) to provide the blocks for his new buildings.

While there would be works throughout Egypt and Nubia, Thebes was to serve as the focus of his construction programme. Tuthmosis III had ruled from Memphis, and his descendants had continued this tradition. Now, with long-term stability in the east, and the continuing growth of the west bank as the élite necropolis, Amenhotep moved his residence to Thebes, leaving Memphis as the northern administrative centre. On the east bank of the Nile the Karnak complex was once again remodelled, with many earlier structures dismantled and used as filing or foundations for the new buildings. Indeed, much of residential Thebes was flattened as the old mud-brick town made way for the ever-expanding complex. The redesigned city, built on lower-level ground, is today lost beneath the groundwater. Karnak received two new gateways: Pylon III was 'a very great gateway before Amen-Re, covered in gold throughout' while the

unfinished Pylon X, decorated with scenes of Amenhotep triumphant, made
a suitable background for two colossal statues of the king. There was a new
temple to Maat, and a major renovation of the temple of Mut. Meanwhile,
at nearby Luxor, the limestone temple built by Hatshepsut and Tuthmosis
III was demolished to make way for a grander sandstone temple.

Over on the west bank at Kom el-Hetan, directly opposite the Luxor
temple, work was underway on the construction of Amenhotep's
magnificent mortuary temple. Close by, he founded the 'Palace of the
Dazzling Aten and House of Rejoicing', an extensive complex known
today as the Malkata Palace. Here was everything a king would ever
need: private apartments, public audience chambers, a festival hall, a
temple dedicated to Amen, rooms for officials and servants and extensive
storage facilities. A nearby village housed the palace servants, while an
artificial harbour provided easy access for goods, and a suitable setting for the
pageantry of Amenhotep's *sed*-festival celebrations in Years 30, 34 and 37. Splendid
though it was, the mud-brick, plaster-coated Malkata Palace was never intended to be
a permanent structure, and it was abandoned soon after Amenhotep's death.

Amenhotep corresponded regularly with his near equals, his brother kings in
Mitanni, Babylon, Assyria, Hatti, Arzawa (western Anatolia) and Alashiya (Cyprus),
and with his inferiors, the vassals whose constant complaints kept the Egyptian
bureaucrats busy. Written in Akkadian, the language of Babylonia, these letters united
his extensive empire. We would know nothing about them, however, were it not for a
chance discovery. In AD 1887 a peasant woman conducted a clandestine excavation at
the ancient site of Amarna, looking for antiquities and for *sebbakh* (decayed ancient
mud-brick), which was valued as a fertilizer. She discovered a collection of baked clay
'bricks' covered in tiny lines and started to sell them on the illegal antiquities market.

Damaged head in yew-wood of Tiy, queen consort of Amenhotep III. Tiy was the subject of numerous depictions: she appeared alongside her husband on public monuments and in private tombs, while her cartouche was linked with his on official inscriptions, as well as on more personal household furniture and fittings.

GILUKHEPA AND TADUKHEPA

Amenhotep's harem housed an estimated 1000 wives, including princesses
from Syria (2), Babylon (2), Arzawa (Anatolia) and Mitanni (2), the last two
being the best known.

Tuthmosis IV had married a princess of Mitanni, but his death broke the
diplomatic bond between the two kingdoms. So, in Year 10, Amenhotep
married Gilukhepa, daughter of Shutturna II of Mitanni. The commemorative
scarab issued at the time tells us that the bride arrived in Egypt accompanied
by a retinue of some 317 attendants. Eventually Shutturna was succeeded
by his son Tushratta. Amenhotep was by this time a sick old man but he
nevertheless started negotiations for the hand of Tushratta's daughter,
Tadukhepa. Amenhotep died just as his new bride arrived in Egypt, and
Tadukhepa was inherited by the new pharaoh, Amenhotep IV.

Initially Egyptologists, unable to read the cuneiform script, dismissed the bricks as forgeries. It was not until a considerable number had been destroyed that it was realized that they were the remains of the royal diplomatic archive preserved on clay tablets. Today we have just over 350 tablets and tablet-fragments, dating from the later part of the reign of Amenhotep III to Year 3 of Tutankhamen.

A LIVING GOD

As chief priest of all religious cults, Amenhotep served all of Egypt's gods. Ptah of Memphis, Re of Heliopolis and Thoth of Hermopolis benefited from his generosity, and we may fairly assume that there were building works at all the regional temples. However, while he scrupulously acknowledged Amen-Re as the patron god of his empire, it seems that Amenhotep felt little personal need of the support of the warrior god who had so inspired the earlier 18th-Dynasty pharaohs. Instead, following the trend set by his father and his grandfather, he developed an interest in the ancient northern sun cults. His new temples included open solar courts that bathed the faithful in sunlight. In particular, he became increasingly fascinated by an old but hitherto rather obscure genderless solar deity named the Aten. The Aten had once taken the form of a falcon but from the time of Amenhotep II onwards it was depicted as a blank, faceless sun's disk radiating long ray-like arms tipped with hands capable of holding religious symbols. Suddenly the Aten was everywhere, and even the king's pleasure barge was named 'The Aten Dazzles'.

At the same time Amenhotep was starting to explore his own divinity. We have already seen his birth story, recorded on the walls of the newly refurbished Luxor temple. The colossal statues of himself, positioned outside the temple gates, were neither enormous works of art nor gigantic, true-to-life portraits. Each statue was a potentially divine being, an intermediary standing partway between mortal man and the remote gods. As such each statue had a name, and each had its own cult following and its own cult priest. Amenhotep was to commission over 1000 free-standing statues of himself, many at a colossal scale suitable for worship.

In front of the eastern gateway of his mortuary temple at Kom el-Hetan, Amenhotep III had two gigantic seated quartzite statues of himself erected. Today, with the temple long since vanished, the two eroded statues, known as the 'Colossi of Memnon', sit in splendid isolation beside the modern road.

His *sed*-festival marked a turning point in his self-presentation. Prior to this, Amenhotep was clearly a man, albeit with divine attributes. Afterwards his identification with the Aten or sun disk was made more obvious as the cult of the Aten was used to develop the cult of the living king. Tradition dictated that pharaoh should become fully divine only at his death, but Amenhotep was already recognized as the living embodiment of Ptah, and worshipped at Memphis in the temple of Nebmaatre-United-with-Ptah. Beyond Egypt's borders he was worshipped as a god in his own right. At Soleb in Nubia Amenhotep built a temple for Amen-Re; at nearby Sedeinga Tiy was given a temple dedicated to a local version of the goddess Hathor. These twin temples were not just built for the royal couple, they were dedicated to them, so that at Soleb we can see Amenhotep offering to his own image, Nebmaatre-Lord-of-Nubia, while Tiy, the earthly manifestation of Hathor-Tefnut, took the form of a sphinx to prowl across the pillars of her Sedeinga temple. After his death, Amenhotep IV would be shown worshipping his father at Soleb while at the Theban tomb of Kheruef, which features Amenhotep III and Tiy linked with various solar deities, a scene shows the king and queen in the evening boat of Re.

PATRON OF THE ARTS

Decades of unprecedented wealth, an abundance of raw materials, contact with neighbouring societies and three *sed*-festivals inspired Egypt's artists and craftsmen. The sculptors, painters, potters, jewellers, glass and faience makers (and, we may reasonably assume, although the evidence is absent, textile workers, joiners, musicians and performers) were stimulated as they had never been before and Amenhotep's new buildings were beautifully decorated and furnished inside and out.

From the very start of the dynastic age pharaoh had traditionally been depicted as a young, healthy, idealized man. But by the end of Amenhotep's long reign, artists were starting to experiment with a different, more fluid style of royal representation. Our last glimpse of Amenhotep is of a bloated king dressed in loose and flimsy robes, slumped in a chair, his seemingly alert and vigorous (but sadly, badly damaged) wife by his side. The intention was perhaps to show Amenhotep in an informal, relaxed setting but many early Egyptologists were deeply unimpressed. Reading the art literally – always a mistake in ancient Egypt – some concluded that Amenhotep must have entered into a premature senility brought about by sexual excess, and that Tiy was now effectively ruling the country on her husband's behalf. Although Tiy did indeed outlive her husband, there is no archaeological or textual evidence to support such an assumption.

Amenhotep's highest recorded date is Year 38. Soon after, at probably less than 50 years of age, he died. He was buried in the tomb abandoned by his father; tomb KV 22 in the Western Valley, an offshoot of the Valley of the Kings. Since his intended heir, Tuthmosis, had predeceased him, he was succeeded by a younger son who took the throne as Amenhotep IV. It has been argued that there may have been a period of co-regency, with the two Amenhoteps ruling together for maybe as little as two years or as long as 12. So far the evidence put forward to support this theory is highly ambiguous.

Now you are asking for my daughter as your bride, but my sister was given to you by my father and is there with you although no one has seen her and no one knows whether she is still alive or dead.

KADESHMAN-ENLIL OF BABYLON SEEKS HIS SISTER (AMARNA LETTER 1)

HIGH NOON
AMENHOTEP IV/AKHENATEN
AND THE AMARNA PERIOD

Late 18th Dynasty c.1352 – 1336 BC

AMENHOTEP IV ('AMEN IS SATISFIED') WAS CROWNED AT THEBES BY AMEN-RE. THE FIRST INDICATION THAT his reign was to be different from all others came in Year 2, with the announcement that a *sed*-festival was to be celebrated next year. The builders were galvanized into action; there were new sun temples at Heliopolis and Memphis, and a new sandstone quarry was opened at Gebel Silsila (north of Aswan). Thebes, the focus of the celebration, received four new temples orientated towards the east and dedicated to the worship of the sun. Among these, situated to the east of the existing Karnak complex, were *Gempaaten* ('the Sun-Disk is found'), an open temple surrounded by a roofed colonnade and decorated with colossal images of the king, and its subsidiary, the *Hwt-Benben* ('Mansion of the *Benben*-Stone'), home to a female-centred solar cult. Neither temple has survived, but archaeologists have recovered thousands of disjointed inscribed sandstone blocks (*talatat* blocks; the dismantled temple walls) from within later walls and gateways and it has proved possible to reconstruct a number of the lost scenes.

The *Gempaaten* blocks confirm that many of the great state gods, including Amen-Re himself, were excluded from the *sed*-celebrations. This deliberate insult was just a foretaste of what was to come. By the end of Year 5 Amenhotep had abolished most of the established pantheon, replacing the multitude of deities with one god, the Aten. The old temples were closed and the court relocated to the new, purpose-built city of Akhetaten (Horizon of the Aten: modern Amarna). Rejecting the name that linked him with the despised Amen, Amenhotep IV became Akhenaten, 'Living Spirit of the Aten'.

Akhenaten offers to the Aten. The pharaoh's androgynous body shape was probably a deliberate icon of his divinity and not, as some recent scholars have speculated, evidence of a genetic disorder or other disfiguring medical condition.

HERETIC OR VISIONARY?

To describe Akhenaten as a heretic is easy but lazy. Argument has raged long and hard over the nature of Akhenaten's inspiration. Was this a genuine religious conversion? Or was it merely an excuse to attack the increasingly powerful state priesthoods? Was Akhenaten a genius, or an unbalanced self-obsessive? Whatever his motivation it is clear that Akhenaten felt entirely free to distance himself from the traditions and expectations of Egyptian monarchy.

Early in his reign Akhenaten took Nefertiti as his consort. The new queen's parents are never named but circumstantial evidence indicates that she was the daughter of

the courtier Ay, who himself is likely to have been a second son of Yuya and Thuya and therefore brother to the king's mother Tiy. If his much-used title of 'god's father' is to be taken literally Ay, like Yuya before him, must have been the father-in-law of the king, and Akhenaten must have married his cousin. Ay's wife, Tey, claims to have been the 'nurse of the king's great wife Nefertiti, nurse of the goddess, ornament of the pharaoh'. This would suggest that Tey was a second wife who raised her deceased predecessor's child. Nefertiti was to give Akhenaten six daughters. The elder three, Meritaten, Meketaten and Ankhesenpaaten were born at Thebes while the younger three, Neferneferuaten-the-Younger, Neferneferure and Setepenre were born at Amarna.

The reconstructed scenes from the *Hwt-Benben* show Nefertiti and Meritaten shaking their sacred rattles beneath the rays of the Aten, and Nefertiti herself making offerings to the Aten, while Akhenaten remains conspicuous by his absence. Meanwhile, blocks recovered from Karnak and Hermopolis show Nefertiti wielding either a mace or a sword to smite a female foe. In all these scenes Nefertiti wears her own unique headdress, a tall, straight-edged, flat-topped blue crown reminiscent of the crown worn by the goddess Tefnut. By Year 5 Nefertiti had been renamed Neferneferuaten-Nefertiti ('Beautiful are the Beauties of the Aten, A Beautiful Woman has Come'), and within her cartouche the name 'Aten' had been reversed to face the determinative sign that indicated her royal status; this was a great honour, which literally allowed the queen to gaze at her god. Later she would occasionally be given two cartouches so that her name resembled that of a pharaoh.

> *Pure of hands, Great King's Wife whom he loves, Lady of the Two Lands Nefertiti, may she live. Beloved of the great living Sun-Disk who is in jubilee ...*
>
> NEFERTITI, DESCRIBED AT THE THEBAN *HWT-BENBEN*

A DISEMBODIED DEITY

Akhenaten worshipped – and expected his people to accept, if not to actively revere – a genderless, faceless disk that shone in the sky above the royal family. Beneath the god stood the king and queen, forming a triad that paralleled the ancient triad formed by Atum and his children Shu and Tefnut. This was a major change. For over 1000 years the Egyptians had respected hundreds of divine beings occupying a series of overlapping religious spheres, ranging from the official state gods celebrated in the great temples to the demigods and spirits who played an important role in the informal religion and magic practised at home. Private individuals revered a highly personal mixture of demigods and regional deities, with family-based cults playing an important if difficult-to-assess part in daily life. The sudden loss of most of the state gods would not have posed too great a problem for a population who had little, if any, connection with the great temples. But the loss of Osiris would certainly have been lamented, as it was he, and he alone, who offered the promise of an afterlife for all. With Osiris banished and his kingdom gone, the Aten assumed responsibility for the deceased. He offered a poor substitute. After death, devotees of the Aten would haunt the altar of the sun temple by day, and sleep the sleep of the dead in their tombs at night. Only the royal family would escape to enjoy an eternal life with their god.

THE SCULPTOR TUTHMOSIS

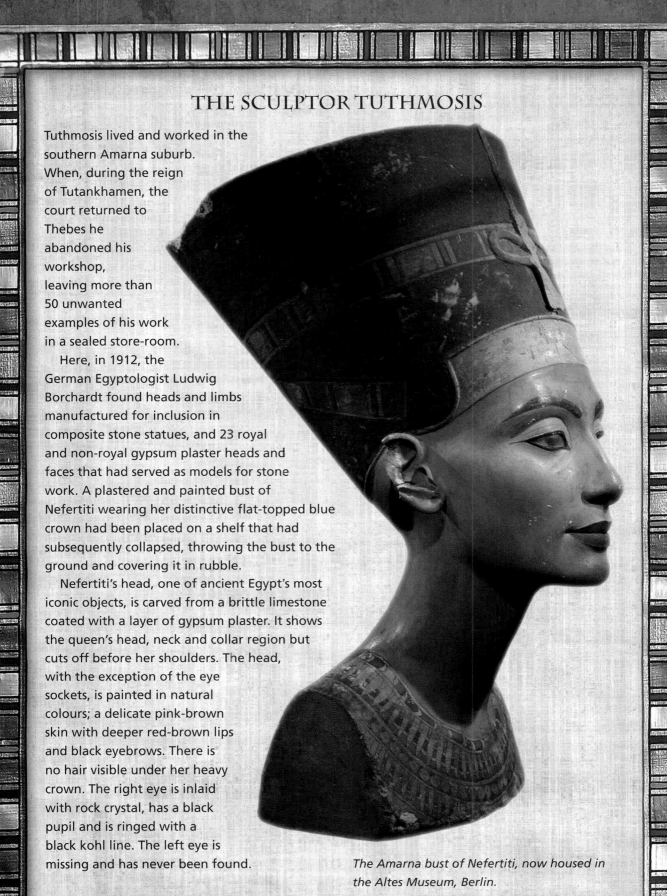

Tuthmosis lived and worked in the southern Amarna suburb. When, during the reign of Tutankhamen, the court returned to Thebes he abandoned his workshop, leaving more than 50 unwanted examples of his work in a sealed store-room.

Here, in 1912, the German Egyptologist Ludwig Borchardt found heads and limbs manufactured for inclusion in composite stone statues, and 23 royal and non-royal gypsum plaster heads and faces that had served as models for stone work. A plastered and painted bust of Nefertiti wearing her distinctive flat-topped blue crown had been placed on a shelf that had subsequently collapsed, throwing the bust to the ground and covering it in rubble.

Nefertiti's head, one of ancient Egypt's most iconic objects, is carved from a brittle limestone coated with a layer of gypsum plaster. It shows the queen's head, neck and collar region but cuts off before her shoulders. The head, with the exception of the eye sockets, is painted in natural colours; a delicate pink-brown skin with deeper red-brown lips and black eyebrows. There is no hair visible under her heavy crown. The right eye is inlaid with rock crystal, has a black pupil and is ringed with a black kohl line. The left eye is missing and has never been found.

The Amarna bust of Nefertiti, now housed in the Altes Museum, Berlin.

A shattered colossal statue of Akhenaten, recovered from the ruins of the Theban Aten temple.

By the end of Year 5 Akhenaten had developed a curiously exaggerated range of features. His face had lengthened and narrowed, and now bore almond-shaped eyes, fleshy earlobes, a long nose, pronounced cheekbones and thick, sensual lips. His shoulders, chest, arms and lower legs were slight and underdeveloped, yet he had voluptuous hips, wide thighs, pronounced breasts, a narrow waist and a rounded stomach. Akhenaten himself must have been the inspiration behind this new androgynous image. No artist would have dared to challenge tradition in such a dramatic way and, indeed the royal artist Bak explains that he was merely 'the pupil whom His Majesty taught'. However, Akhenaten was not so much inventing a new style as speeding up a natural evolution and, just as his religious 'revolution' was rooted in the solar-based theology of his father and grandfather, so several of his artistic innovations may be traced back to the artistic changes seen towards the end of his father's reign.

AMARNA: HORIZON OF THE ATEN

Egypt's new capital was situated on the east bank of the Nile in Middle Egypt, its limits defined by a series of stelae carved into the cliffs of the east and west banks. The first three boundary stelae detail the founding of the city on a virgin site. Construction had started during Year 5, and by the end of that year the royal family were settled in temporary quarters while they waited for their palace to be built. By Year 6 a further 11 stelae had been carved, and Akhenaten had sworn an oath of dedication. His oath was renewed in Year 8 when he inspected his boundaries. By Year 9, the city was fully functional.

Amarna included a full range of amenities: two Aten temples, several palaces, workshops, offices, a harbour, barracks, élite villas, a workman's village, rock-cut tombs for the rich and desert cemeteries for the poor. A long, broad road ran through the city, parallel to the river, linking the North Riverside Palace, the private home of the royal family, to the North Palace, the northern suburbs and city centre which housed the main religious and administrative buildings. Continuing southwards, passing again through suburbs and narrowing, the road eventually reached the isolated Maru-Aten cult centre, a religious complex provided for the royal women. The workmen's village housed the artisans, imported from Deir el-Medina (see pages 100–101), who worked in the rock-cut tombs. Like Deir el-Medina, the village was laid out with a strict regularity: 73 houses built in six straight terraces faced onto five narrow streets and were enclosed by a wall with a single guarded gate. The élite tombs were located in the cliffs to the east of the city, in the land of the rising, rather than the setting, sun. They fell into two groups to the north (18 tombs) and south (27 tombs) of the *wadi* housing the royal tomb.

Inscriptions recovered from Maru-Aten show the name and titles of the eldest royal daughter, Meritaten, carved on top of the name of another woman. The original name and titles belong to a secondary queen named Kiya, 'wife and greatly beloved of the king of Upper and Lower Egypt living on truth, lord of the Two Lands Neferkheperure Waenre'. Kiya's name has been found on a handful of objects from Amarna and on blocks recovered from Hermopolis. Her origins, however, are obscure, and it seems likely that 'Kiya' was a contraction of either a longer Egyptian name or a foreign name; it may even be that in Kiya we have found the missing Tadukhepa of Mitanni.

Behold Akhetaten [Amarna], which the Aten desires me to make for him as a monument in his name for ever. It was the Aten my father that brought me to Akhetaten. Not a noble directed me to it saying 'it is fitting for his majesty to make Akhetaten in this place'. It was the Aten my father who directed me to it, to make it for him as Akhetaten.

FROM THE AMARNA BOUNDARY STELAE

AMENHOTEP IV/
AKHENATEN

Dynasty: 18th
Father: Amenhotep III
Mother: Tiy
Consort: Nefertiti
Burial place: Amarna
   Royal Tomb
Successor:
   Smenkhkare?/
   Tutankhamen

Although Kiya never became a 'great wife', she was allowed to participate in the rituals of Aten worship which had until now been confined to Akhenaten and Nefertiti, and there is strong circumstantial evidence to suggest that she bore Akhenaten several children. We have no confirmed portrait of Kiya in the round, but her two-dimensional image has survived, enabling us to recognize her smiling face, her short bobbed wig and her large, round earrings.

THE REVOLUTION ENDS

Akhenaten pursued a dangerously blinkered path. Isolated at Amarna, he felt himself invulnerable, and what military action he did sanction was simply too little, too late. Although he welcomed the taxes and tribute supplied by his vassals he was curiously reluctant to play any active role in international affairs and he failed to recognize a potentially serious threat to his eastern territories. Suppululiumas, king of the Hittites, had spotted a weakness. Mitanni had suffered greatly from political in-fighting. Suppululiumas now intervened to back the rebel government against Tushratta, brother-in-law of Akhenaten. Tushratta struggled alone while Akhenaten established a friendly correspondence with Suppululiumas. The campaign ended with Tushratta dead, Mitanni split into two ineffective, kingdoms, and the Hittites in possession of Syrian lands as far south as the River Orontes. The balance of power had shifted. Many of Akhenaten's Syrian vassals had already expressed their loyalty to Suppululiumas. Others, sensing weakness, indulged in minor rebellions and inter-city feuding. Egypt lost the tribute paid by these vassals and, denied access to the Levantine ports, was unable to import timber. Meanwhile Nubia, too, had sensed weakness. In Year 12 Akhenaten was forced to dispatch troops south to quash a rebellion.

Year 12 saw splendid celebrations as ambassadors from 'all foreign countries' – Egypt's vassal states in the near East, Libya and Nubia – arrived at Amarna to bow low and present generous gifts. Within four years Tiy, Nefertiti, Kiya, Meketaten, Neferneferuaten, Neferneferure and Setepenre had vanished; the obvious assumption is that they had died and been buried in the royal *wadi*. This assumption is in part supported by poignant scenes, carved in the royal tomb, which show Akhenaten and Nefertiti mourning over the body of their second-born daughter, and the dead

A tomb shall be made for me in the eastern mountain of Akhetaten, and my burial shall be performed in it with a multitude of festivals that the Aten has ordered for me. If the Great Queen Nefertiti who lives, should die in any town of north, south, west or east, she shall be brought and buried at Akhetaten. If the king's daughter Meritaten should die in any city of north, south, west or east, she shall be brought and buried in Akhetaten.

FROM THE AMARNA BOUNDARY STELAE

Akhenaten with his consort Nefertiti and their daughters Meritaten, Meketaten and Ankhesenpaaten. The family group is, characteristically, positioned beneath the sun disk on this limestone altar recovered from Amarna.

Meketaten standing before her grieving family in a garlanded bower. As this was a time of plague in the Near East, it seems that Akhenaten's guests may have brought more than tribute to Amarna. Alternatively, some of the royal women may have died in childbirth. The only evidence for Nefertiti's burial at Amarna comes from the fragments of a single inscribed shabti figure. This has led to the suggestion, accepted by some Egyptologists, that Nefertiti survived to rule Egypt, first as co-regent to her husband, then as an independent king.

Akhenaten's final years saw an intensified campaign against the traditional gods. His last recorded date is Year 17; no official record of his death has survived but it seems reasonable to assume that he died soon after and was buried in the unfinished royal tomb.

SUNSET
THE EXPERIMENT FAILS

❦

Late 18th Dynasty c.1338 – 1295 BC

S MENKHKARE'S NAME AND IMAGE APPEAR FLEETINGLY TOWARDS THE END OF AKHENATEN'S REIGN. A GRAFFITO scribbled by the workman Pawah in the Theban tomb of Pere, provides us with a reference to Year 3 of a king 'Ankhkheperure beloved of the Aten, the son of Re: Neferneferuaten beloved of Waenre'. The decorated Amarna tomb of the courtier Meryre II actually shows this new king. The south and east walls of the main chamber display Akhenaten, Nefertiti and their daughters, but an unfinished and damaged image on the north wall shows a royal couple standing beneath the rays of the Aten. They look like Akhenaten and Nefertiti, and may well have started out as the old king and queen, but their cartouches belong to the 'pharaoh of Upper and Lower Egypt, Ankhkeperure son of Re, Smenkhkare' and the 'king's great wife Meritaten'.

These cartouches were recorded during the late 19th century; more recently, thieves have hacked the king's cartouche off the wall and it is now lost. Nevertheless, from this evidence it is possible to suggest that Smenkhkare was a son of Akhenaten born either to Nefertiti or to a secondary queen (Kiya?) who served as co-regent and/or short-lived successor to Akhenaten. He is also likely to have been the husband of the eldest royal daughter, Meritaten, who, at the end of her father's reign, became a King's Great Wife and started to write her name in a cartouche. Meritaten may have survived her father and husband to rule Egypt briefly as the ephemeral female pharaoh Neferneferuaten. Alternatively, but perhaps less likely, Neferneferuaten may have been Meritaten's mother Nefertiti.

THE MYSTERIOUS TOMB KV 55

KV 55 was discovered during the 1906–7 season of excavation in the Valley of the Kings, financed by retired American lawyer Theodore M. Davis and led by British archaeologist Edward Ayrton. The tomb was a simple one. A flight of steps dropped down to a sealed door that opened into a sloping, rubble-filled corridor leading to an undecorated burial chamber. The tomb was in a state of total disarray. The grave goods were a curious mixture of objects taken from various Amarna burials and brought together to create a parody of a royal burial. They included the gilded shrine provided by Akhenaten for the burial of Queen Tiy which was discovered, dismantled, in the corridor, the funerary bricks prepared for Akhenaten's own funeral which were found in the burial chamber, and a set of canopic jars in a niche (possibly an unfinished second chamber) whose bases belonged originally to Kiya, but whose human-headed

One of four alabaster canopic jars found in tomb KV 55, believed to represent either Akhenaten's secondary wife Kiya or his daughter Meritaten.

SMENKHKARE

Dynasty: 18th

Father: Amenhotep
  IV/Akhenaten?

Mother: Kiya?

Consort: Meritaten?

Burial place:
  Amarna/KV 55?

Successor:
  Tutankhamen

stoppers may have been carved for Meritaten. There was no stone sarcophagus but there was an elaborate gilded and inlaid anthropoid coffin, and a body within the coffin. There had been water damage and the ceiling had partially collapsed, but there was no sign that the tomb had been robbed. And, as Tutankhamen's was the last name recorded in the tomb, it seems safe to assume that it had been sealed in his reign.

The wooden coffin had suffered from damp and falling rocks. By the time Davis had recovered it from the tomb it had splintered into hundreds of pieces; it was later reassembled in Cairo Museum. The bands of hieroglyphs which decorated the coffin were words spoken by a woman who could be described as the '[wife and greatly beloved of] the king of Upper and Lower Egypt, living in order, lord of the Two Lands [Neferkheperure Waenre], the perfect little one of the living disk, who shall be alive continuously forever'. Experts agree that this woman must have been Kiya. However, some time after its manufacture Kiya's coffin was fitted with a beard and uraeus that made it suitable for the burial of a royal male. At the same time, the inscriptions were altered from feminine to masculine, and Kiya's name was replaced by a name in a cartouche. Following the burial both the uraeus and the gold mask covering the face were torn away and the royal name was removed from the cartouche.

As Davis tore the bandages from the mummy he discovered a small body, with 'a delicate head and hands' and a perfect set of teeth (one of which Davis immediately broke by hitting it to test its strength). The left arm was bent with the hand on the breast and the straight right arm rested on the thigh. Unfortunately the unwrapping was not properly recorded and no photographs were taken as the body was rapidly stripped to the bone.

A local doctor and an obstetrician who happened to be holidaying in Luxor were called in to pronounce the remains female. No observer since has ever doubted that the bones are male. Where observers have varied is in their assessment of the age of the bones. Elliot Smith found them to be the remains of a young man of about 25 years of age; he later agreed that they could be slightly older, and could therefore represent Akhenaten. In the late 1920s Professor Douglas Derry examined the remains and decided that unfused epiphyses and an interrupted right upper third molar indicated an age of no more than 25 years old at death. Subsequent investigators have agreed that the bones represent a young male who died in his late teens or early twenties, and who was closely related to Tutankhamen. The person who best fits this description is Tutankhamen's assumed brother, the ephemeral Smenkhkare. How the young king's remains came to be buried on the Valley of the Kings, some 200 miles (320 km) upriver of Amarna, is not known.

TUTANKHAMEN

Dynasty: 18th

Father: Akhenaten?

Mother: Kiya?

Consort:
  Ankhesenamen

Burial place: KV 62

Successor: Ay

THE 'BOY PHARAOH'

Tutankhaten acceded to the throne and married Ankhesenpaaten, the only surviving Amarna princess. Soon after, the royal couple changed their names to remove all reference to the Aten, becoming Tutankh-amen ('Living image of Amen') and Ankhesen-amen ('Living through Amen').

Who was the new pharaoh? Given that he was less than ten years old at his accession, we must assume that he inherited his throne rather than won it. He is coy about his parentage (one might assume, with good reason), but an inscription recovered from Soleb speaks of 'he who renewed the monument for his father, pharaoh of Upper and Lower Egypt, Lord of the Two Lands, Nebmaatre, image of Re, son of Re, Amenhotep ruler of Thebes'. At first reading this seems to leave no room for doubt: Tutankhamen is the son of Amenhotep III. However, nothing is ever simple in Egyptology. 'Father' can also mean ancestor, and the text was inscribed relatively late in Tutankhamen's reign, at a time when he may well have wished to disassociate himself from Akhenaten. Indirect but compelling evidence for Tutankhamen's parentage is provided by the reliefs in the Amarna royal tomb. Here two scenes tell a continuous story. The first is set in the palace. We see Akhenaten and Nefertiti with their right arms raised to their heads in grief as they face a now-vanished image. Outside the room a woman is cradling a baby, an attendant holds an open fan over the child, women lament, and a group of courtiers raise their arms in sorrow. In the scene below we see Akhenaten and Nefertiti grieving.

Rock-cut tombs in the necropolis at Amarna. The city of Amarna was abandoned some 20 years after its foundation.

over the body of a woman lying on a bier. It seems that a mother has died giving birth to a child There is no obvious father present, unless Akhenaten himself is the father, and the presence of the queen consort in her distinctive blue crown rules Nefertiti out as the mother. It therefore seems likely that the scene shows a beloved secondary queen (Kiya?) dying as she gave birth to Akhenaten's child (Tutankhamen?).

ATTEMPTS AT RESTORATION

Tutankhamen abandoned Amarna within four years of his accession. Thebes would once again serve as Egypt's religious capital, while the civil service was based at Memphis. A significant population remained at Amarna, but when it became clear that the court would not return numbers dwindled, the stone blocks were salvaged for reuse at nearby Hermopolis, and the mud-brick city crumbled. The workmen's village, in contrast, was reoccupied and even expanded before being abandoned during the reign of Horemheb.

Outside Amarna the chief of the treasury Maya was charged with reopening (and taxing) the traditional state temples from Elephantine to the Delta. The priesthoods were re-established with compensation for past wrongs, and refurbished shrines and new statues were provided. Lest there should be any doubt, a decree, issued from Memphis, detailed Tutankhamen's reinstatement of the old order: 'He restored what was ruined, creating everlasting monuments. Truth is back in her proper place, for he put an end to wrongdoing throughout Egypt …' Tutankhamen had become a 'repeater of births'; a king who inaugurates a new age. Even in Egypt, however, history could not be so easily rewritten. Tutankhamen was strongly connected to the Amarna heresy and Akhenaten, Smenkhkare, Tutankhamen and Tutankhamen's successor Ay would all be omitted from the official king lists, which passed straight from Amenhotep III to Ay's successor Horemheb.

A TROUBLESOME LETTER

At the end of Tutankhamen's reign Suppiluliumas, king of the Hittites, received a letter from a widowed queen of Egypt:

My husband has died and I do not have a son. But, they say, you have many sons. If you would give me one of your sons he would become my husband. Never shall I pick out a servant of mine and make him my husband.

Sadly the surviving cuneiform copy of the letter is undated and the queen's name, given as Dahamunzu, is unrecognizable. We cannot be certain that Ankhesenamen wrote it (there remains the outside possibility that it may have been written by her widowed sister Meritaten or even by her mother Nefertiti) and we do not know if the letter is genuine, or a trick designed (by Ay? Or Horemheb?) to allow the Egyptians to capture a valuable Hittite hostage.

Suppiluliumas was extremely suspicious. He knew that Egyptian queens did not marry outside their own family. But Egypt was a great prize. After extensive enquiries, Prince Zinanza was dispatched to marry the anonymous queen. Unfortunately the bridegroom disappeared on the way to his wedding – it is not known whether he fell victim to assassins or to the plague – and relations between the Egyptians and the Hittites plunged to a new low.

The exquisite inlaid gold funerary mask of Tutankhamen is the most instantly recognizable of all Egyptian artefacts. Some of Tutankhamen's burial equipment, including one of his golden coffins, was made for the funeral of Smenkhkare.

It proved less easy to restore the eastern empire, which had dwindled through years of neglect. The Hittites, now Egypt's most powerful rival, had seized Kadesh. In Year 9 Tutankhamen's troops failed to retake the city, allowing Suppiluliumas to consolidate his hold on northern Syria. Further battles may have followed but, before he could father a living heir, Tutankhamen died unexpectedly in his late teens or early twenties. His body is in a bad condition, but the evidence of damage to the chest and legs suggests – while by no means proving – that he may have died as the result of an impact, possibly sustained during a chariot or boating accident. As Tutankhamen's tomb was unfinished, his successor Ay interred him in KV 62, a modest private tomb (possibly Ay's own) hastily adapted to accommodate a pharaoh.

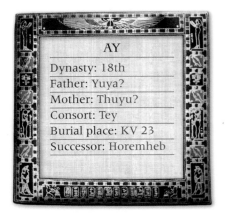

AY

Dynasty: 18th
Father: Yuya?
Mother: Thuyu?
Consort: Tey
Burial place: KV 23
Successor: Horemheb

GOD'S FATHER AY

The elderly and highly experienced courtier Ay, putative brother of Queen Tiy and father of Nefertiti, had become 'God's father Ay, Divine ruler of Thebes, beloved of Amen' while Nefertiti's former nurse Tey had taken her place as queen of Egypt. Given his advanced years, Ay could never have expected to enjoy a long reign. His highest year date is Year 4. He was buried in KV 23, probably the tomb originally intended for Tutankhamen and, as his intended heir, his son or grandson Nakhtmin, had predeceased him, he was succeeded by the great general of the army, Horemheb.

HOREMHEB: THE FIRST RAMESSIDE KING?

Horemheb is a man of obscure origins, although his second wife, Mutnodjmet, may be the identically named sister of Nefertiti; if this identification is correct, it would make Horemheb Ay's probable son-in-law. Horemheb maintained a low profile during the Amarna period, then served with distinction under Tutankhamen when he held, amongst others, the offices of 'pharaoh's deputy in every place', 'overseer of the generals of the lord of the Two Lands' and 'hereditary prince of southern and northern Egypt'. Given this impressive string of titles, it is perhaps surprising that he did not inherit Tutankhamen's throne; it may be that Ay was able to bury the young king, and assume control of the country, because Horemheb was away fighting the Hittites at the time of Tutankhamen's death.

Horemheb usurped many of Tutankhamen's monuments and claimed Ay's mortuary temple as his own. Continuing a process which had started during Tutankhamen's reign he dismantled and reused the Karnak's Aten temples; Akhenaten's *talatat* blocks were now used to build Pylons II, IX and X. The falcon-headed Horus of Hutnesu was both his local god and his namesake (Horemheb literally means 'Horus is in Festival') and we are told that it was this version of Horus who crowned Horemheb in the presence of Amen. But Horemheb was too wise to confine his attentions to just one deity. All the major state temples benefited from his generosity, and there was a new temple to Seth at Avaris. At Gebel Silsila he started, but did not finish, a rock-cut chapel dedicated to seven deities: Sobek, Amen, Mut, Khonsu, Taweret, Thoth and the deified Horemheb himself.

Ruling from Memphis, he launched a much-needed reform of the civil service. Years of neglect had allowed Egypt's bureaucrats to grow complacent and inefficient.

HOREMHEB

Dynasty: 18th
Father: unknown
Mother: unknown
Consort: Mutnodjmet
Burial place: KV 57
Successor: Ramesses I

I have shunned wrongdoing, I never did evil since my birth; indeed I am a gentle one before god. One wise, one calm, who listens to maat.

PRAYER OF GENERAL HOREMHEB

The legal system was corrupt, and the treasury was suffering. Horemheb issued a decree outlining a programme of reforms designed to streamline the legal and administrative systems and overhaul the palace administration. The text is today badly damaged, but it is clear that the penalties for those who disobeyed pharaoh's laws were swift and brutal, and included beatings, cuttings. the amputation of extremities and banishment to the eastern border town of Sile (from whence, presumably, they were liable to be sent to the Sinai mines).

The army, too was to be reformed. Regrouped into two separate divisions, north and south, each under its own commander, the newly motivated troops were set to work in Nubia and Syria. Given that Horemheb's Ramesside successors would be forced to deal immediately with unrest on Egypt's western border, we must assume that his campaigns were less effective than he hoped.

Horemheb had prepared a beautifully decorated private tomb at Sakkara; it is here that we learn about Tutankhamen's unspectacular military campaigns in Syria and Nubia. This tomb was abandoned as Horemheb prepared the first full-sized royal tomb to be built in the Valley of the Kings since the time of Amenhotep III. But Horemheb was over-ambitious and his reign – which, although Manetho allows him just four years and one month, seems to have lasted for somewhere between 13 and 20 years – was not long enough to complete his plans. When General Paramessu buried Horemheb in KV 57, the tomb was incomplete.

Much of Horemheb's reign had been spent distancing himself from the Amarna Age. This was recognized by the Ramesside kings, who acknowledged him as the founder of their line and included him in their king lists. Manetho, however, classified Horemheb, whom he knew as Oros, as the last king of the 18th Dynasty, allowing Horemheb's chosen successor, Ramesses I, to become the founder of the 19th.

Horemheb and the falcon deity Horus (Kunsthistorisches Museum, Vienna).

THE RAMESSIDE PHARAOHS

C.1295–1069 BC

*Ramesses II ('the Great') fought a series of successful
military campaigns to subdue Egypt's neighbours. On this
painted relief, a larger-than-life Ramesses is seen smiting
Nubian, Libyan and Syrian prisoners.*

A NEW BEGINNING
GENERAL RAMESSES AND HIS SON

❦

Early 19th Dynasty c.1295–1279 BC

THE 19TH DYNASTY PHARAOHS WERE ARRIVISTES WHO HAILED FROM AVARIS IN THE EASTERN DELTA, AND WERE proud of it. Their red hair – analysis of his mummy suggests that Ramesses II 'the Great' was auburn-headed – and their personal names were a constant celebration of their northern roots: 'Ramesses' (Born of the god Re) links the family with Re of Heliopolis while 'Seti' (Man of Seth) indicates a loyalty to the unpredictable Seth of Avaris, whom the Ramessides revered as an ancestor. As northerners, the Ramesside kings felt little personal loyalty to either Amen-Re or Thebes and so, while the Karnak complex and the west bank necropolis retained their important religious roles, there was increased political and religious activity in the north. However, in spite of, or maybe because of, their relatively humble origins, the Ramesside kings displayed a keen interest in Egypt's past and took every opportunity to prove their right to rule by remembering history, reinterpreting it, and linking their own deeds with the achievements of the more prestigious of their royal 'ancestors'.

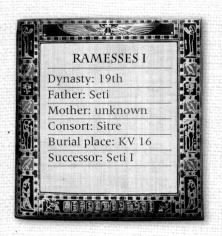

RAMESSES I
Dynasty: 19th
Father: Seti
Mother: unknown
Consort: Sitre
Burial place: KV 16
Successor: Seti I

Ramesses I, in his tomb in the Valley of the Kings (KV 16), is pictured between the gods Horus (left) and Anubis (right).

Paramessu, son of General Seti, had served both as general and vizier to Horemheb. He was already an elderly man but his experience as a soldier and a statesman, and the fact that he had not only a healthy son but also a healthy grandson, made him an ideal choice as pharaoh. Not since the reigns of Amenhotep III/Amenhotep IV had the crown passed from father to son in a straightforward manner, and the abrupt changes of ruling family were, to the superstitious, a sign that the gods were not best pleased with Egypt. Ramesses I looked back to the glorious days of the early 18th Dynasty and, for his coronation, selected simple titles emulating those chosen by Ahmose two and a half centuries earlier. He knew that a new pharaoh – particularly a pharaoh of non-royal birth – would have to prove himself to his foreign subjects, as any sign of weakness would invariably be interpreted as a signal to revolt. And, after serving as commander of the Sile fortress on Egypt's eastern border, he knew where Egypt was most vulnerable. A brief period of military training was followed by an aggressive raid on Canaan, which sent a clear warning message to the potentially disloyal Levantine states.

Back home building work started with ambitious plans to convert an open court built at Karnak by Horemheb into a columned (hypostyle) hall. But Ramesses died just 16 months later. His tomb (KV 16) was unfinished; only two stairways linked by a corridor and leading to a single room had been cut. This room had to serve as a burial chamber and the red granite sarcophagus had to be painted rather than carved with hieroglyphs which, due to their speedy preparation, included a number of errors.

19TH DYNASTY RULERS

*c.*1295 BC Ramesses I
(Menpehtyre)

*c.*1294 BC Seti I
(Menmaatre)

*c.*1279 BC Ramesses II
(Usermaatre Setepenre)

*c.*1213 BC Merenptah
(Baenre)

*c.*1203 BC Amenmessu
(Menmire)

*c.*1200 BC Seti II
(Userkheperure Setepenre)

*c.*1194 BC Siptah
(Akhenresetepenre)

*c.*1188 BC Tawosret
(Sitremeritamen) (female
pharaoh)

ANOTHER COMMONER ON THE THRONE

Seti I became the fourth successive commoner to ascend the throne. He had been well prepared for his new role, having served as priest of Seth, as general, as vizier and finally as co-regent during his father's brief reign. As pharaoh, he chose titles that would link him with the mighty warrior Tuthmosis III and the great builder Amenhotep III.

Despite the best efforts of Horemheb and Ramesses I, Egypt's eastern vassals were still proving troublesome. Year 1 saw a brief campaign to reassert control over the Bedouin who were threatening the all-important trade route over the Sinai land bridge. Later in the same year Seti travelled further north to quell disturbances in the Jordan Valley and a stela celebrating his victory was erected in the garrison city of Beth-Shan. This was just the beginning. Over the next few years Seti returned to Canaan and the northern province of Upi, advancing as far as Damascus before securing the ports of Tyre, Sidon, Byblos and Simyra. Details of these campaigns are preserved on the walls of the Karnak temple of Amen-Re. It seems that Seti had determined to challenge the growing might of the Hittite empire but, before the situation could come to a head, he was forced to return home to defend the Delta against the Libyan tribes.

Northern Egypt was being increasingly troubled by bands of pirates, the 'Sherden', who were pillaging the villages of the Delta coast. This problem was left for Prince Ramesses to solve. Posting troops at strategic points along the coast, he simply waited; when the Sherden appeared they were captured and enlisted in the pharaoh's army. Soon after, a defensive line of forts was established along the northwest Delta edge. The remains of three of these forts have been discovered to the west of Alexandria, at Gharbaniyat, el-Alamein and Zawiyet Umm el-Rakham, with a further two in the western Delta at Tell Abqa'in and Kom el-Hisn. The forts had a dual purpose. They dominated the coastline, serving as a welcome landmark and providing provisions and protection for trade boats sailing from Crete to Memphis, and they offered a defence against invasion.

Having secured his western border Seti turned his attention again to the east, and to the Hittites. However his rhythm had been broken and, although his army was able to erect a triumphal stela in Kadesh, there was no great decisive battle. Instead an agreement was reached and Kadesh and Amurru reverted to Hittite control while Egypt retained her hold on the ports.

Now, as for this king, he rejoices at the beginning of battle. He delights to enter a fight and his heart is gratified at the sight of blood. He cuts off the heads of the dissidents. More than the day of rejoicing he loves the moment of crushing the enemy. His Majesty slays them at one stroke. He leaves them no heirs, and whoever escapes his hand is brought as prisoner to Egypt.

FROM THE KARNAK BATTLE INSCRIPTIONS OF SETI I

SETI'S 'HANDS-ON' RULE

To the south, Seti's rule went largely unopposed. In Year 8, rumours of a planned insurrection beyond the Third Cataract had met with such a quick response that few subsequently cared to challenge the pharaoh's authority. Five years later a minor revolt in Lower Nubia was crushed by Prince Ramesses who took two of his sons – Khaemwaset and Amenhirwenemef – into battle with him. It is unlikely that the boys were more than five or six years old at this time.

The prisoners captured in Nubia were deployed as cheap labour on Seti's many building projects. Throughout Egypt, workmen were still engaged in restoring and re-carving the inscriptions defaced by Akhenaten. The temples of Re at Heliopolis and Ptah at Memphis received some refurbishment, while the temple of Seth

Some of the finest New Kingdom reliefs are found in the temple of Seti I at Abydos. Seti (middle) is supported by the goddesses of Upper and Lower Egypt.

SETI I	
Dynasty:	19th
Father:	Ramesses I
Mother:	Sitre
Consort:	Mut-Tuya
Burial place:	KV 17
Successor:	Ramesses II

As to any keeper of cattle, any keeper of hounds, any herdsman ... who shall give any head of animals belonging to the House by defalcation to another ... punishment shall be done to him by casting him down and impaling him on a stake, forfeiting his wife and children and all his property to the House and extracting the herd of animals from him to whom he shall have given it at the rate of a hundred to one ...

THE ABYDOS DECREE OF SETI I AT NAURI

at Avaris was expanded. Within the Karnak temple of Amen-Re the great hypostyle hall, now decorated with an elegant raised relief, was renamed 'Glorious is Seti in the Domain of Amen', with no reference whatsoever to Ramesses I.

Meanwhile, on the Theban west bank, work had started on the construction of Seti's mortuary temple at Qurna and on the excavation of his tomb in the Valley of the Kings. Seti also built a lavish summer palace in the eastern Delta, near to the old Hyksos city of Avaris, and a magnificent temple at Abydos. To fund his Abydos temple in perpetuity, Seti donated lands whose income would now go directly to the temple. Included among these was a Nubian estate. High in the cliff face at Nauri (Nubia), Seti carved an 'exemption decree', outlining the penalties for those who might be tempted to steal from the estate: a serious crime that would be interpreted as stealing directly from the Abydos temple.

As to any Viceroy of Kush, any foreign chief, any mayor, any inspector or any person who shall take any individual belonging to the House ... punishment shall be done to him by beating him with two hundred blows and five open wounds, together with exacting the work of the individual belonging to the Residence from him for every day that he shall spend with him, to be given to the House ...

Seti took a 'hands-on' approach to his reign. An inscription at Silsila records how, in Year 6, he improved the wages of the stonemasons, a highly popular move that ensured each man a daily ration of bread, roast meat and assorted vegetables plus two monthly sacks of grain. Three years later, while inspecting the gold mines in the Eastern Desert, he ordered that a well be dug: this brought comfort to those forced to travel across the desert, while protecting the supply of gold destined for the Abydos temple. That same year he visited the Aswan granite quarries on a quest for good-quality stone suitable for the production of colossal statues.

After 10–16 years on the throne, and probably no more than four years of co-regency with his son Ramesses, Seti died at Avaris. Ramesses sailed south with his father's mummy to Thebes. Here Seti was interred in the longest, deepest and most beautifully decorated tomb in the Valley (KV 17).

THE TEMPLE OF SETI AT ABYDOS

Abydos had long been recognized as the burial place of Osiris, king of the dead. By the New Kingdom Abydos had become a place of pilgrimage with many Egyptians visiting the site to dedicate either statues or *mahat* (mud brick shrines holding limestone stelae). The Middle-Kingdom pharaoh Senwosret III had constructed an Abydene cenotaph temple which may even have replaced his Dahshur pyramid as his final burial place. Ahmose had continued this tradition with his cenotaph for Tetisheri and other 18th Dynasty kings had followed suit, although most of their monuments are now lost. The most impressive surviving temples are those built by the early 19th Dynasty kings.

Seti's enormous Abydos temple can be seen as the direct counterpart of his mortuary temple at Qurna, but with one important difference. At Thebes, Amen, Mut and Khonsu were the primary

View of the second pillared hall (hypostyle) of Seti's temple at Abydos. The roof of this hall is supported on 36 massive columns with capitals in the form of lotus buds.

deities. At Abydos, the family of Osiris took over this role. Uniquely, the Abydos temple has seven sanctuaries dedicated to Osiris, Isis, Horus, Amen-Re, Re-Harakhty, Ptah and the deified Seti.

Seti built not only a dummy mortuary temple, but also a dummy tomb. Immediately to the west of his temple he excavated a hall whose granite roof was supported by giant pillars. This structure is today known as the Osireion. A room opening from the central hall was designed with the shape and decoration of an enormous sarcophagus, while a channel surrounding the hall formed a groundwater moat, allowing the hall to represent the mound of creation.

MASTER OF PROPAGANDA
RAMESSES II

Mid-19th Dynasty *c.*1279–1213 BC

USERMAATRE RAMESSES BECAME SOLE RULER OF EGYPT ON DAY 27 OF THE THIRD MONTH OF SUMMER. By Year 2 he had revised his name; he was now Usermaatre Setepenre Ramesses ['Strong in Truth is Re, Chosen of Re, Born of the God Re'], a name that emphasized his interest in the cult of Re of Heliopolis. Soon after his father's death Ramesses converted Seti's northern summer palace into a splendid new city. Pi-Ramesse Aa-nakhtu (the House of Ramesses-Great-of-Victories: modern Qantir) would become his main residence although, unlike Akhenaten before him, Ramesses was well aware of the danger of settling permanently in one city and he continued the tradition of travelling the length and breadth of his land.

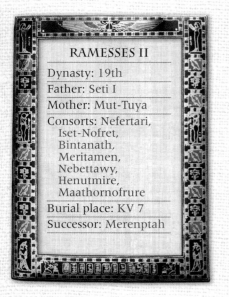

RAMESSES II

Dynasty: 19th

Father: Seti I

Mother: Mut-Tuya

Consorts: Nefertari, Iset-Nofret, Bintanath, Meritamen, Nebettawy, Henutmire, Maathornofrure

Burial place: KV 7

Successor: Merenptah

Pi-Ramesse would continue in use throughout the 20th Dynasty, until the Pelusiac branch of the Nile started to silt up and the harbour became unusable. Eventually, at the end of the 21st Dynasty, the city was abandoned and the royal residence was relocated to nearby Tanis (modern San el-Hagar; ancient Djanet; Biblical Zoan). Much of the old city was dismantled, its masonry and statuary transported to Tanis for reuse, so that today there is nothing of the once-splendid city visible.

Ramesses commissioned at least 50 life-sized or larger portrait statues for his new capital. These statues, each of them named, stood either in front of the temple pylons or within the first, public, temple courtyard where they were accessible to the general public. Nor were the statues confined to Pi-Ramesse. Thebes, too, has yielded enormous versions of Ramesses, many of which were usurped from Amenhotep III and the 12th Dynasty pharaohs, while at least 11 colossi – whole or in pieces – have been recovered from the ruins of the Ptah temple at Memphis. Whether these 'borrowings' should be seen as canny cost-cutting exercises designed to fill the land with monumental images of Ramesses at minimum expense, or whether they should be seen as a recognition of the enduring cyclical nature of kingship, and a particular tribute to Amenhotep III and the 12th Dynasty kings, is not now clear.

THE BATTLE OF KADESH

Ramesses had determined to stamp his authority on his eastern vassals by recapturing Kadesh. Year 4 saw the 'campaign of victory'. Ramesses led his army across the Sinai land bridge and along the coast to confirm Egypt's hold over Canaan and the Phoenician ports. He then turned inland and regained Amurru. Ramesses returned home in triumph leaving a division of élite soldiers behind. Next year he rode east at the head of an army of 20,000 soldiers sub-divided into four divisions of 5000, each

'Re of the Rulers'. One of a pair of colossal seated statues of Ramesses II that flank the entrance to the processional colonnade of Amenhotep III at the Luxor temple.

a mixture of infantry and chariotry marching under the standard of a protective god; Amen Division (soldiers recruited from Thebes), Re Division (Heliopolis), Ptah Division (Memphis) and Seth or Sutekh Division (northeast Delta region). They took one month to pass through Canaan and south Syria and, making use of the Bekaa Valley, to approach Kadesh from the south. Meanwhile the élite force left in Amurru in Year 4 had started to move.

Having reached the Wood of Labwi, some 10 miles (16 km) to the south of Kadesh, the Egyptian soldiers were about to cross the River Orontes when their guards discovered two Hittite deserters skulking around the Egyptian camp. The 'deserters' (who were actually Hittite spies) reported that the Hittites were too frightened to

EXODUS

The Bible tells us that the city of 'Raamses' [Pi-Ramesse] was built by Hebrew slaves:

There arose up a new king over Egypt, which knew not Joseph, and he said unto his people 'Behold! The people of the children of Israel are more and mightier than we are ...' Therefore they did set over them taskmasters to afflict them with their burdens. And they built for the Pharaoh treasure cities, Pithom and Raamses ...

(Exodus 1:8)

Ramesside Egypt did include a significant minority of foreigners and the Delta was home to settled Semitic-Egyptian communities. There is no Egyptian record of mass enslavement but, like the rest of the population, these settlers were liable to be summoned to work for the state under the corvée system. The Bible continues with the story of Moses and the freeing of the Hebrew slaves:

And Moses stretched out his hand over the sea; and the Lord caused the sea to go back by a strong east wind all that night, and made the sea dry land, and all the waters were divided. And the children of Israel went into the midst of the sea upon the dry ground: and the waters were a wall unto them on their right hand, and on their left. And the Egyptians pursued, and went in after them to the midst of the sea, even all Pharaoh's horses, his chariots and his horsemen ... And Moses stretched forth his hand over the sea, and the sea returned to his strength ... and the waters returned and covered the chariots and the horsemen, and all the hosts of Pharaoh that came into the sea after them; there remained not so much as one of them.

(Exodus 14:21-27)

The pharaoh of this story is unnamed, although the name of his city, 'Raamses', provides a major clue. If this is a real event rather than a legend, the Exodus must have occurred either during Ramesses' reign or during that of his son, Merenptah. There is no Ramesside record of any mass departure from the Delta.

approach the mighty Ramesses, and were cowering over 100 miles (160 km) away. On the strength of this dubious information, Ramesses decided to head straight for Kadesh. The army split into its four divisions and Ramesses, riding with Amen Division, forded the river and set up camp on the high ground to the northwest of the city. Re Division followed close behind, leaving Ptah and Seth on the opposite bank of the river. The plan was to reunite the troops in time for a morning assault on the city. But things did not go according to plan. The capture of two more Hittite spies and their confessions – encouraged by a sound beating – made the truth horribly clear. Muwatallis was already stationed at Kadesh and was poised for an immediate attack. After a frantic council of war, the vizier was sent to summon the missing divisions, and the vulnerable royal family, who had accompanied Ramesses to observe his victories, were hurried to a position of safety.

Charioteers at the Battle of Kadesh. This scene appears on the pylon (gateway) to the Ramesseum. Egyptian propaganda presented the engagement as a great victory. Later scholars, however, believe that the outcome was far less clear-cut.

A NARROW ESCAPE

Suddenly the Hittites launched a chariot attack on the isolated Re Division. The Egyptian soldiers, taken completely by surprise, fled northwards, leading the enemy straight to Amen Division. As his soldiers ran away, the brave Ramesses found himself surrounded by Hittites. Only his shield-bearer Menna, who rode beside him in the royal chariot, could help him now. Quickly Ramesses sent a desperate prayer to Amen-Re who, although many miles away in his Theban temple, helped him by making him

Although I prayed in a distant land my prayer was heard in Thebes. Amen came when I called to him; he gave me his hand and I rejoiced ... I found that my heart grew stout and my breast swelled with joy. Everything which I attempted I succeeded ... I was before the enemy like Seth in his moment. I found the enemy chariots scattering before my horses. Not one of them could fight me. Their hearts quaked with fear when they saw me and their arms went limp so they could not shoot. They did not have the heart to hold their spears. I made them plunge into the water like crocodiles. They fell on their faces, one on top of another. I slaughtered them at my will ... Those who fell down did not rise ...

RAMESSES CALLS UPON AMEN-RE AT THE BATTLE OF KADESH

stronger and fiercer than any other man. Egypt's gods were, of course, stronger than the gods of any other nations. Single-handedly (or so he would have us believe), Ramesses defeated the entire Hittite army.

Muwatallis had made a grave tactical error. He had not committed his full infantry to the ambush on Re Division, and most of the Hittite army remained on the east bank of the Orontes. The arrival of the Egyptian élite troops from Amurru came as a shock. Reinforced, Ramesses was able to push back the Hittite chariots who suddenly turned tail and fled. As the Hittites struggled to swim across the Orontes, Ptah Division arrived and the deserters of Re and Amen returned. Finally Seth Division appeared on the scene, and the Egyptian camp settled down for the night.

It is not obvious what happened next morning, as the texts are somewhat ambiguous, but it is clear that more blood was spilt. Was there more fighting? Or did Ramesses punish his own deserters? Next, according to the Egyptian records, Muwatallis sent a letter to Ramesses, pleading for peace. Negotiators were summoned and a truce was agreed although pride forbade Ramesses to sign a formal treaty. He returned home once again in triumph, and retold his story in prose, poetry and relief on Egypt's temple walls. But, unseen by Ramesses, the Hittite records, recovered from Bogazköy in Anatolia (Turkey), tell a very different tale, which ends with a humiliated Ramesses forced to retreat. History tends to support the Hittite version of events. With Ramesses gone, the Hittites were able to reinforce their hold on Kadesh and to regain control of Amurru. They then pushed south through the Bekaa Valley to secure Upi which was placed under the control of Muwatallis's brother Hattusilis. Kadesh was to be Egypt's last 'traditional' battle against a fellow superpower.

The Kadesh débâcle inspired several local rulers to try their luck against the Egyptians and Ramesses was forced to reassert his authority in Canaan, Syria and Amurru. Years 8 and 9 saw him campaigning in Galilee before moving east to occupy the cities of Dapur and Tunip which had been lost to Egypt for over a century. There was more campaigning in Phoenicia in Year 10 while Syria was targeted intermittently between Years 10 and 18. In Hatti, meanwhile, things were not going well. Muwatallis had died, leaving his young son Urhi-Teshub to take the throne as Mursilis III. After seven years Hattusilis staged a successful coup. The deposed king was banished first to Syria then to Cyprus. Finally Urhi-Teshub sought refuge in Egypt and Ramesses refused to return him to his uncle. War seemed imminent until Hattusilis suggested that a formal peace treaty would prove mutually beneficial. Year 21 saw the arrival of the Hittite diplomat Tili-Teshub, bringing a letter from the Hittite king. Ramesses entered into lengthy negotiations and terms were settled. In an agreement intended to last beyond the death of either monarch the two nations were now pledged to defend each other against enemy attack.

BUILDING WORKS

Ramesses kept his builders busy. There were substantial improvements to the temple of Ptah at Memphis, which soon rivalled in size and beauty the complex of Amen-Re at Thebes, and a new cenotaph temple at Abydos, smaller than the temple of Seti I. While smaller local temples benefited from the pharaoh's generosity, his workmen were demolishing the last remaining buildings at Amarna and transporting the stone across the river so that it could be reused in building works at Hermopolis.

At Thebes, the temple of Amen-Re acquired a peristyle courtyard and pylon. The magnificent hypostyle hall was, inevitably, renamed 'glorious is Ramesses II in the domain of Amen'. Building work had already finished and the hall was a tall and gloomy forest of 134 papyrus-style columns arranged in rows. Seti had started to decorate the hall in raised relief; this stopped as Ramesses' workmen adopted the faster, cruder and harder to erase sunken relief which decorates almost all of his monuments. The exterior was eventually to be embellished with battle scenes, including the Kadesh triumph, plus a copy of the Hittite peace treaty. At the nearby Luxor temple, Seti had planned an

---

THE HITTITE KING REQUESTS A DOCTOR FOR HIS SISTER

Ramesses and Hattusilis corresponded regularly, and exchanged gifts. Knowing Egyptian doctors to be the most skilful in the world, Hattusilis requested a physician who could cure his sister's infertility. Ramesses sent a rather tactless reply:

As for Matanazi, my brother's sister, the king your brother knows her. Fifty years old, you say? Never! She is certainly sixty! No one can produce medicine to make her fertile. But, of course, if Re and the Weather-God should wish it ... I will send a good magician and an able physician and they will prepare some fertility drugs for her anyway.

Fragment of one of the cuneiform-inscribed tablets found at Bogazköy. It records correspondence from Hattusilis III to Ramesses II, concerning the impending marriage of one of the Hittite king's daughters to the pharaoh.

impressive project: a pylon and forecourt enhanced by mighty obelisks and colossal statues. These were taken over by Ramesses, with the work being substantially completed by Year 3. With Seti's founding role forgotten the exterior face of the pylon now showed Kadesh battle scenes, while two red granite obelisks stood before the pylon. The forecourt included a triple shrine to Amen, Mut and Khonsu which, originally built by Hatshepsut and Tuthmosis III , was substantially rebuilt by Ramesses, and within the forecourt there were yet more colossal statues of the king.

Meanwhile, over on the west bank, Seti's mortuary temple had to be completed, and Ramesses needed to start making preparations for his own death. His mortuary temple, the 'Mansion of Millions of Years, United-with-Thebes' was called the 'Memnonium' or 'Tomb of Ozymandias', by the Greeks, and is today known as the Ramesseum. It lies on the edge of the desert between the 18th Dynasty temples of Amenhotep II and Tuthmosis IV, and is orientated towards the Luxor temple.

Some time around Year 21 Ramesses crushed a minor Nubian rebellion. Some 7000 rebels were captured and the victory was commemorated on the main gate of Amara West. His Nubian victory seems to have sparked an interest in temple-building. There were to be at least seven new Nubian temples, while several older foundations were restored. Many of the new temples were cut into the living rock, with their sanctuaries hidden deep inside the Nubian cliffs; all were ornamented with colossal images of Ramesses. Ramesses' best known Nubian monuments are the two temples built on the west bank of the Nile at Abu Simbel, 175 miles (280 km) south of the Egyptian border at Aswan. The temples were started early in his reign and were dedicated during Year 24 although they were not finished for at least another decade. Abu Simbel was a remote and sparsely populated location, at first sight a curious choice for a major building project. It seems likely that Ramesses was inspired by the local geography, which allowed him to cut twin temples into sandstone cliffs so that just twice each year, on 21 February and 21 October, the rising sun would pierce the dark interior of the Great Temple to illuminate the four divine figures – Ptah of Memphis, Amen-Re of Thebes, Re-Harakhty of Heliopolis and Ramesses of Pi-Ramesse – who sat facing the boat shrine at the back of the sanctuary.

THE ROYAL FAMILY

Ramesses was the first member of his family to marry knowing that his wife would be queen of Egypt. He had married Nefertari, and fathered his first son, Amenhirwenemef, before Seti's death. Nefertari was to give him ten children, including his third son Prehirwenemef and one of his favourite daughters, Meritamen. She was alive in Year 24, when the royal family attended the inauguration of the Abu Simbel temples, but may have already been ill, as her eldest daughter Meritamen served as her deputy during the ceremony. She was absent from the jubilee celebrations of Year 30, and had presumably died.

Nefertari's place was filled by Iset-Nofret, a secondary wife of long standing who had born at least four children: Princess Ramesses, Khaemwaset and Merenptah, and Ramesses' eldest daughter Bintanath. Iset-Nofret appears as consort with Ramesses and their children on stelae erected by Khaemwaset at Aswan (Year 24–30) and in the

THE ABU SIMBEL TEMPLES

No one could be in any doubt that the Great Temple of Abu Simbel belonged to Ramesses. Two colossal statues of the pharaoh sat on either side of the central doorway, dwarfing the figure of the god above the door. Here stood Re-Harakhty, the goddess Maat by his left leg and the hieroglyphic sign for 'User' by his right, so that he could be read as a rebus: 'User-Maat-Re'.

Beyond the façade the temple extended almost 50 metres (160 ft) into the cliff. The great hall, bisected by two rows of Osiriform pillars, was decorated with scenes of the victorious Ramesses displaying his earthly triumphs before the gods. A doorway, guarded by two hawk-

The façade of the Great Temple. Between 1964 and 1968, the entire structure was moved 200 metres (656 ft) to a higher site to save it from the rising waters of the new Aswan High Dam.

headed sphinxes, led to a second pillared hall decorated with images of the pharaoh performing rituals and offering to himself.

The Small Abu Simbel Temple, dedicated to a local form of Hathor, was strongly identified with the queen consort Nefertari. The façade was decorated with six colossal standing figures; two of Nefertari wearing the cow-horns and carrying the sistrum of Hathor, and four of Ramesses.

Sandstone relief of Nefertari, consort of Ramesses II, forms part of the central doorway at the Great Temple of Abu Simbel.

temple of Horemheb at Gebel Silsila (Year 33–34) where the fact that she is carrying an *ankh* suggests that she may already be dead. Her tomb has yet to be discovered.

Ramesses married at least three of his daughters, Bintanath, Meritamen and Nebettawi, plus a lady named Henuttawi who was either his daughter or his sister. These new queens were acquired while the old queens were still living, and never took

The Great King of Hatti wrote year after year seeking to appease His Majesty, but never would he listen to them. So that when they saw their land in a miserable state under the great powers of the Lord of the Two Lands, then the King of Hatti said to his soldiers and courtiers: 'Look! Our land is devastated … Let us strip ourselves of all our possessions, and with my oldest daughter in front of them, let us carry peace offerings to the King of Egypt so that he may give us peace and we may live.' Then he caused his oldest daughter to be brought, the costly tribute before her consisting of gold, silver, ores, countless horses, cattle, sheep and goats.

RAMESSES TELLS HOW HE ACQUIRED A NEW BRIDE

precedence over them; indeed, there are images of Nefertari and Meritaten, and possibly Iset-Nofret and Bintanath, acting as queens together. It seems that they acted as deputy consorts, standing in for their mothers whenever required; this suggests that the 'marriages' were not necessarily consummated unions.

Five official consorts were not enough: Ramesses also married Hattusilis's daughter. The anonymous princess, accompanied by her retinue, her dowry and her mother, travelled to southern Syria where she was received by the Egyptian authorities. A long journey through Canaan and across Sinai followed. Worried that bad weather might delay the bridal party, Ramesses made a special offering to Seth. His offering was accepted and, with the Levant experiencing an unprecedented spell of good winter weather, the princess arrived safely at Pi-Ramesse. She was renamed Maathorneferure ('the One who sees Horus, the Visible Splendour of Re') and given the title of queen consort, an unprecedented honour for a foreign queen. Maathorneferure bore her husband at least one child, a daughter, before fading into obscurity. Ten years after the first marriage, with Maathorneferure presumably dead, Hattusilis agreed to send a second wife to Ramesses. The name of this new bride went unrecorded, and her fate is unknown.

HINTS OF DECLINE

Towards the end of Ramesses' reign there are hints of economic instability: this is most obvious in the now much-reduced building programme, which showed an increasing use of recycled building materials and shoddy construction techniques. It seems that Egypt was feeling the growing insecurity that was afflicting the wider Mediterranean world. As he grew older, and in greater need of rejuvenation, Ramesses' jubilees – celebrated in years 30, 33/34, 36/37, 40, 42/3, 45/46, 48/49, 51/52, 54/5, 57/8, 60/61, 63/64 and 66/67 – became almost annual events. He never appointed a formal co-regent but, gradually and unofficially his eldest surviving son, the thirteenth-born Merenptah, started to take over the running of the country. No official document preserves the details of his passing, but it seems that Ramesses II died at Pi-Ramesse during the August of his 67th regnal year. He was buried in KV 7, near the entrance to the Valley of the Kings.

KV 5: THE TOMB OF THE ROYAL SONS

Tomb KV 5 had been included on some of the earliest sketch maps of the Valley, and had been explored by the British traveller James Burton in 1825. The tomb doorway, which bore the cartouche of Ramesses II, was recorded in 1850 and cleared in 1902. But the doorway had then vanished beneath tons of debris from Howard Carter's excavations. When it was realized that a road-widening scheme might destroy KV 5, the Theban Mapping Project (1987–94), led by American Egyptologist Kent Weeks, determined to rescue the lost tomb.

The tomb was found to be completely blocked by compacted rubble deposited by floodwater. But an exploratory channel, cut by Burton over a century earlier, was still in place and it was possible to crawl through to the tomb interior. The blocked chambers and passages were then slowly cleared. In 1995 a long corridor was discovered beyond the first hall. Opening off this corridor were doorways, ten on each side, while the lowest two doorways led to more corridors with more small side-chambers until over 150 passageways and chambers had been found. The tomb, a usurped 18th-Dynasty tomb, had been extended into a catacomb to house the burials of the sons and perhaps some of the daughters of Ramesses II.

The tomb had been thoroughly looted in antiquity. However, the recovery of some human skeletal material (three skulls and a fragile complete skeleton) from a pit in one of the chambers, offers hope that more remains are yet to be found.

AN INEXTRICABLE DECLINE

FROM MERENPTAH TO TAWOSRET

Late 19th Dynasty c.1213 – 1186 BC

EGYPT'S NEW PHARAOH, MERENPTAH SON OF ISET-NOFRET, APPEARS IN OFFICIAL PORTRAITS AS A YOUNG AND vigorous man. In fact, he was already in his 60s and had effectively been Egypt's ruler for several years. The international unrest evident at the end of his father's reign continued, as a combination of circumstances – including the weak Mycenaean economy, crop failure, famine in Greece and Anatolia and an outbreak of plague – caused population shifts that disrupted the eastern Mediterranean world. As the peace treaty with the Hatti remained, Merenptah sent grain to the starving Hittites, but the Hittites had been weakened by a series of natural disasters and territorial disputes, and could no longer be regarded as powerful allies.

MERENPTAH
Dynasty: 19th
Father: Ramesses II
Mother: Iset-Nofret I
Consort: Iset-Nofret II
Burial place: KV 8
Successor: Amenmesse

A deceptively youthful Merenptah is depicted in a granite statue from his mortuary temple at Thebes. He was over 60 by the time he ascended the throne, and by the end of his reign was afflicted by arthritis and arteriosclerosis.

Sometime between Years 1 and 5 Merenptah subdued Ashkalon, Gezer and Yenoam. The eastern empire was, for the time being, secure. The west, however, was another matter. The Libyan nomads, led by their chief Meryey, were now allied with the 'Sea Peoples', an ill-defined band of seaborne itinerants and pirates who, quick to capitalize on the widespread unease, were plaguing the eastern Mediterranean. Together they had raised an army of 16,000 men and, as a preliminary to the invasion and colonization of the Delta, the Libyans had sent messengers southwards in an attempt to provoke a Nubian rebellion. Fortunately, in Year 5, Merenptah's spies learned of the Libyan plans. The Egyptian army, inspired this time by Ptah of Memphis, defeated the enemy in a six-hour battle that claimed the lives of over 6200 Libyans, including Meryey's sons and close relations (Merenptah tells us that his troops collected their uncircumcised penises to aid the count), and many more captured and set to work for the Egyptian state. Meanwhile the Nubians did indeed revolt, but it was a case of 'too little, too late', and Merenptah was able to put down the insurrection with relative ease.

Pi-Ramesse remained Egypt's capital city, but Merenptah built a new ceremonial palace close to the Ptah temple at Memphis. He did not attempt to replicate his father's extensive building programme, but he built, completed and usurped monuments at Hermopolis, el-Sirirya, Dendera, Abydos and Gebel Silsila. At Thebes his mortuary temple, which stood between the temples of Ramesses II and Amenhotep III, was built using blocks recycled from the partially ruined Amenhotep III temple. His tomb, KV 8,

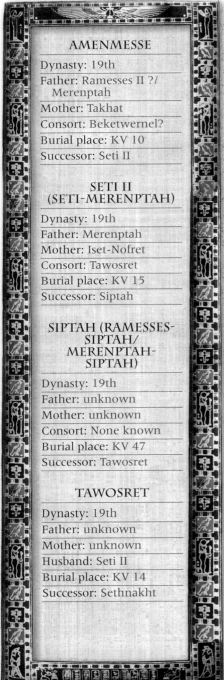

AMENMESSE

Dynasty: 19th
Father: Ramesses II ?/ Merenptah
Mother: Takhat
Consort: Beketwernel?
Burial place: KV 10
Successor: Seti II

SETI II (SETI-MERENPTAH)

Dynasty: 19th
Father: Merenptah
Mother: Iset-Nofret
Consort: Tawosret
Burial place: KV 15
Successor: Siptah

SIPTAH (RAMESSES-SIPTAH/ MERENPTAH-SIPTAH)

Dynasty: 19th
Father: unknown
Mother: unknown
Consort: None known
Burial place: KV 47
Successor: Tawosret

TAWOSRET

Dynasty: 19th
Father: unknown
Mother: unknown
Husband: Seti II
Burial place: KV 14
Successor: Sethnakht

was a simplified version of the tombs prepared for his father and his grandfather. Here, after a ten-year reign, Merenptah was buried. He had already chosen his successor: Seti-Merenptah, son of Iset-Nofret II, 'heir of the Two Lands, generalissimo and senior prince'. However, his wishes were ignored, as Merenptah was actually succeeded by the hitherto unknown Amenmesse.

THE USURPER

Amenmesse is likely to have been a member of the royal family which, thanks to the 100-plus children of Ramesses II, many of whom by now had produced children and grandchildren of their own, was dangerously large. He may well be identical with the viceroy of Nubia, Messuy, who served under Merenptah. His mother, Takhat, originally claimed the simple title of 'King's Mother', although some of her statuary was later altered to suggest that she had been a 'King's Wife'.

The precise sequence of events following Merenptah's death is unclear, but it is possible that the death occurred unexpectedly when Seti-Merenptah was absent from court and that, in his absence, Amenmesse was proclaimed pharaoh. Alternatively, it may be that Seti-Merenptah did claim his throne, only to be temporarily deposed, in the south if not throughout Egypt, by Amenmesse between Years 3 and 5. It is unlikely that Amenmesse would have been able to succeed had Egypt not already been suffering the first effects of what was to be a long-term crisis. The instability in the eastern Mediterranean, which had grown worse since the time of Merenptah, was starting to interrupt the royal cash flow, and the civil service was, slowly but surely, becoming inefficient and corrupt.

The new pharaoh enjoyed an ill-documented four-year reign. He was buried in KV 10, where he shared his tomb with two women: his mother Takhat and the 'King's Great Wife' Baketwerel, who is generally believed to have been his consort, although it is possible that she might have been a late 20th Dynasty tomb usurper.

Amenmesse was succeeded by Seti II, who is likely to be the displaced Seti-Merenptah, eldest son of Merenptah. The new pharaoh attempted to erase all trace of his predecessor, 'the enemy', from the archaeological record, recarving his cartouches and usurping his monument. There is very little evidence for his own six-year reign. Although he gave himself a string of impressive military titles there is no evidence that Seti fought any major battles, and his principal monuments are a small triple shrine in the Karnak complex, his mortuary temple and his unfinished tomb (KV 15). As the heir apparent, Crown Prince Seti-Merenptah, had predeceased him, the throne passed to a boy whom historians have variously identified as a son of Ramesses II, Merenptah, Amenmesse or, most likely Seti II.

Ramesses-Siptah started his rule under the joint guardianship of his stepmother Tawosret and the mysterious 'Chancellor of the Whole Land' Bay. By Year 3 the young pharaoh had changed his name to Merenptah-Siptah; to avoid confusion, historians generally refer to him as Siptah. Siptah's mummy, recovered as part of the KV 35 royal cache, shows that the young king had a distorted left foot and an atrophied lower leg, possibly the result of cerebral palsy. This is not shown in any of his portraits, where he appears as a physically perfect pharaoh.

Chancellor Bay is an intriguing but sadly ill-documented character. His unusual name suggests that he may have been born into a family of Syrian extraction. His title 'he who established the king on his father's throne', usually reserved for the gods, suggests that he played an important role in ensuring that Siptah inherited and retained his throne. This in turn suggests that there was some opposition to Siptah's rule. Bay was clearly a person of great importance, with a close personal link to both the king and the dowager queen. He was depicted standing behind Siptah's throne, an unusual honour for a non-royal, was mentioned in the foundation deposits of Siptah's mortuary temple and was allowed to build his own tomb in the Valley of the Kings (KV 13). However, an ostracon tells us that he was executed for unspecified crimes during Siptah's Year 5, leaving Tawosret as sole regent.

Siptah's six-year reign was plagued by economic instability and by the Libyan tribes who were crossing the border to settle in the western Delta in ever increasing numbers. He built a Theban mortuary temple and a tomb in the Valley of the Kings, but Thebes was no longer secure. The corrupt and inefficient civil service were unwilling, or unable, to police the necropolis and, as official rations were in short supply and the royal workmen were hungry, the tombs and temples were suffering from sporadic outbursts of looting. When Siptah died in his late teens or early twenties, without a consort and without an heir, Tawosret assumed a full royal titulary and, continuing Siptah's regnal years, claimed the throne as the female pharaoh 'daughter of Re, lady of Ta-merit, Tawosret chosen of Mut'.

Wall painting from the tomb of Seti II showing showing the king offering maat *to Osiris.*

TAWOSRET: DAUGHTER OF RE

Tawosret's parents go unrecorded and she does not claim the claim the title 'King's Daughter', but it seems reasonable to assume that she too was one of the many descendants of Ramesses II. She was the consort of Seti II and the mother of his intended successor Seti-Merenptah; a small cache of 19th Dynasty jewellery recovered from a pit in the Valley of the Kings (KV 56: widely but erroneously known as the 'Golden Tomb') may represent the burial of a young daughter of Tawosret and Seti II Manetho remembers her as 'King Thuoris, who in Homer is called Polybus, husband of Alcandara, and in whose time Troy was taken.'

Tawosret's only substantial monuments are her unfinished mortuary temple and her tomb (KV 14) which, started during the reign of Seti II, extended during Siptah's reign and extended again during her own reign, remained unfinished at her death. After a two-year reign, Tawosret disappeared from the archaeological record and is presumed to have either died or been deposed. The end of her reign marks the end of the 19th Dynasty.

RISE AND FALL
EIGHT KINGS NAMED RAMESSES

20th Dynasty c.1186–1069 BC

MANETHO CLASSIFIED EGYPT'S NEXT PHARAOH, SETHNAKHT, AS THE FOUNDER OF DYNASTY 20, SUGGESTING that he was regarded as different from the pharaohs who had gone before. Yet, despite the fact that he apparently emerged from nowhere after a brief period of civil unrest, it seems likely that he was connected with the wider Ramesside family. His son, Ramesses III, modelled his reign on that of Ramesses II but never claimed direct descent from him, while Sethnakht himself tells us, on a stele carved at Elephantine during Year 2, that he came to the throne via a divine oracle, and that he brought *maat* to a land troubled by chaos by purging Egypt of the foreign 'rebels' who were inflicting misery on the people. The Great Harris Papyrus, a lengthy and heavily biased history written during the reign of his grandson Ramesses IV, elaborates: here we read how years of near-anarchy culminated in the unwelcome reign of the Syrian Irsu (literally 'one who made himself': a false name) and how the gods then chose Sethnakht to end this humiliating period of foreign rule.

SETHNAKHT

Dynasty: 20th
Father: unknown
Mother: unknown
Consort: Tiy-Merenese
Burial place: KV 10
Successor:
    Ramesses III

Sethnakht reigned for just two years leaving no substantial monuments. His original tomb (KV 11) had been abandoned when it cut into the tomb of Amenmesse (KV 10), and so Sethnakht was buried in Tawosret's remodelled tomb (KV 14). Having erased the queen's name and image from the walls, he extended her tomb so that it became one of the longest in the Valley of the Kings.

RAMESSES III AND THE ROYAL ASSASSINS

Ramesses III inherited an invitingly fertile land with insecure borders: the wide, flat Delta with its lengthy coast was particularly tempting to disadvantaged foreigners. Libyan nomads had taken full advantage of Egypt's preoccupation with internal affairs and, from the time of Siptah onwards, had been gradually colonizing the western Delta. Now the situation had become intolerable. A minor revolt, sparked by Ramesses' interference in Libyan politics, gave him an excuse to take action, and Year 5 saw successful campaigns against three Libyan tribes, the Libu, the Meshwesh and the Seped, who were temporarily pushed westwards, out of the Delta.

Three years later Ramesses was again preparing for war. The Sea Peoples had already devastated the eastern Mediterranean world: they had caused the collapse of the Hittite empire, overwhelmed Cyprus and sacked, among many other towns and cities, Ugarit and Alalakh. Now, from a temporary base in northern Syria, they started to move southwards by land and boat, bringing their women and children with the express intention of settling in the Delta. Ramesses faced a two-pronged attack. In Year

Ramesses III vanquishes people from 'all foreign lands'.

RAMESSES III

Dynasty: 20th

Father: Sethnakht

Mother: Tiy-Merenese

Consort:
Iset Ta-Hemdjert

Burial place: KV 11

Successor:
Ramesses IV

8 he responded with a fierce battle in Canaan and a naval battle fought off the eastern Delta coast. Again he was victorious; again there was much bloodshed.

Finally, in Year 11, came more conflict on the western border. Libyan settlers had once again infiltrated Egypt to the west of the Canopic branch of the Nile and were now, again allied with the Sea Peoples, preparing to take over the Delta. Again, Ramesses responded with efficient brutality. Those Libyans who escaped death and capture were evicted westwards while the Sea Peoples retreated to settle on the Levantine coast. Detailed scenes of Ramesses' three great triumphs were recorded on the walls of his Medinet Habu mortuary temple, where the various enemy tribes can be identified by their clothing and weapons, and the dead enemy can be identified by their uncircumcised penises.

The wars of the first 11 years gave way to two decades of peace and superficial prosperity. The Great Harris Papyrus tells us that there were building works at Pi-Ramesse and at the Delta city of Tell el-Yahudiya, a successful trading mission to Punt and the resumption of expeditions to the copper and turquoise mines. Meanwhile, at Medinet Habu on the Theban west bank, Ramesses was building a magnificent mortuary temple, taking as his inspiration the nearby Ramesseum.

This appearance of prosperity was, however, deceptive. Three defensive campaigns in seven years had been a huge drain on resources at a time when tribute from the eastern vassals was failing and trade routes were collapsing. Now poor harvests were depleting the grain stores and the unwieldy bureaucracy and inefficient land management were contributing to the growing sense of crisis. Ramesses made things worse by making major

donations of land to the state and local cults, so that the temples now controlled almost a third of Egypt's agricultural land. With high inflation causing nationwide discontent, and delays in the payment of rations, the Deir el-Medina workmen went on strike. Fully aware of the threat that this posed to the royal tombs, Ramesses sent officials to negotiate with the ringleaders. The outstanding rations were paid, and the crisis was temporarily averted. All too soon, however, things took a turn for the worse as Libyan nomads started to attack the Theban west bank settlements. Deir el-Medina, isolated and completely dependent upon state rations, was uneasy and, as was inevitable, this

The fortified eastern gate ('Migdol gate') into the enclosure surrounding Ramesses III's mortuary temple at Medinet Habu. A canal from the Nile originally led to a landing quay just below this gate.

unease coincided with an outbreak of thefts from the royal monuments, including an attempted robbery at the tombs of Ramesses II and his sons.

The growing feeling of dissatisfaction may explain why, after 35 relatively successful years on the throne, Ramesses fell victim to a harem plot. The conspirators, a group of court officials and harem women, had determined to replace the pharaoh and his chosen heir, Ramesses IV son of Iset Ta-Hemdjert, with 'Pentaweret' (literally 'He of the Great One': a made-up name), son of the secondary wife Tiy. Their first attempt, which involved the making and cursing of wax figures, would have seemed entirely logical in a land that accepted magic as a valid means of killing remote enemies, but it failed. Their second attempt, a more practical assassination probably involving knives hidden in baskets during the celebration of the Opet Festival at Medinet Habu, was partially successful; the king was almost certainly killed, but the conspirators were caught and put on trial. Court papers tell us that the plot involved six harem wives and 31 male conspirators, and further complications arose when five of the trial judges were also arrested, accused of gross misconduct with the harem women. The punishments meted out to the guilty were severe; Tiy's fate is uncertain, but we know that Pentaweret was allowed the privilege of death by suicide.

THE MUMMY OF RAMESSES III

Ramesses III was buried in tomb KV 11, the tomb started and abandoned by his father Sethnakht. The king's mummy was discovered in 1871, as part of the Deir el-Bahri cache. His beautifully mummified head was unwrapped in Cairo by Egyptologist Gaston Maspero on 1 June 1886, but his body remains bandaged, making it difficult to determine whether he had been physically attacked. His head has served as the model for a number of mummy-based horror films, including the 1932 classic *The Mummy*, starring Boris Karloff.

THE LAST RAMESSIDES

Ramesses III was followed by a further seven Ramesses, a confusing and occasionally overlapping succession of fathers, sons, uncles and nephews, all descended from Ramesses III. These were potentially strong kings who knew how a traditional pharaoh should act. They mined, built tombs and mortuary temples, raised statues and occasionally campaigned against the Libyans, but their reigns were increasingly

I have made other countries afraid to remember Egypt. At the mere mention of my name, they are immediately scorched. Since my reign began ... I have not allowed any foreign land to look at the borders of Egypt with greedy eyes ... On the contrary, it is I who have seized their lands and added their territory to my own. Their rulers and people are in awe of me ... so, Egypt, let the sound of your rejoicing reach the heights of heaven, now that I am ruler of the Two Lands ...

RAMESSES III FIGHTS THE SEA PEOPLES

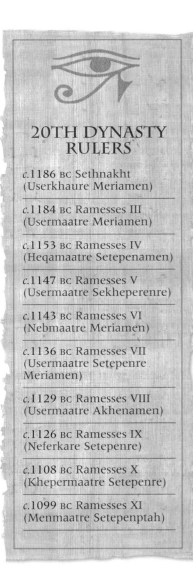

20TH DYNASTY RULERS

*c.*1186 BC Sethnakht
(Userkhaure Meriamen)

*c.*1184 BC Ramesses III
(Usermaatre Meriamen)

*c.*1153 BC Ramesses IV
(Heqamaatre Setepenamen)

*c.*1147 BC Ramesses V
(Usermaatre Sekheperenre)

*c.*1143 BC Ramesses VI
(Nebmaatre Meriamen)

*c.*1136 BC Ramesses VII
(Usermaatre Setepenre
Meriamen)

*c.*1129 BC Ramesses VIII
(Usermaatre Akhenamen)

*c.*1126 BC Ramesses IX
(Neferkare Setepenre)

*c.*1108 BC Ramesses X
(Khepermaatre Setepenre)

*c.*1099 BC Ramesses XI
(Menmaatre Setepenptah)

troubled by a relentless cycle of drought in northeast Africa, low Nile levels, poor harvests, inflation, civil unrest, bureaucratic incompetence and tomb robbery. Slowly but surely Egypt's borders, and income, shrank. When inter-family feuding was added to the mixture, the situation became irretrievable.

After the relatively brief and undistinguished reigns of Ramesses IV (6 years), V (4 years), VI (8 years), VII (7 years), VIII (3 years), the 18-year reign of Ramesses IX brought a welcome stability. But corruption was rife, there was a wave of robberies at Thebes, and no one was above suspicion. So concerned was Ramesses that he sent a team of government inspectors to report on the condition of the west bank tombs. These inspectors, led by Paser, mayor of eastern Thebes, examined both royal and private tombs from the 11th to the 18th Dynasties. Unexpectedly, and almost certainly incorrectly, they concluded that, although the royal burials were still substantially intact, many of the private burials had been desecrated. The finger of suspicion pointed firmly towards Paweraa, mayor of western Thebes. However, it proved impossible to corroborate Paweraa's involvement, and when Paser mysteriously disappeared soon after filing his report the case was, as far as we can tell, closed.

Ramesses IX built at Heliopolis and excavated a long tomb in the Valley of the Kings (KV 6). His successor, Ramesses X, reigned for somewhere between three and nine years before becoming the last pharaoh to be interred in the Valley of the Kings.

As the unpaid workmen of Thebes looted the temples and tombs of the west bank more or less unchecked, Ramesses XI prudently abandoned his partially built tomb in the Valley of the Kings (KV 4) and made a permanent move northwards, to Pi-Ramesse. Year 8 or 9 saw increased tensions in the Theban region as the high priest of Amen, Amenhotep, was deposed. Three years later, Panehsy, viceroy of Nubia, led his troops northwards to fight in support of Amenhotep. The high priest was restored, but Panehsy was rewarded with the position of 'overseer of the granaries', an office that brought him into increasingly acrimonious conflict with Amenhotep, whose temple owned most of the grain in Thebes.

Remnants of the granite sarcophagus of Ramesses VI in his tomb in the Valley of the Kings. Soon after burial, his body was targeted by grave robbers.

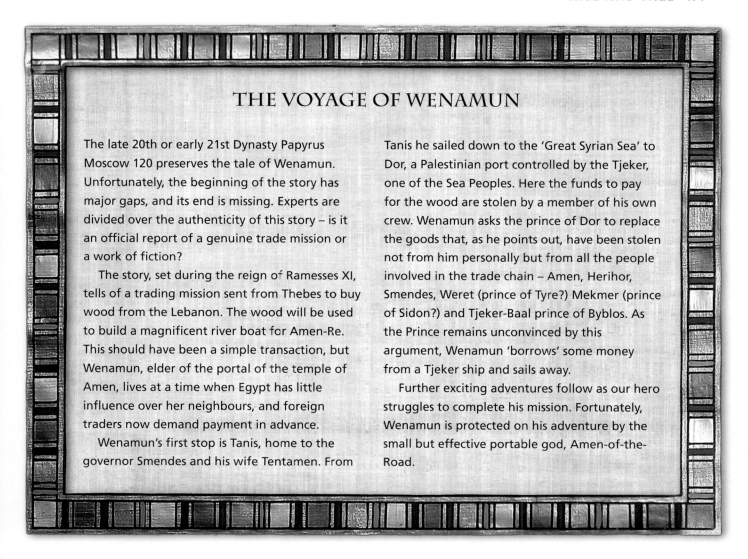

THE VOYAGE OF WENAMUN

The late 20th or early 21st Dynasty Papyrus Moscow 120 preserves the tale of Wenamun. Unfortunately, the beginning of the story has major gaps, and its end is missing. Experts are divided over the authenticity of this story – is it an official report of a genuine trade mission or a work of fiction?

The story, set during the reign of Ramesses XI, tells of a trading mission sent from Thebes to buy wood from the Lebanon. The wood will be used to build a magnificent river boat for Amen-Re. This should have been a simple transaction, but Wenamun, elder of the portal of the temple of Amen, lives at a time when Egypt has little influence over her neighbours, and foreign traders now demand payment in advance.

Wenamun's first stop is Tanis, home to the governor Smendes and his wife Tentamen. From Tanis he sailed down to the 'Great Syrian Sea' to Dor, a Palestinian port controlled by the Tjeker, one of the Sea Peoples. Here the funds to pay for the wood are stolen by a member of his own crew. Wenamun asks the prince of Dor to replace the goods that, as he points out, have been stolen not from him personally but from all the people involved in the trade chain – Amen, Herihor, Smendes, Weret (prince of Tyre?) Mekmer (prince of Sidon?) and Tjeker-Baal prince of Byblos. As the Prince remains unconvinced by this argument, Wenamun 'borrows' some money from a Tjeker ship and sails away.

Further exciting adventures follow as our hero struggles to complete his mission. Fortunately, Wenamun is protected on his adventure by the small but effective portable god, Amen-of-the-Road.

THE LOSS OF NUBIA AND THEBES

Not long after his restoration, Amenhotep found himself under siege at Medinet Habu. When Ramesses expressed his support for Amenhotep, events escalated into civil war. Ramesses' troops, led by General Piankh, were able to push Panehsy southwards into Nubia but they could not entirely crush him, and Nubia and her valuable gold resources passed outside Egyptian control. Meanwhile Piankh, now based at Thebes, assumed Panehsy's titles and, following the death of Amenhotep, pronounced himself high priest of Amen. To celebrate his own achievements he proclaimed a *wehem mesut* ['Renaissance'] and started his own year numbering system. He in turn was succeeded by generalissimo and former vizier Herihor, a High Priest who had the temerity to use the cartouches and regalia of a pharaoh. Thebes had become a state within a state.

Throughout his reign, which lasted for 27 to 30 years, Ramesses claimed sovereignty over the entire land. But this was a convenient fiction. Panehsy controlled Nubia, Herihor and his descendants ruled southern Egypt as the High Priests of Amen, and the influential local governor Smendes effectively ruled northern Egypt from Tanis. Following the death of Ramesses XI, Smendes formally claimed his throne. The New Kingdom had ended.

PHARAOHS AND FOREIGNERS

C.1069–332 BC

Detail of a mural from the palace of Xerxes at Persepolis,
ceremonial capital of the Achaemenid empire of Persia.
When an early ruler of this dynasty, Cambyses II, conquered
Egypt in 525 BC, he became the first in a line of Persian
overlords. Persian hegemony over Egypt was to last,
sporadically, for almost 200 years until Alexander the
Great gained control of the country in 332 BC.

DIVIDED RULE
TANIS AND THEBES

21st Dynasty c.1069–945 BC

THE THIRD INTERMEDIATE PERIOD (DYNASTIES 21–25) WAS A TIME OF HEREDITARY PRIESTHOODS, decentralization and population movement that saw large numbers of Libyans settle in Egypt. But, despite the obvious problems, it was for many a period of relative peace and prosperity, characterized by the perfection of the art of mummification. Unfortunately, our understanding of Third Intermediate Period history is limited by the paucity of the written record, and by the poor survival of archaeological sites in the Delta. The capital cities of Pi-Ramesse, Tanis and Bubastis (modern Zagazig) once rivalled Thebes in size, if not in architectural sophistication, but today Pi-Ramesse is all but invisible, the stone temples and statues dismantled and reused at later sites and the mud-brick buildings dissolved into the fertile Delta soil. Tanis and Bubastis have fared better, but have few immediately visible monuments and are still in the process of excavation.

Fragments of colossal statues and building blocks lie strewn around the site of the city of Tanis (modern San el-Hagar) in the Nile Delta, residence of kings of the 21st and 22nd Dynasties.

The local governor Smendes, probable son-in-law to Ramesses XI, had become the pharaoh Smendes. He was to rule northern Egypt for 26 ill-recorded years. His court was based at Tanis, a city that, due to the decentralized administration that made large-scale planning difficult, was largely built from materials recycled from earlier sites. However, while Tanis was developed as a cult centre, royal residence and burial ground, Memphis maintained its traditional role as the northern administrative centre.

MAINTAINING CLOSE TIES

Meanwhile, the high priests of Amen controlled Egypt to the south of the entrance to the Faiyum (modern el-Hiba). This was not an acrimonious division of political or religious power. The close links that the two courts maintained and their repeated intermarriages meant that they were effectively two branches of the same family. The high priests adopted the northern regnal dating system, the Theban triad of Amen, Mut and Khonsu was worshipped at Tanis, and Smendes financed restoration work at the Karnak temple complex.

The precise sequence of events at Thebes is the subject of fierce debate. Manetho records seven 21st Dynasty kings reigning for 130 years. We know that Smendes was succeeded by Amenemnisu, a short-lived and ill-documented king of unknown parentage, and that he in turn was succeeded by Pasebkhanut I, son of the high priest of Amen Pinodjem I and brother and father-in-law of the high priest Menkheperre. We do not know the parentage of Amenemope, successor to Pasebkhanut.

Egypt's next pharaoh, Osorkon the Elder, was the son of Shoshenq, the chief of the Libyan Meshwesh tribe. His successor, Siamun, ruled for almost 20 years, during which he extended the Tanis temple of Amen. It was during his reign that Egyptian princesses were, for the first time, allowed to marry foreign kings. The final pharaoh of the dynasty, Pasebkhanut (Psusennes) II, was almost certainly the shadowy high priest of Amen Psusennes 'III'. He ruled for 14 years and at his death the throne passed to a king of Libyan extraction, Shoshenq I, nephew of Osorkon the Elder.

HIGH PRIESTS OF THEBES

Some 400 miles (640 km) away, in Thebes, the high priests, who now controlled an estimated two-thirds of all temple-owned assets (not only land, but also mines, shipping and factories throughout Egypt), were developing a parallel 'royal family'. General Piankh, now high priest of Amen, had married Nodjmet, putative daughter of the high priest Amenhotep. Hrere, Nodjmet's mother, bears the title 'King's Mother' and, although her son goes unnamed, this suggests that she may also have been the mother of Smendes. Nodjmet was to give Piankh four sons, including the future high priest Pinodjem I. A short time after Piankh's death, the new high priest Herihor, another former general, married a woman named Nodjmet; it seems reasonable to speculate that the widowed Nodjmet had married her late husband's successor.

Herihor, 'high priest of Amen, generalissimo, army-chief and captain at the forefront of the army of all Egypt', made improvements to the Khonsu temple at Karnak, building a forecourt and pylons. Here we see him using the royal titulary and cartouche, and here we see his children: 19 named sons and 5 named daughters. As the presentation of the children is clearly modelled on scenes carved by Ramesses II and III, and as it seems unlikely that Nodjmet would have given her new husband 24 children, it seems that Herihor may have assumed another royal privilege, and acquired a harem.

Pinodjem I son of Piankh succeeded his stepfather Herihor as high priest. Pinodjem's wife, Henttawy was another possible daughter of Ramesses XI. She bore the future pharaoh Pasebkhanut I, the next two high priests of Amen (Masaharta and Menkheperre), and the divine adoratrice and god's wife of Amen, Maatkare. Smendes II succeeded his father Menkheperre, and he in turn was succeeded by his brother Pinodjem II. Pinodjem's tomb, cut high in the Deir el-Bahri cliff (DB 320), housed his family burials. Later it would be extended to house a cache of New Kingdom royal mummies 'restored' by the high priests. The gold and other valuables recovered from these stripped mummies made a welcome contribution to Theban finances, while the experience of unwrapping and examining the bodies may well have led to the improvements in mummification techniques obvious at this time.

Pinodjem's successor, the high priest Pasebkhanut 'III', is ill recorded but is likely to be identical with the northern king Pasebkhanut II.

21ST DYNASTY RULERS

*c.*1069 BC Smendes
(Hedjkheperre Setepenre)

*c.*1043 BC Amenemnisu
(Neferkare)

*c.*1039 BC Pasebkhanut
[Psusennes] I (Akheperre
Setepenamen)

*c.*993 BC Amenemope
(Usermaatre Setepenamen)

*c.*984 BC Osorkon the Elder
(Akheperre Setepenre)

*c.*978 BC Siamun
(Netjerkheperre
Setepenamen)

*c.*959 BC Pasebkhanut II
(Titkheperure Setepenre)

THE ROYAL TOMBS OF TANIS

The 21st and 22nd Dynasty pharaohs built a complex of subterranean tombs inside their temple precincts. Here they could lie in close proximity to the gods, and be guarded night and day. Reusing materials salvaged from earlier buildings, the pharaohs were interred in limestone and granite-lined chambers built within a large pit. The pit was then filled in and covered, during the 22nd Dynasty reign of Shoshenq III, by a low, flat, *mastaba*-like structure. A series of shafts allowed access to the burials. Eventually the pharaohs were forgotten, the mud-brick structure was demolished, and a series of Ptolemaic workshops was built on top of the tombs.

On 27 February 1939, while excavating beneath the pavement in the smaller Mut temple of Tanis, French Egyptologist Pierre Montet found the looted multi-chambered tomb of Osorkon II; also included in this tomb were Shoshenq III, Takeloth II (who had been interred in a recycled sarcophagus), and Osorkon's son Prince Hornakht. On 17 March the burials of Shoshenq II, Siamun and Pasebkhanut II were discovered.

A massive granite plug made from a Ramesside obelisk hid the entrance to the intact burial of Pasebkhanut I; the only Egyptian king to be recovered in an intact burial. The king wore a gold face mask, and lay in a solid silver anthropoid coffin inside a black granite anthropoid sarcophagus recycled from a 19th Dynasty burial, which was itself housed in the red granite sarcophagus of the

The gold burial mask of Pasebkhanut I. Although the tomb was found intact, only the more durable objects had survived; the damp soil of Lower Egypt had destroyed wooden and cloth artefacts.

19th Dynasty pharaoh Merenptah. A second chamber held the intact burial of Amenemope. Two more chambers were subsequently discovered, housing the burials of Generals Ankhefenmut and Wendjebauendjedet.

CHAOS AND CONFUSION
THE LIBYAN PHARAOHS

22nd–24th Dynasties c.945–715 BC

S HOSHENQ I CAME FROM ONE OF THE MANY LIBYAN FAMILIES WHO HAD SETTLED IN THE DELTA TO MAKE A success of life in Egypt. His uncle, Osorkon the Elder, had already served as pharaoh, he himself had worked under Pasebkhanut II and his wife was probably Pasebkhanut's daughter. Shoshenq looked back to the glories of the New Kingdom; a time when priests were subservient to kings, when priestly titles were not hereditary, and pharaohs ruled an undivided land. Recognizing that the role of the Theban high priest had to be restricted, Shoshenq appointed his second-born son Iuput simultaneously high priest of Amen, commander-in-chief of the armies and governor of Upper Egypt. Other family members were used as a check to growing local autonomy. It may be argued, however, that these measures had precisely the opposite effect to that intended; that they promoted, rather than hindered, decentralization.

Ruling from the Delta city of Bubastis, mid-way between Memphis and Tanis, Shoshenq reopened the Gebel Silsila sandstone quarries and started to construct an ambitious new colonnaded forecourt in the Karnak temple of Amen and an equivalent court and gateway at the Memphite temple of Ptah. Smaller-scale building works occurred at Tanis, Bubastis and Pithom. In Year 10 he raised an army that, so the Bible tells us, included over 1000 chariots and both Libyan and Nubian soldiers and, taking advantage of the confusion caused by the death of Solomon of Israel, launched a campaign that ended with the defeat of both Israel and Judah. Having raised a victory stela at Megiddo, Shoshenq returned to Egypt with all of Solomon's treasures, except the Ark of the Covenant. His triumph was recorded on his new gateway (the 'Bubastite Portal'; the only part of his Karnak building works to be completed) at the temple of Amen. This may have been intended to be the first of many Palestinian campaigns, but Shoshenq died soon after his return and was buried within the precincts of the Mut temple at Tanis.

Serried ranks of Semitic prisoners are portrayed on this relief panel from the temple of Amen at Karnak, which celebrates the victories of Shoshenq I in his campaign against Philistia, Judah and Israel in 924 BC.

Shoshenq was succeeded by his son Osorkon I, who made his heir and co-regent, Shoshenq II, high priest of Amen. The early death of Shoshenq II saw the throne pass to his brother Takeloth I and then, after 15 ill-recorded years, to Osorkon II. The adoption of royal titles by the high priests of Amen at this time (always a worrying sign) has confused our understanding of the succession, and for some years the high priest Harsiese was accepted as a full pharaoh ruling between Osorkon II and Takeloth II. Realizing the danger of growing Theban independence, Osorkon II restored royal control by appointing his son Nimlot high priest of Amen at Thebes, while his son

And it came to pass in the fifth year of king Rehoboam, that Shishak [Shoshenq] king of Egypt came up against Jerusalem. And he took away the treasures of the house of the Lord, and the treasures of the king's house; he took away everything. He also took away all the shields of gold which Solomon had made.

1 KINGS 14: 25–6

22ND (LIBYAN) DYNASTY RULERS

*c.*945 BC Shoshenq I
(Hedjkheperre)

*c.*924 BC Osorkon I
(Sekhemkheperre)

*c.*890 BC Shoshenq II
(Heqakheperre)

*c.*889 BC Takeloth I

*c.*874 BC Osorkon II
(Usermaatre)

*c.*850 BC Takeloth II
(Hedjkheperre)

*c.*825 BC Shoshenq III
(Usermaatre)

*c.*773 BC Pimay
(Usermaatre)

*c.*767 BC Shoshenq V
(Aakheperre)

*c.*730 BC Osorkon IV
(Aakheperre)

Shoshenq became high priest of Ptah at Memphis. A pious prayer addressed to Amen, that 'brother should not be jealous of brother', indicates a sensible awareness that danger could come from within, as well as without, the royal family. Osorkon II was able to finance a traditional building programme, and there were new projects at Bubastis, Tanis, Memphis, Thebes and Leontopolis (modern Tell Muqdam). But a powerful new enemy had awoken in the east, and Osorkon's Palestinian campaigns were defensive rather than offensive. In 853 BC Egypt fought alongside Israel and her allies at the Battle of Qarqar; together they were able to ward off the advancing Assyrian army, led by Shalmaneser III.

THE GROWING NORTH–SOUTH DIVIDE

Takeloth II, successor to Osorkon II, was the half-brother and son-in-law of the of the high priest of Amen Nimlot, while Nimlot's son, Ptahwedjankhef, was governor of Herakleopolis. With one extended family controlling the major secular and political hot-spots, Egypt enjoyed 11 years of peace until the death of Nimlot shattered the fragile unity. Takeloth had chosen his son Osorkon as the next high priest of Amen, but this appointment was challenged by the Theban Harsiese, a descendant of the counter-pharaoh Harsiese. Takeloth's troops pushed southwards, through the lands controlled by Ptahwedjankhef, and in a brief, brutal campaign, temporarily reasserted royal control over Thebes. Trouble flared again four years later; this time, it took almost ten years to reassert royal authority over Thebes.

With the heir to the throne, Osorkon, pushed to one side, Takeloth II was succeeded by a younger son, Shoshenq III. The new pharaoh was to rule for 53 years of diminishing royal authority which would see not only a widening north–south divide – the appointment of Harsiese as high priest of Amen confirms Thebes's growing independence – but also a growing division between the eastern Delta court of Tanis, and the central Delta city of Leontopolis. Egypt continued to fragment during the reigns of Pimay and Shoshenq V, until the final king of the 22nd Dynasty (whom some Egyptologists would classify as a 23rd-Dynasty pharaoh), Osorkon IV, was defeated by the Nubian invader Piye.

The 23rd and 24th Dynasties are local rulers, and are partially or wholly contemporary with the late 22nd and early 25th Dynasties. The 23rd Dynasty was a line of kings of Libyan ancestry from Leontopolis; the Thebans chose to recognize these kings in preference to the 22nd Dynasty.

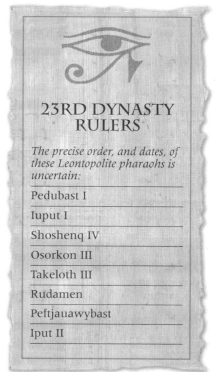

23RD DYNASTY RULERS

The precise order, and dates, of these Leontopolite pharaohs is uncertain:

Pedubast I
Iuput I
Shoshenq IV
Osorkon III
Takeloth III
Rudamen
Peftjauawybast
Iput II

Osorkon I presided over a largely uneventful period of peace at the end of the ninth century BC. This broken statue was consecrated by his vassal Elibaal, ruler of the Phoenician city-port of Byblos.

The 24th Dynasty was a brief coalition of the northern independent kings, based at the Delta city of Sais. Only two 24th-Dynasty pharaohs, the 'Prince of the West' Tefnakht and his successor Bakenrenef (Bocchoris), are known. Herodotus tells us, almost certainly erroneously, that the dynasty ended when Bakenrenef was captured by the Nubian pharaoh Shabako and burned alive. Alongside these recognized dynasties, other major cities developed their own semi-formal lines of local rulers.

BRIEF STABILITY
THE NUBIAN PHARAOHS

25th Dynasty c.747–656 BC

From around 747 BC Piye, son of Kashta, ruled Kush from Napata (modern Gebel Barkal), below the fourth cataract. In his Year 20 he sailed north to halt Tefnakht's expansionist plans. Details of Piye's campaign were recorded on a 'Victory Stela' erected in the temple of Amen at Napata; similar stelae were doubtless put up throughout Egypt, but were later destroyed.

25TH (NUBIAN) DYNASTY RULERS

c.747 BC Piye
(Menkheperre)

c.716 BC Shabako
(Neferkare)

c.702 BC Shebitko
(Djedkaure)

c.690 BC Taharka
(Khunefertemre)

c.664 BC Tanutamani
(Bakara)

The Kushite pharaoh Shabako extended Nubian control over Egypt from the south to the Nile Delta. This pink granite statue shows him wearing the nemes *headcloth.*

Piye's first major victory – moreover, one in which he encountered little or no resistance – was at Thebes, where he reinforced his position by insisting that the god's wife of Amen, Shepenwepet I, adopt his sister Amenirdis I as her successor. Having celebrated the Opet Festival at the temple of Amen, Piye continued northwards, defeating the local kings, including the 'Four Great Chiefs of the Ma [Meshwesh]' and taking Memphis by force. Only the 'Western Kingdom' – namely, the Delta lands controlled by rulers of Libyan descent – remained outside his control.

Following a pilgrimage to the unplundered temples of Memphis and Heliopolis, Piye was acknowledged by the defeated local rulers; all submitted in person except for the bitter Tefnakht, who sent a representative. Gathering the spoils of war, Piye withdrew to rule from Napata, allowing the local rulers to govern Egypt in his absence. To all intents and purposes, it was as if the Nubian invasion had never been, and Tefnakht was soon claiming a local kingship. Piye died without returning to Egypt.

PIYE'S SUCCESSORS

Following Nubian tradition, Piye's throne passed to his brother, Shabako. The new pharaoh returned – or reinvaded – to execute Bakenrenef. This great victory was celebrated on a commemorative scarab: 'He has slaughtered those who rebelled against him in both South and North, and in every foreign land.' Ruling from Memphis, Shabako enjoyed a 14-year reign, and his building works stretched from the southern Delta to el-Kurru. A skilled diplomat, he managed to maintain friendly terms with the Assyrians, and it was almost certainly during his reign that Iamani, rebel prince of

It is the year for making an end, for putting the fear of me into Lower Egypt, and inflicting upon them a great and severe beating.

PIYE ADDRESSES HIS TROOPS (VICTORY STELA)

Thus did I come from Nubia among the brothers of pharaoh
that His Majesty had summoned ... I was crowned in Memphis
after the falcon rose into heaven.

TAHARKA INHERITS THE THRONE OF EGYPT (STELA V; KAWA TEMPLE OF AMEN)

Ashdod, fled to Egypt and was handed back to the Assyrians by an anonymous king who ruled both Egypt and Nubia.

Shabako's successor, his nephew and perhaps co-regent Shebitko, was less of a diplomat. Having adopted a series of aggressive titles, he most unwisely became involved in an attempted Palestinian rebellion against the Assyrian king Sennacherib. The rebellion failed, the Assyrians took Jerusalem, and Sennacherib henceforth came to regard Egypt as an enemy. Shabako built at Memphis, Thebes and el-Kurru.

Shebitko's brother, Taharka, ruled Egypt from Memphis and, perhaps, Tanis. His Year 6 brought a good omen: an abnormally high Nile flood that virtually wiped out Egypt's large rat and mouse population, and led to a larger than usual harvest. That same year the queen mother travelled from Nubia to visit her son. Taharka had the resources to build extensively both in Egypt (at Karnak, Medinet Habu, Memphis) and Nubia (at Kawa, Gebel Barkel, Buhen, Semna, Kasr Ibrim), but the second half of his 26-year reign was increasingly troubled. An inscription, carved on the rear of the wall of the Hall of Annals of Tuthmosis III at Karnak during Year 15, mentions dwindling eastern tribute.

Diorite head of Taharka. For his tenacious defence of Egypt against the powerful Assyrian empire, the first-century BC Greek writer Strabo lauded him as one of the foremost military tacticians of the ancient world.

THE SHABAKO STONE

During Shabako's reign a scribe claimed to have copied an Old Kingdom text onto a black granite slab. As the text explains, this was done because the pharaoh found the original, which was presumably written on a papyrus or leather scroll, to be 'a work of the ancestors that was worm-eaten'. However, it seems equally likely that this is an 'archaizing text', a contemporary text written so as to appear old. The lengthy text explains the theology of priests of Ptah at Memphis.

It is said of Ptah: 'He [it is] who made all things and created all gods. He is Ta-tenen who gave birth to the gods, and from whom everything came forth: food, provisions, divine offerings and everything good ...'

THE DAHSHUR RUNNING STELA

The Nubian kings were fiercely militaristic and took pride in the physical prowess of their soldiers. The Dahshur Running Stela records details of a race by army units who were required to run from Memphis across the desert to the Faiyum and back – an exhausting 65 miles (104 km). Watched by Taharka, who provided prizes for the winners, and who even joined the runners for a short distance, the victor covered the first leg of the run in an impressive four hours.

Meanwhile, the Assyrian king Esarhaddon became convinced that Egypt was interfering to too great an extent in foreign affairs.

ENTER THE ASSYRIANS

In 674 BC Taharka's forces repelled the Assyrians at the border city of Ashkalon. Two years later the Assyrians reached Memphis and captured and deported most of the royal family including, as Esarhaddon recorded in his *Annals*, Taharka's 'consort, his harem, his heir Ushankhuru, his sons and daughters'. As Taharka retreated to mourn his family in Thebes, the Assyrians removed the local officials and appointed their own men to govern on their behalf. Esarhaddon died in 669 BC, and was succeeded by his son Ashurbanipal. Two years later, a short-lived Egyptian recovery was followed by the fall of Memphis, the surrender of Thebes and the execution of many of the Assyrian-appointed governors who were found to be plotting against their masters. Taharka fled to Napata and died soon after. He was buried at Nuri.

For the first time in its long history, Egypt was ruled by a remote, foreign king who showed no interest in behaving like a conventional pharaoh. Meanwhile, in Nubia, Taharka's cousin (or nephew) and successor, Tanutamani, was inspired by a dream of military greatness. Sailing north from Napata, restoring temples and making divine vows as he went, he was able to recapture Aswan, Thebes and Memphis where he accepted the surrender of the Delta rulers.

Ashurbanipal wasted no time in delivering his response, and in 664 BC Tanutamani's dream of a resurgent Egypt became a nightmare as the Assyrians arrived in force, Thebes fell, the temple of Amen was sacked, and Tanutamani was forced into permanent exile in Nubia. Like Piye, Shabako and Shebitko before him, he was eventually buried in the el-Kurru cemetery.

PIYE

Dynasty: 25th
Father: Kashta
Mother: Pebatjma
Consorts: Tabiry, Abar, Khensa, Peksater
Burial place: Nubia
Successor: Shabako

SHABAKO

Dynasty: 25th
Father: Kashta
Mother: Pebatjma?
Consort: Qalhata
Burial place: Nubia
Successor: Shebitko

SHEBITKO

Dynasty: 25th
Father: Piye
Mother: unknown
Consort: Arty
Burial place: Nubia
Successor: Taharka

TAHARKA

Dynasty: 25th
Father: Piye
Mother: Abar
Consort: Atakhebasken
Burial place: Nubia
Successor: Tanutamani

TANUTAMANI

Dynasty: 25th
Father: Shabako?
Mother: Qalhata?
Consort: Piankharty
Burial place: Nubia

A BACKWARDS GLANCE
THE SAITE PHARAOHS

26th Dynasty c.664–525 BC

THE LATE PERIOD (DYNASTIES 26–31) IS RELATIVELY WELL DOCUMENTED NOT ONLY WITHIN EGYPT, WHERE writings survive in hieroglyphs, hieratic, demotic, Greek and Aramaic, but also in the writings of the Classical authors. Most notable among these is Herodotus of Halicarnassus (modern Bodrum), who visited northern Egypt in approximately 450 BC. Herodotus proved to be a gullible tourist who believed almost everything that he was told, no matter how implausible. Nevertheless, his *Histories* (Book II) offers an engaging eyewitness account of the minutiae of Late Period life. In contrast, the archaeology of the Late Period is ill understood and, again with the emphasis on Delta sites, ill preserved.

This was a time of prosperity and increasing Greek, Carian (from the Asian mainland near the island of Rhodes), Cypriot, Phoenician and Jewish immigration. The Egyptians were, to a large extent, tolerant of the new arrivals, but it is no coincidence that the Late Period is characterized by a renaissance of Egypt's cultural heritage with deliberate artistic, architectural and linguistic references to Egypt's glorious past.

The 26th Dynasty is generally recognized as the opening dynasty of the Late Period. However, the distinction between the Third Intermediate Period and the Late Period is less than clear-cut, and many experts would also include within the latter era the 25th Dynasty, a time when Egypt had an acknowledged dynasty of pharaohs ruling alongside a series of powerful local rulers.

Esarhaddon of Assyria had spared Nakau of Sais and installed him as a puppet king to rule Memphis and the western Delta. At the same time Nekau's son, Psamtek, was allowed to rule from the Delta city of Athribis. In 664 BC, when the Nubians made their final attempt to reclaim Egypt, Tanutamani's army killed the collaborator Nekau. Psamtek, however, escaped, returning only when Tanutamani had retreated.

HIS OWN MAN

Psamtek ruled around half of the Delta as an Assyrian client king. But this was not enough. He risked alienating the *machimoi* (the Egyptian soldier classes) by recruiting a large mercenary army, and started to expand his territories. By 660 BC Psamtek ruled the entire Delta from Sais; four years later he had broken away from the Assyrians to claim sovereignty over a gradually reunited land. He was to rule for 54 years.

Strengthened trade links with the Mediterranean boosted Egypt's economy, with the new wealth being used to build new temples and repair or improve older buildings.

A Late Period figure, carved in basalt, of the goddess Isis.

... the Egyptians themselves in their manners and customs seem to have reversed the ordinary practices of mankind. For instance, women attend markets and are employed in trade, while men stay at home and do the weaving ... Men in Egypt carry loads on their heads, women on their shoulders; women urinate standing up, men sitting down. To ease themselves they go indoors, but eat outside in the streets, on the theory that what is unseemly but necessary should be done in private, and what is not unseemly should be done openly.

HERODOTUS (*HISTORIES* II: 35)

Psamtek constructed the south pylon at the Memphite temple of Ptah, built for the cult of the Apis bull. Meanwhile, a series of military campaigns in Nubia, Palestine and on the western border, offered a fleeting reminder of Egypt's glorious past. Not everything went to plan, however: Herodotus tells us that during Psamtek's reign 240,000 *machimoi* deserted and fled to Nubia because they had not been relieved for three years. Psamtek chased after his men and tried to reason with them. Yet when he accused them of deserting their gods, along with their wives and children, 'one of them pointed to his genitals and said that wherever these went, there would be no shortage of wives and children'.

The Assyrians were no longer considered a serious threat; indeed, in 616 BC Psamtek's army supported them to the east of the Euphrates, as they attempted to push back the increasingly powerful Babylonians (Chaldaeans). This was too little, too late. In 612 BC the Assyrian empire fell to a joint Scythian and Persian army, leaving a dangerous power vacuum.

INCURSIONS INTO NUBIA

Nekau II, son of Psamtek, was another brave soldier intent on recovering some of Egypt's lost territories. In 609 BC he defeated Josiah of Judah and established a base at Carchemish; in 605 BC, however, he was forced to retreat and the Babylonians followed him to Egypt's eastern border. Meanwhile, a successful Nubian campaign nipped an incipient rebellion in the bud. Nekau, too, built for the Apis bull. More unusually, he gave generous donations to major shrines in eastern Greece; this would, presumably, have pleased the Greeks who played an important role in his mercenary army and his newly inaugurated navy. Nekau constructed a fleet of ramming warships, and cut, or partially cut, a canal linking the Pelusiac branch of the Nile to the Red Sea.

The six-year reign of Psamtek II saw a brief Palestinian campaign and a far larger Nubian war. Stelae recovered from Tanis, Karnak and Shellal, as well as graffiti scratched on the legs of the statues fronting the Great Temple at Abu

26TH (SAITE) DYNASTY RULERS

672 BC Nekau I

664 BC Psamtek [Psammetichus] I (Wahibre)

610 BC Nekau II (Wehemibre)

595 BC Psamtek II (Neferibre)

589 BC Wahibre [Apries] (Haaibre)

570 BC Ahmose II [Amasis] (Khemibre)

526 BC Psamtek III (Ankhkaenre)

THE 'GOD'S WIVES OF AMEN'

The Late Period 'God's Wives of Amen' were celibate. Their freedom from the perils of pregnancy and childbirth may explain why they enjoyed such unusually long lives.

Piye's sister, Amenirdis I, served as God's Wife through the reigns of Shabako and Shebitko, and was eventually buried alongside her predecessor Shepenwepet I, daughter of Osorkon III, in a tomb-chapel at Medinet Habu. Her successor, Shepenwepet II daughter of Piye, outlasted her dynasty and died during the Saite reign of Psamtek I. The next God's Wife should have been Taharka's daughter Amenirdis II, but Amenirdis passed the title straight on to her adopted successor Nitocris I, daughter of Psamtek I. Details of this arrangement are preserved on a stela erected in the Karnak temple of Amen:

> I [Psamtek] have given to him [Amen] my daughter to be a God's Wife, and have endowed her better than those who were before her. Surely he will be gratified with her worship, and protect the land of he that gave her to him … .

Nitocris I was God's Wife for almost 70 years, outliving her intended successor, her niece Shepenwepet. The office then fell to her great-niece Ankhenesneferibre, daughter of Psamtek II. Ankhenesneferibre served as God's Wife for over 60 years. She had followed custom, and adopted a successor, but the Persian invasion brought a halt to the reign of Nitocris II, daughter of Ahmose II. There would be no further God's Wives of Amen.

Amenirdis I, daughter of the Nubian king Kashta; the opulence of her tomb at Medinet Habu attests the high status of the office of God's Wife.

NEKAU BUILDS A CANAL

It was Necos [Nekau] who began the construction of the canal to the Arabian Gulf ... the length of the canal is four days' journey by boat, while its breadth is sufficient to allow two triremes to be rowed abreast ... The construction of the canal cost the lives of 120,000 Egyptians. Necos did not complete the work; he stopped in deference to an oracle that warned him that his work was all for the benefit of the 'barbarians' – the Egyptians' term for anyone who does not speak their language.

Herodotus (*Histories* II: 158)

Simbel, confirm that Psamtek had mustered a large expeditionary force of Egyptian, Phoenician, Greek and Jewish soldiers and defeated a rebellion. Back home he defaced the statuary and reliefs of the Nubian pharaohs. Herodotus confirms the Nubian campaign as the most important event of Psamtek's reign, and adds that the king was asked to give his advice on the organization of the Olympic Games.

Wahibre, son of Psamtek II, campaigned successfully against the Babylonians, and against Cyprus and Phoenicia. But his problems were closer to home. There was trouble at Aswan, where the garrison was on the verge of mutiny, as well as on the western border, where the Libyans were being menaced by Greek invaders. With the *machimoi* troubled by the increasingly influential foreign mercenaries civil war broke out, and Wahibre was killed in battle (possibly drowned during an expedition to capture Cyrene) in 570 BC.

THE MILITARY'S CHOICE

Ahmose II was a former general, possibly of Libyan descent, who was chosen as pharaoh by the army and who therefore had the support of the *machimoi*. Herodotus preserves the memory of a somewhat lightweight king, the soldier's friend prone to 'frivolous amusements, drinking and joking with friends', but history does not bear this analysis out. Ahmose was able to thwart a Babylonian invasion during Year 4 and then, recognizing the growing might of Persia, forged a short-lived diplomatic alliance with the Greek state of Lydia, the island of Samos and the Babylonians. The Persians, led by Cyrus the Great, would destroy Lydia in 546 BC and Babylon in 538 BC, leaving Egypt isolated. Meanwhile, Ahmose reformed the Egyptian judicial system and, recognizing the importance of international trade, re-established the city of Naukratis as a Greek

The Nubians of every hill-country rose up against him, their hearts full of rage against him. The attack took place, and it was misery for the rebels. His majesty has done a fighter's work ... One waded in their blood as in water ...

PSAMTEK DEFEATS THE NUBIANS (VICTORY STELA, SHELLEL)

Cambyses and Psamtek, *a painting by the French Romantic artist Adrien Guignet (1816–54), shows the pharaoh being deposed by the Persian king after the Battle of Pelusium.*

polis – a Greek trading centre governed by Greek laws – on the Canopic branch of the Nile, near Sais. Ahmose was a wealthy and enthusiastic builder, and is credited with making major improvements to the temple of Neith at Sais, and building a temple of Isis and erecting colossi at Memphis.

Within a year of succeeding to his father's throne, Psamtek III was required to show his mettle. In 525 BC the Egyptians met the Persians, now led by Cambyses, at Pelusium, gateway to the eastern Delta. Herodotus claims that the Persians were helped by the defecting mercenary general Phanes of Halicarnasus. It was apparently Phanes who suggested that the Persians should ask the Bedouin the best way of crossing the desert: as punishment, Phanes was forced to watch as the Egyptian army killed his sons and drank their blood. Egypt lost the battle but the hapless Psamtek was captured and sent to Susa, capital city of the Persian empire.

HERODOTUS VISITS THE BATTLEFIELD AT PELUSIUM

At the place where the battle occurred I saw a great marvel that the natives had told me about. The bones still lay there, those of the Persians separate from those of the Egyptians ... and I noticed that the skulls of the Persians are so thin that the merest touch with a pebble will pierce them, while those of the Egyptians are so tough that it is hardly possible to break them with a blow from a stone. I was told that the reason was that the Egyptians shave their heads from childhood, so that the bone of the skull is hardened by the action of the sun – this is also why they hardly ever go bald, baldness being rarer in Egypt than anywhere else ...

Herodotus (*Histories* III: 12)

A HATED OVERLORD
TWO PERSIAN INVASIONS

27th–31st Dynasties c.525–332 BC

FOR OVER A CENTURY A SERIES OF SATRAPS (VICEROYS) RAN EGYPT ON BEHALF OF THE ABSENT PERSIAN GREAT Kings. Herodotus tells of unspeakable horrors at this time – the sacking of cities, desecration of the royal burials, murder of the sacred Apis bull and grave insults to the royal family – but as a Greek, Herodotus is biased against the Persians, and there is no evidence of these traumas in the archaeological or written record.

Indeed, it seems that the Persian pharaohs, Cambyses and Darius I in particular, tried to conform to local ideas of kingship by adopting cartouches, respecting local gods, restoring the temples and allowing the Egyptians to play a part in running their own country. While Egypt was expected to make a significant contribution to the Persian empire – its soldiers and sailors now fought alongside the Persians against the Greeks – the bureaucratic infrastructure was left largely intact beneath a tier of Persian administrators. Despite occasional revolts, life for most people continued much as it had before.

NATIONAL RULE REVIVED

Eventually, after over a century of remote rule from Susa, one of the revolts succeeded. Amyrtaios of Sais claimed a brief period of independent, nationwide rule as the only pharaoh of the 28th Dynasty, before being deposed by the marginally longer-lived, ill-documented 29th Dynasty.

Having moved the capital from Sais to the more central Delta city of Mendes, Nefarud I had the resources to start a building programme extending from the Delta to Thebes, and to maintain the cult of the Apis bull at Sakkara. His death in 292 BC sparked civil unrest, which ended when the apparently unrelated Hakor seized the throne. Hakor's 14-year reign brought a welcome stability to Egypt. Once again the masons took up their chisels, as pharaoh funded building works throughout the Nile Valley. Allying himself with the Greeks, sworn enemies to the Persians, Hakor was able to ward off several threatened Persian invasions. But after his death in 380 BC, his son and chosen successor Nefarud II was deposed after just a few months' rule.

The 30th Dynasty was founded by the former general Nakhtnebef, governor of the Delta city of Sebennytos. In 375 BC, after seven peaceful years, Nakhtnebef saw off a combined Persian–Athenian invasionary force that had launched an attack on the western Nile Delta, but which had been thwarted by the unanticipated annual Nile flooding. Nathtnebef interpreted the reprieve as divine intervention, and hastened to make a military alliance with Sparta and Athens. Much of his stable 18-year reign would be devoted to a high-quality, country-wide temple restoration programme.

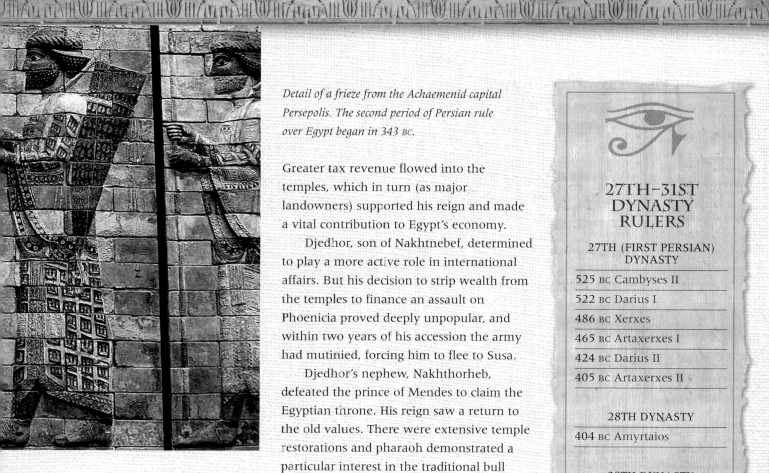
Detail of a frieze from the Achaemenid capital Persepolis. The second period of Persian rule over Egypt began in 343 BC.

Greater tax revenue flowed into the temples, which in turn (as major landowners) supported his reign and made a vital contribution to Egypt's economy.

Djedhor, son of Nakhtnebef, determined to play a more active role in international affairs. But his decision to strip wealth from the temples to finance an assault on Phoenicia proved deeply unpopular, and within two years of his accession the army had mutinied, forcing him to flee to Susa.

Djedhor's nephew, Nakhthorheb, defeated the prince of Mendes to claim the Egyptian throne. His reign saw a return to the old values. There were extensive temple restorations and pharaoh demonstrated a particular interest in the traditional bull cults by promoting the Buchis bull of Armant and participating in the burial of the Apis at Sakkara. Nakhthorheb was even more concerned to establish his own divinity. The cult of Nakhthorheb the Falcon (Horus) was widely promoted, and Egypt's temples now included royal statues which had their own priesthoods, and which were financed by their own endowments.

Unfortunately Nakhthorheb did not have his grandfather's military prowess. In 351 BC he managed to repel a Persian invasion led by Artaxerxes III but when, in 343 BC, Artaxerxes tried again, he was defeated at Pelusium. Egypt's last native pharaoh fled to Nubia. Vanishing from recorded history, he promptly reappeared in popular mythology as a semi-legendary figure whose story grew with time. Nakhthorheb appears in the *Alexander Romance*, a fictional account of the life of Alexander the Great written 500 years after his death, as a magician who turns himself into a snake, sleeps with Queen Olympias of Macedonia and fathers Alexander.

THE SECOND PERSIAN PERIOD

The Second Persian Period began with Artaxerxes III ruling from Persia. If the pro-Greek historians are to be believed, the ensuing decade saw the demolition of defences, the desecration of the major temples and the slaughter of the Apis bull and the sacred ram of Mendes. To a certain extent archaeology confirms this, and excavations at Mendes have yielded evidence of destruction at this time.

In 336 BC a period of unrest and regicide in Persia was brought to an end when Darius III seized the throne. He was to rule for just four years before the satrap Mazakes allowed Alexander the Great to take Egypt without bloodshed.

27TH–31ST DYNASTY RULERS

27TH (FIRST PERSIAN) DYNASTY

525 BC	Cambyses II
522 BC	Darius I
486 BC	Xerxes
465 BC	Artaxerxes I
424 BC	Darius II
405 BC	Artaxerxes II

28TH DYNASTY

404 BC	Amyrtaios

29TH DYNASTY

399 BC	Nefarud I
393 BC	Hakor
380 BC	Nefarud II

30TH DYNASTY

380 BC	Nakhtnebef [Nectanebo I]
362 BC	Djedhor [Teos]
360 BC	Nakhthorheb [Nectanebo II]

31ST (SECOND PERSIAN) DYNASTY

343 BC	Artaxerxes III
338 BC	Arses
336 BC	Darius III

THE FINAL
PHARAOHS

332–30 BC

*Part of the temple complex on the island of Philae near
Aswan. Construction here began in the reign of Nekhtnebef
and continued throughout the period of Ptolemaic rule, as
the site became an important shrine to the goddess Isis.*

SALVATION
THE MACEDONIAN PHARAOHS

332–305 BC

EGYPT'S LAST PHARAOHS RULED THE MOST DENSELY POPULATED LAND IN THE MEDITERRANEAN WORLD. THERE are no precise statistics but the Greek historian Diodorus Siculus, who visited in 60 BC, estimated a population of about three million. The vast majority of these were native Egyptians, but over 10 percent were of Greek heritage, and there was also a large Jewish community. These groups co-existed in parallel worlds with their own languages, legal systems and gods. Egypt was still divided into around 40 nomes, but the nomes now had Greek names, while the traditional nomarch was replaced by a Greek *strategos* (literally 'general'). Gradually the Greeks started to take over the important administrative posts, while the Egyptians filled the bulk of the menial jobs.

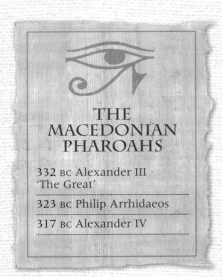

THE MACEDONIAN PHAROAHS

332 BC Alexander III 'The Great'

323 BC Philip Arrhidaeos

317 BC Alexander IV

The people of Alexandria considered themselves an important and distinct cultural group. While the reigns of some of the earlier Ptolemies would be marred by Theban uprisings, the reigns of the later Ptolemies would be influenced by the Alexandrian king-makers, who believed they had a god-given right to choose their own pharaoh.

THE ALL-CONQUERING ALEXANDER

In the winter of 333 BC Alexander III defeated Darius III in the Battle of Issos. The next year, after a lengthy siege, Tyre was taken. Alexander then turned towards Egypt. Only Gaza was foolish enough to resist; the city eventually fell after two months under siege. When Alexander set up camp at Pelusium, the Persian satrap Mazakes welcomed him. Legend maintains that Alexander was crowned pharaoh in the temple of Ptah at Memphis. He visited the Apis bull, and the temple of Re at Heliopolis, then made a 300-mile (480-km) trek to consult the oracle of Zeus-Ammon in the Siwa Oasis. Here Alexander was recognized as a living god.

In 331 BC Alexander founded a new city near the old port of Rhakotis in the western Delta. Rhakotis lay on a strip of land running between the Mediterranean to the north and Lake Canopus to the south. This was an ideal location: the sea would allow close contact with the Hellenistic world, while canals running into the lake would allow contact with the Nile and southern Egypt. Isolated from the

ALEXANDER III 'THE GREAT'

Dynasty: Macedonian

Father: Philip II of Macedon

Mother: Olympias of Epiros

Consort: Roxane

Burial place: Alexandria?

Successor: Philip Arrhidaeos

traditional Egyptian cities, Alexandria was Hellenistic in style and culture, and populated by a volatile mixture of Egyptians, Greeks and Jews. While the army was placed under the command of Macedonian and Greek officers, the civil service was controlled by two former nomarchs, the Persian Doloaspis and the Egyptian Peteisis. When Peteisis resigned, Doloaspis took sole control. Meanwhile Kleomenes of Naukratis became both finance minister and minister in charge of developing Alexandria.

Alexander left Egypt in May 331 BC, fully intending to return. However, on 10 June 323 BC he died in Nebuchadnezzar's palace in Babylon. As his generals quarrelled over his empire, Egyptian embalmers prepared Alexander for his last journey. Two years later, his cortège set off for the Macedonian burial ground of Aegae (modern Vergina). But when it reached Damascus, the body was seized by Ptolemy, governor of Egypt. It went first to Memphis then, probably during the reign of Ptolemy II, to Alexandria, where it became an object of pilgrimage. The tomb and body were lost in the late third or early fourth centuries AD.

AN UNCERTAIN LEGACY

Alexander left a pregnant widow, Roxane. Until the child was born his empire passed to his half-brother, Philip III Arrhidaeos, and the highly ambitious Macedonian general Ptolemy, son of Lagos, took over the day-to-day running of Egypt. Arrhidaeos was mentally incompetent, perhaps the result of a poisoning attempt by the dowager queen Olympias. Meanwhile Roxane gave birth to a son, Alexander IV, who became co-regent with Arrhidaeos. Roxane and her son were murdered in Macedon in 310 BC. Neither Arrhidaeos nor Alexander ever visited Egypt. The building works that bear their names – temple restorations at the Karnak complex and Hermopolis Magna (Arrhidaeos) and work at the Elephantine temple of Khnum (Alexander IV) – were almost certainly started by Alexander III, and finished on their behalf by the satrap Ptolemy.

ALEXANDER DREAMS OF FOUNDING A CITY

As he lay asleep he saw a wonderful vision. A man with very hoary locks and of a venerable aspect appeared to stand by his side and recite these verses: 'Now, there is an island in the swelling sea, in front of Egypt; Pharos is what men call it.' Accordingly, he rose up at once and went to Pharos, which at that time was still an island, a little above the Canopic mouth of the Nile, but now it has been joined to the mainland by a causeway. And when he saw a site of surpassing natural advantages (for it is a strip of land like enough to a broad isthmus, extending between a great lagoon and a stretch of sea which terminates in a large harbour), he said he saw now that Homer was not only admirable in other ways, but also a very wise architect, and ordered the plan of the city to be drawn in conformity with this site.

Plutarch, *Life of Alexander*: 26 (The 'venerable' man whom Plutarch refers to was Alexander's great hero, Homer)

Alexander III. Throughout his vast empire, which stretched from Macedonia to India, the great general founded at least 17 cities named after himself. Alexandria in Egypt remains the most famous.

A NEW EMPIRE
PTOLEMY I TO PTOLEMY III

The early Ptolemaic period c.304–221 BC

IT IS EASY TO DISMISS THE PTOLEMAIC DYNASTY AS A TRANSITIONAL AND THEREFORE SOMEHOW TRIVIAL STAGE linking the traditional dynasties to the modern, Roman age. At first glance this appears to be a time of immense cultural confusion: a time when Greek-speaking pharaohs of Macedonian heritage wore traditional pharaonic regalia to offer to hybrid Greek-Egyptian gods. However, the Ptolemies themselves believed that they were the legitimate, divine pharaohs of a land that could be great once again. And, for a brief time, it looked as if they might be right.

'Dysfunctional' barely describes a family that so ruthlessly and repeatedly eliminated those who stood in their way. The private history of the Ptolemies is one of adultery, assassination and ambition; the citizens of Alexandria brought rebellion and murder to the mix. Survival of the fittest was a brutal fact of life for Egypt's last dynasty.

THE 'SAVIOUR' FOUNDS HIS EMPIRE

Ptolemy was present when Alexander took Egypt in 332 BC, and present again when he marched across the desert to Siwa. In the course of his campaigns in the East, he captured Bessus, satrap of Bactria and assassin of Darius III, in 329 BC, while two years later he was fighting in Pakistan, where he commanded a third of Alexander's army. In 323 BC he returned to become satrap of Egypt. Having removed the hated Kleomenes, he ruled first on behalf of Philip Arrhidaeos, then on behalf of Alexander IV. His military days, however, were far from over. In 322 BC Ptolemy annexed Cyrenaica. The next year his kidnapping of Alexander's body sparked a war which saw Alexander's former general and bodyguard, Perdikkas, invade the Delta. Having suffered two defeats, Perdikkas was murdered by his officers and the subsequent settlement of Triparadeisos saw Ptolemy confirmed in his role of satrap of Egypt and Cyrenaica. Ptolemy next fought, successfully, in the Successor Wars of 319–315 BC and 314–311 BC. He ruled Cyprus from 313–306 BC, and led a campaign in Asia Minor in 309 BC.

When, in 310 BC, Alexander IV was murdered, Egypt behaved as if nothing had happened; Ptolemy retained his role as satrap and Alexander's regnal years continued. In late 306 BC Ptolemy lost a sea battle (and half the fleet) but fought off an invasion led by another of Alexander's ex-generals, Antigonos I Monophthalmos and his son Demetrios Poliorketes. Soon after Antigonos claimed the Macedonian title *basileos* (king). In response Ptolemy, too, was declared king by his troops (he was dubbed Soter ['Saviour'] by the Rhodians for lifting a siege of the island in 306). Finally, in 304 BC, Ptolemy was crowned pharaoh. Alexander's empire had collapsed, and the

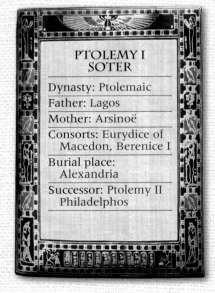

PTOLEMY I
SOTER

Dynasty: Ptolemaic

Father: Lagos

Mother: Arsinoë

Consorts: Eurydice of
Macedon, Berenice I

Burial place:
Alexandria

Successor: Ptolemy II
Philadelphos

Mediterranean world was dominated by three independent Hellenistic kingdoms with Macedonian roots: the Antigonid empire of Macedon and mainland Greece ruled by Antigonos, the Seleucid empire of Syria and Mesopotamia ruled by Seleukos I, and the Ptolemaic or Lagid empire of Egypt and Cyrenaica (Libya), ruled by Ptolemy I.

Still there was more fighting. In 303–301 BC Ptolemy occupied Byblos and much of Coele-Syria (literally 'Hollow Syria': much of the modern states of Israel, Jordan, Lebanon and southern Syria). In 295–294 BC he added Cyprus and the ports of Sidon and Tyre to his territories. Finally, in 287 BC, Egyptian troops took part in an Athenian rebellion against Demetrios Poliorketes. Showing a flash of financial brilliance, Ptolemy would later decree that all his grain-bearing lands should share one currency. Travellers and traders were now forced to accept his state-controlled rate of exchange.

Back home, Ptolemy promoted Alexandria as an international centre of learning, establishing the Museion and its Library and, by 311 BC, making it his capital city.

A tetradrachm silver coin with the head of Ptolemy I Soter. One of Alexander the Great's most trusted generals, Ptolemy fought a series of campaigns to establish his power base in Egypt.

Outside Alexandria, he instigated a programme of temple building and restoration which, initially confined to northern Egypt, soon spread southwards as Ptolemy sought to legitimize his rule. New temples were raised at Terenuthis (Hathor), Naukratis (Amen), Kom el-Ahmar (Osiris) and Tebtunis (Soknebtynis) and the new Greek city of Ptolemais Hormou (modern el-Mansha, near Sohag) was founded to replace Thinis as an administrative centre and, perhaps, serve as a check to the rebellion-prone Thebes.

The pharaohs of Egypt, like the kings of Macedon, had been polygamous. But the Ptolemies and their subjects practised serial monogamy, taking one wife at a time, remarrying after death or divorce and maintaining mistresses whose children were considered illegitimate. The thrice-married Ptolemy I was no stranger to family strife. Controversially bypassing the legitimate sons born to his wife Eurydice, Ptolemy chose the illegitimate son of his mistress and eventual wife, Berenice I, as his co-regent. Ptolemy I and Ptolemy II ruled together for three years before Ptolemy's death in 285 BC.

FIGHTING ON MANY FRONTS

The accession of Ptolemy II was challenged by those who would have preferred the children of Eurydice to inherit Egypt. But once this crisis was past, his reign developed into a time of internal peace and sporadic foreign campaigns which saw first an expansion, then a contraction, of Egypt's territories. His early campaigns are ill-documented, but in 280–279 BC Ptolemy was able to occupy the island of Samos and extend his control over Asia Minor. Meanwhile Ptolemy's half-brother and son of Eurydice, Magas of Cyrene, had determined to seize the land he regarded as rightfully his. In around 275 BC he marched on Alexandria but was forced to return home to quash a rebellion amongst the Libyan tribes. Ptolemy, too, was facing rebellion: a revolt among his Celtic soldiers was resolved with a mass execution. Magas and Ptolemy were eventually reconciled, and family relationships were re-established with a marriage between Magas's daughter Berenice II and the heir to the throne, Ptolemy III.

The ill-conceived First Syrian War (274–271 BC) began with an Egyptian invasion of Syria but ended with a rapid retreat and the urgent defence of Egypt's borders as the Syrians threatened to invade the Delta. Ptolemy was saved, not because of his military skills but because the Syrians were unable to complete their planned invasion. Soon after, Ptolemy committed his navy to a campaign in the Black Sea in support of Byzantium. Having formed an alliance with Athens and Sparta, the Chremondean War (267–261 BC) saw the Ptolemaic fleet pitted against the Macedonian navy while the Macedonian army fought the unified Athenians and Spartans. While the alliance lost, and Athens fell, the Egyptians were able to establish a series of useful island bases.

The Second Syrian War (260–253 BC) saw Ptolemy fighting an alliance of Syria and Rhodes. The Egyptian navy suffered heavy defeats at

PTOLEMY II PHILADELPHOS

Dynasty: Ptolemaic

Father: Ptolemy I

Mother: Berenice I

Consorts: Arsinoë I, Arsinoë II

Burial place: Alexandria

Successor: Ptolemy III Euergetes I

THE PHAROS OF ALEXANDRIA

The Pharos of Alexandria was designed and perhaps financed by Sostratos of Knidos, who worked first for Ptolemy I and then for his son Ptolemy II. The first-century BC Greek geographer Strabo, an occasional resident of Alexandria, wrote that the lighthouse tower was made of marble and that it had many tiers, although given the shortage of local marble, it is more likely to have been built of polished limestone.

Contemporary illustrations suggest that there were just three tiers: a rectangular tower followed by an octagonal tower and surmounted by a cylindrical tower. The lighthouse apparently stood over 120 metres (394 ft) tall. On top of the highest tier was a statue of Zeus the Saviour and a beacon whose constantly burning light was focused by huge bronze mirrors.

The imposing Pharos of Alexandria, as fancifully depicted in 1721 by the Austrian architect Fischer von Erlach (1656–1723).

The lighthouse was completed in around 280 BC and remained substant ally intact until the Middle Ages. In AD 796 the ruined top tower collapsed; a century later a mosque was built on top of the middle tower. When, in 1326, the Arab traveller and scholar Ibn Battuta visited Alexandria he noted that the lighthouse was damaged but more or less ntact. Revisiting the lighthouse 23 years later, he found that it '… had fallen into so ruinous a condition that it was not possible to enter it or climb up to the door'. Today the fort of the Mamluke sultan Qa'it Bey, built in AD 1477, stands in its place.

Cameo in onyx showing the theoi adelphoi ('brother-sister gods') Ptolemy II and his sister/wife Arsinoë II.

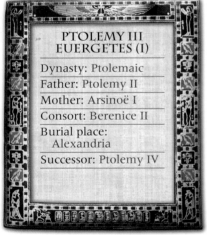

PTOLEMY III EUERGETES (I)

Dynasty:	Ptolemaic
Father:	Ptolemy II
Mother:	Arsinoë I
Consort:	Berenice II
Burial place:	Alexandria
Successor:	Ptolemy IV

Ephesos and Kos, and Egypt's island influence was much reduced. The dispute finally ended with peace and, in 253 BC, the marriage of Ptolemy's daughter Berenice to the Syrian king Antiochus II.

War was always expensive. Ptolemy honed Egypt's already efficient taxation structure, making it one of the most punitive in the world. Some of the revenue raised was used to maintain the army, the rest was needed to finish his father's building projects including the Museion and the lighthouse. Ptolemy's own works included improvements to the Karnak temple complex, the construction of a *naos* (inner sanctuary) at the Philae temple of Isis, and an extension to the birth house in the

The second king of Egypt, Ptolemy Philadelphos by name … had a great many mistresses – namely Didyma, who was a native of the country and very beautiful; and Bilistiche; and beside them, Agathoclea; and Stratonice, who had a great monument on the seashore near Eleusis; and Myrtium; and a great many more; he was a man excessively addicted to amatory pleasures.

GREEK RHETORICIAN ATHENAEUS (*DEIPNOSOPHISTAE* XIII: 37) LATE SECOND CENTURY AD

Dendera temple. Ptolemy also restored the canal linking the eastern Delta to the Gulf of Suez, and founded the city of Arsinoë at its southern end. Land reclamation and improvements to irrigation in the Faiyum brought an increased agricultural yield, and the papyrus and grain industries flourished.

Following the birth of his children Ptolemy divorced his first wife, Arsinoë I daughter of Lysimachos of Thrace, and married his full sister, Arsinoë II, widow of Lysimachos of Thrace and ex-wife of their half-brother Ptolemy Ceraunos, king of Macedon. This incestuous union was considered shocking outside Egypt, but within the country there was ample precedent for such an arrangement, which Ptolemy considered politically expedient. Not only did his marriage link him with the great pharaohs of old, it mimicked the divine union of Osiris and Isis, and of Zeus and Hera. This was important, as Ptolemy had determined to develop the divinity of the royal family as a means of channelling the loyalty of the Graeco-Macedonian élite. In 272–271 BC Ptolemy II and Arsinoë II became officially divine. They were now worshipped as the 'brother-sister gods'.

SUCCESS ABROAD, STRIFE AT HOME

On the death of his father in 246 BC, Ptolemy III ascended the thrones of both Egypt and Cyrenaica. No sooner had he taken power than the Third Syrian War (246–241 BC) broke out, when Berenice, sister of Ptolemy III and widow of Antiochos II, appealed to her brother for help in establishing her young son (name unknown) on the Syrian throne. Berenice and her son were murdered early in the campaign, and the throne passed to Seleukos II, a son born to the former queen Laodice. Ptolemy resolved to continue his campaign and, almost entirely unopposed, reached Mesopotamia, acquiring a vast treasure on the way. The war ended with Ptolemy ruling an empire whose sphere of influence extended from the River Euphrates to Libya, as far north as Thrace and as far south as northern Nubia. He could perhaps have continued, but the situation at home demanded his return.

In many respects, Ptolemy III was a successful pharaoh; a conqueror and a builder whose achievements included the founding of the temple of Horus at Edfu and the construction of the Alexandria Serapeum. Nevertheless, the end of his reign was marred by a native uprising; a response, it seems, to the high levels of taxation imposed to pay for the various Ptolemaic wars, and to the growing economic differences between the native Egyptians and the immigrant Greeks. This situation was made worse by the severe flooding of the Lower Nile in 245 BC, which devastated the harvest and compelled Egypt, the 'breadbasket of the world', to actually import grain.

THE PTOLEMAIA OF ALEXANDRIA

Alexandria was famed for spectacular religious festivals and processions. The historian Athenaeus preserves a description of the celebration, during the reign of Ptolemy II, of the four-yearly Ptolemaia, a festival dedicated to the god Dionysos who, in Egypt, was identified with the god Osiris.

The celebrations started with sacrifices, and with a generous feast. Next day came 'the procession of the morning star', the procession dedicated to the parents of the king, and the procession 'of all the gods'. Towards the front came two enormous statues of Dionysos, one pouring libations out of a golden goblet, and one riding an elephant. Next came displays of treasure, including the crown of Ptolemy I made from 'ten thousand pieces of gold money', floats presenting tableaux, exotic wild animals, actors and musicians, divine and royal statues and, most remarkably, automated statues which awed the watching crowds with their movements. There was even a 55-metre (180-ft) long giant phallus with a star on one end. The military procession, with 57,600 foot soldiers and 23,200 cavalry, was held on the following day.

CHANGE
THE BEGINNING OF THE END

The mid-Ptolemaic period c.221 – 51 BC

THE CITIZENS OF ALEXANDRIA HAD COME TO BELIEVE THAT THEY HAD THE RIGHT TO CHOOSE THEIR OWN pharaoh. The need to please the mob was becoming an important political consideration. Meanwhile, the Egyptians living outside Alexandria were finding it increasingly difficult to accept their foreign overlords. Years of high taxation and hunger led to strikes, occasional local wars and the emergence of local or counter-pharaohs at Thebes. Beyond Egypt's borders, the political map was changing. The Macedonian kingdom would vanish in 167 BC, while the Seleucid kingdom would go in 64 BC. Meanwhile Rome, considered an equal rather than a threat during the reign of Ptolemy II, was starting to play an increasingly prominent role in Egyptian affairs.

THE 'FATHER-LOVING' PHARAOH

Ptolemy IV has acquired an unenviable reputation as a drunkard who watched, unflinching, as the influential courtier Sosibios ruthlessly eliminated all potential opposition to his rule by murdering his brother Magas, his uncle Lysimachos and his mother Berenice II. His tireless dedication to the Greek concept of *tryphe* – boundless, undisciplined indulgence and ostentatious display as a manifestation of power – did little to endear him to his more abstemious contemporaries. Consistently unpopular, Ptolemy's reign witnessed a series of revolts that included civil war in the Delta and the emergence of the Egyptian counter-pharaoh, Harwennefer, who ruled southern Egypt from Thebes from 206 to 200 BC.

The Fourth Syrian War (219–217 BC), which had started with an invasion of Coele-Syria by Antiochos III, ended at the Battle of Raphia (southwest of Gaza) on 22 June 217 BC. Here 70,000 foot soldiers and 5000 cavalry – including, for the first time, 20,000 native Egyptians, assisted by 73 African elephants – fought a combined army of 68,000 Syrians plus 102 Indian elephants. Ptolemy returned home in triumph, to devote himself to more peaceful pursuits. There were building works at many temples, a cult dedicated to Homer at Alexandria, and the temple of Horus at Edfu was completed.

Low-relief carving from the Ptolemaic temple at Deir el-Medina of Ptolemy IV Philopator. This deeply unpopular ruler is seen wearing the double crown (pschent) of Upper and Lower Egypt.

Ptolemy had taken his sister, Arsinoë III, as his queen, but his affections lay with his mistress Agathocleia. This formidable lady bore him at least one child before, allegedly, poisoning first the king and then the queen.

THE 'MANIFEST GOD'

Ptolemy V became pharaoh at just six years old. But with his mother murdered, there was no obvious regent to rule on his behalf. His father's will, almost certainly forged, named Sosibios and Agathocles, brother of Agathocleia, as his guardians, and the child

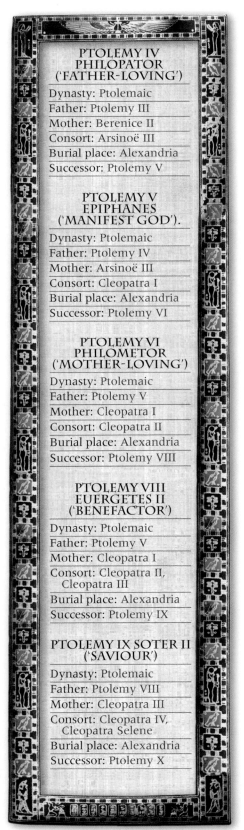

PTOLEMY IV PHILOPATOR ('FATHER-LOVING')

Dynasty: Ptolemaic
Father: Ptolemy III
Mother: Berenice II
Consort: Arsinoë III
Burial place: Alexandria
Successor: Ptolemy V

PTOLEMY V EPIPHANES ('MANIFEST GOD').

Dynasty: Ptolemaic
Father: Ptolemy IV
Mother: Arsinoë III
Consort: Cleopatra I
Burial place: Alexandria
Successor: Ptolemy VI

PTOLEMY VI PHILOMETOR ('MOTHER-LOVING')

Dynasty: Ptolemaic
Father: Ptolemy V
Mother: Cleopatra I
Consort: Cleopatra II
Burial place: Alexandria
Successor: Ptolemy VIII

PTOLEMY VIII EUERGETES II ('BENEFACTOR')

Dynasty: Ptolemaic
Father: Ptolemy V
Mother: Cleopatra I
Consort: Cleopatra II, Cleopatra III
Burial place: Alexandria
Successor: Ptolemy IX

PTOLEMY IX SOTER II ('SAVIOUR')

Dynasty: Ptolemaic
Father: Ptolemy VIII
Mother: Cleopatra III
Consort: Cleopatra IV, Cleopatra Selene
Burial place: Alexandria
Successor: Ptolemy X

was put into the care of Agathocleia and her mother Oinanthe. When Sosibios died with a suspicious suddenness, Agathocles became sole guardian until, in 203 BC, his entire family was murdered by an angry Alexandrian mob bent on avenging the much-loved Arsinoë III. As successive guardians rushed to help the young king, Egypt was essentially ruled by élite Alexandrians.

The Fifth Syrian War (202–193 BC) saw Antiochos III annexing Egyptian territories as far south as Gaza. Egypt immediately appealed to Rome for support. As Philip V of Macedon had also determined to seize Ptolemaic lands, Rome dealt first with the Macedonians, then negotiated peace between Egypt and Syria. The matter was sealed with a diplomatic marriage between the 16-year-old Ptolemy and the 10-year-old Cleopatra I 'the Syrian', daughter of Antiochos III. Egypt had by now lost many foreign territories and the empire essentially comprised Cyprus, Cyrenaica and a handful of Aegean posts. Greek immigration into Egypt slowed to a trickle and, deprived of constant renewed contact with their homeland, the Egyptian Greeks finally started to assimilate.

Outside Alexandria the people were still unhappy with their foreign pharaohs and their expensive, seemingly endless military campaigns. In 200 BC Harwennefer was succeeded by a second counter-pharaoh, Ankhwennefer, who was to rule southern Egypt for four years. Ptolemy died at about 30 years of age, in 181 BC, amid rumours that he had been poisoned by his generals. His widow, Cleopatra I, died four years later.

THE 'MOTHER-LOVING' PHARAOH

The orphaned Ptolemy VI came under the control of the eunuch Eulaios and the Syrian ex-slave Lenaios, who together decided that the young king, who was still underage, should marry his even younger sister Cleopatra II.

Their next decision was a disastrous attempt to reclaim Coele-Syria by provoking the Sixth Syrian War (170–168 BC). At the same time, in an ill-judged move intended to strengthen national unity, they announced that the kingship was to be shared between Ptolemy VI, Cleopatra II and their brother Ptolemy VIII. The war went badly, leaving the Syrians in control of much of northern Egypt. Ptolemy VI was captured by his Syrian uncle, Antiochos IV, Eulaios and Lenaios disappeared, and the Alexandrians proclaimed Cleopatra II and Ptolemy VIII their queen and king. Now Egypt had two rival courts; one based at Memphis ruled by Ptolemy VI under the control of Antiochos IV and one at Alexandria ruled by Ptolemy VIII and Cleopatra II under the control of the Alexandrian élite. When Antiochos returned to Syria, Ptolemy VI joined his siblings in Alexandria. Angered by his nephew's defection, Antiochos marched west while his fleet captured Cyprus. Once again Syria controlled most of the Delta, and only direct Roman intervention prevented Alexandria from falling. Antiochos finally left Egypt in 168 BC, leaving Egypt under a great debt to Rome.

In 164 BC, with Ptolemy VI distracted by civil unrest sparked by the worsening economic plight of the native Egyptians, Ptolemy VIII seized the throne and, as his brother fled, ruled alongside Cleopatra II. The Alexandrian mob soon turned against

All of them were handed together to the mob, and some began to bite them, others to stab them and gouge out their eyes. As soon as any of them fell the body was torn limb from limb …

POLYBIUS DESCRIBES THE DEATH OF AGATHOCLES AND HIS FAMILY

their new pharaoh, and in 163 BC Ptolemy VI was invited back to rule alongside his sister-wife. Growing stability brought increased prosperity to Egypt, and there was an impressive programme of temple restorations. In 145 BC, after regaining many of Egypt's lost territories, Ptolemy VI died in battle in Syria.

A SECOND 'BENEFACTOR'

In 163 BC, exiled from Alexandria, Ptolemy VIII had became king of Cyrenaica. Unhappy with his situation he persistently petitioned Rome, demanding support for his right to rule Cyprus as well. The Romans gave little practical help but they did acknowledge him as a formal 'friend and ally' (*amicus et socius*). Following an attempted assassination in 156 BC, Ptolemy repaid their support by making a will leaving his 'kingdom' (extent unspecified) to Rome should he die without a legitimate heir.

In 145 BC Ptolemy returned to Alexandria and married his widowed sister Cleopatra II. On their wedding day he murdered his nephew, Ptolemy VII, in his mother's arms. A purge of the Jews of Alexandria and of the Museion and Library followed, and many of the scholars fled. In 144 BC Cleopatra gave birth to his son, Ptolemy Memphites. A year later Ptolemy scandalously fathered a son, Ptolemy IX, by his stepdaughter, Cleopatra III. A marriage followed, but there had been no divorce. Cleopatra II refused to stand aside for her daughter and, with no obvious solution, the three found themselves locked together in an uneasy triumvirate. The Alexandrians supported Cleopatra II, as ominous rumblings of discontent grew in the city. In 131 BC, the royal palace burned down, and Ptolemy VIII fled, taking Cleopatra III with him. Settled in Cyprus he sent for his 14-year-old son Memphites, and had him murdered: the boy's dismembered body was sent home to his mother in a chest.

The people of Alexandria had chosen Cleopatra II as sole ruler of Egypt. But the native Egyptians favoured Ptolemy VII who had allowed them privileges that his predecessors had denied them. There were rumbling rebellions, and in 131 BC Harsiese proclaimed himself counter-pharaoh, ruling from Thebes.

In 130 BC Ptolemy returned to Egypt and Cleopatra II fled to Syria. She returned in 124 BC and brother and sister were reluctantly reconciled, neither being capable of raising the support needed to rule alone. Ptolemy VIII died in 116 BC, leaving Cleopatra II, Cleopatra III and Ptolemy IX to rule Egypt and her surviving territories of northern Nubia, Cyrenaica and Cyprus.

Coin with the portrait of Cleopatra I 'the Syrian'. In the four years between the murder of her husband Ptolemy V and her own death, she exercised sole power in Egypt as guardian of her underaged son Ptolemy VI.

Ptolemy IX Soter II receiving the two crowns of Egypt from the country's tutelary deities. On the left Wadjet places the red crown (deshret) of Lower Egypt on his head, while on the right, Nekhbet gives him the white crown (hedjet) of Upper Egypt. Relief from the Horus temple at Edfu.

ANOTHER 'SAVIOUR'

Cleopatra II outlived her husband-brother by just a few months. Her death left Cleopatra III regent for her two sons, Ptolemy IX and Ptolemy X. Under the terms of her husband's will, Cleopatra was to decide which son should become her co-ruler. There was no mention of who was to inherit Cyprus, but the five Greek towns of Cyrenaica were to pass to Ptolemy Apion, the son of Ptolemy VIII by his mistress Eirene. Following Apion's death, in 96 BC, Cyrenaica would pass to Rome.

Cleopatra and her sons ruled together in complete disharmony, with first one brother then the other being forced into exile. Finally, in 107 BC, Ptolemy IX established himself as king of Cyprus, where, after an abortive attempt to retake Egypt, he lived peacefully until 88 BC, when he returned to rule Egypt. Meanwhile, Cleopatra and Ptolemy X ruled together until, in 101 BC, Ptolemy murdered his mother. Marrying his niece, Berenice III, Ptolemy X ruled for a decade of declining prosperity and native unrest which culminated in a Theban rebellion (90–88 BC). When the anti-Semitic Alexandrians took exception to his favourable treatment of the Jews, he was forced to

His body had become corrupted by fat and a belly of such size that it would have been hard to measure it with one's arms.

ATHENAEUS DESCRIBES PTOLEMY VIII (*DEIPNOSOPHISTAE* XII 184)

flee. In revenge, he willed the Egyptian empire to the Romans. He died in 88 BC, attempting to take Cyprus from his brother.

Ptolemy IX returned home to be re-crowned by the high priest of Ptah in Memphis. His daughter, Berenice III, was to act as his consort. Ptolemy ruled Egypt for a further seven years, during which he was able to restore control over Thebes. Much of Nubia, however, was irretrievably lost.

THE 'FLUTE-PLAYER'

Berenice III, daughter of Ptolemy IX and widow of Ptolemy X, inherited her father's crown. Six months later she married her stepson, Ptolemy XI, and wife and husband started to rule together. But Ptolemy, as the natural son of Ptolemy X, believed that he should be pharaoh in his own right. Underestimating his wife's popularity, he had Berenice murdered. The very next day he was snatched by an enraged Alexandrian mob, dragged to the gymnasium and butchered.

THE 'NEW DIONYSOS'

The double murders plunged the royal family into crisis. Years of vicious feuds had caused a shortage of legitimate male Ptolemies, but it was important that a pharaoh be found to prevent the Romans from seizing Egypt under the terms of the will of Ptolemy X. In 76 BC, Ptolemy XII, illegitimate son of Ptolemy IX, was crowned by the high priest of Ptah at Memphis.

Egypt's days of independence were clearly numbered. Fully aware of his precarious position, Ptolemy started to bribe Roman senators for their support. In 60 BC three influential Romans, Pompey, Crassus and Caesar, united to form a triumvirate. Ptolemy offered Pompey and Caesar 6000 silver talents in exchange for recognition as Egypt's true pharaoh. They accepted and Ptolemy, having borrowed heavily from the Roman moneylender Rabirius, finally became a 'friend and ally'. Ptolemy was a friend but his brother Ptolemy, king of Cyprus, was not. In 58 BC Cyprus was annexed and King Ptolemy committed suicide. As Alexandria's people rioted, Ptolemy XII fled to Pompey's villa in Rome. In his absence his eldest daughter, Berenice IV, proclaimed herself queen and married her cousin Seleucos, whom she murdered within a week of their wedding. In his place she married Archelaos of Pontus, and the couple ruled for two years supported by the Alexandrians.

Ptolemy's exile continued until early 55 BC, when he paid Gabinius, governor of Syria, to give him military support. Later that year Gabinius's army occupied Alexandria. Ptolemy returned home to execute Berenice and her supporters and their property was used to repay Rabirius, who for one exploitative year became Egypt's finance minister. Eventually Rabirius returned to Rome, where he agreed that Caesar should take over the collection of his outstanding Egyptian debt. The 'Gabinians', the remnants of Gabinius's army, remained in Egypt.

Ptolemy XII died in 51 BC and the throne passed to his 18-year-old daughter Cleopatra VII and her eldest brother, the 10-year-old Ptolemy XIII. His will appointed the people of Rome guardians of Egypt's new king and queen and protectors of the Ptolemaic dynasty.

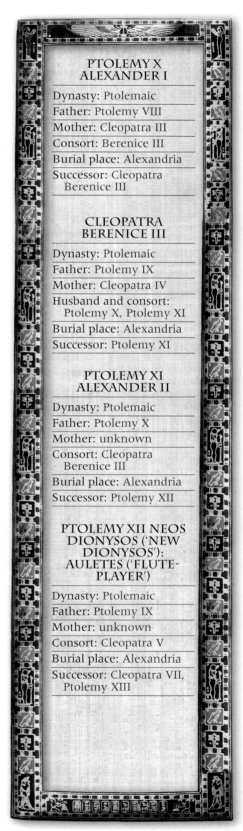

PTOLEMY X ALEXANDER I
Dynasty: Ptolemaic
Father: Ptolemy VIII
Mother: Cleopatra III
Consort: Berenice III
Burial place: Alexandria
Successor: Cleopatra Berenice III

CLEOPATRA BERENICE III
Dynasty: Ptolemaic
Father: Ptolemy IX
Mother: Cleopatra IV
Husband and consort: Ptolemy X, Ptolemy XI
Burial place: Alexandria
Successor: Ptolemy XI

PTOLEMY XI ALEXANDER II
Dynasty: Ptolemaic
Father: Ptolemy X
Mother: unknown
Consort: Cleopatra Berenice III
Burial place: Alexandria
Successor: Ptolemy XII

PTOLEMY XII NEOS DIONYSOS ('NEW DIONYSOS'): AULETES ('FLUTE-PLAYER')
Dynasty: Ptolemaic
Father: Ptolemy IX
Mother: unknown
Consort: Cleopatra V
Burial place: Alexandria
Successor: Cleopatra VII, Ptolemy XIII

THE LAST PHARAOHS
THE FALL OF THE HOUSE OF PTOLEMY

The late Ptolemaic period 51 – 30 BC

For a year and a half Cleopatra VII was able to push her younger brother into the background as she effectively ruled alone. This left Ptolemy vulnerable to a band of courtiers, including his tutor Theodotos, General Achillas and the eunuch Pothinos. All the while, Egypt was being dragged, unwillingly, into Roman affairs. In late 51 BC Bibulus, Roman governor of Syria, sent his two sons to Egypt to ask the Gabinians to return home and protect his land. Rather than negotiate, the Gabinians killed the messengers. Cleopatra and Ptolemy had the murderers deported to Syria.

Two years later Caesar led his army across the Rubicon, effectively declaring war on Pompey. When Pompey's son Gnaius arrived to beg for help Egypt supplied him with wheat, soldiers and warships. This was a joint decision, but the Alexandrians blamed Cleopatra for siding with the Romans. Taking full advantage of his sister's unpopularity, Ptolemy started to assert his independence. In the summer of 49 BC Cleopatra's name disappeared from all official documents. Soon after she fled to Syria and started to raise a mercenary army.

On 9 August 48 BC Caesar defeated Pompey at the Battle of Pharsalus. Pompey fled, and made his way to Egypt, where he expected to receive help from the son of his old friend Ptolemy XII. Encamped just outside Pelusium, Ptolemy XIII and his army were awaiting the arrival of Cleopatra's troops when messengers announced Pompey's arrival. Ptolemy was uncertain how to proceed. Some of his advisors argued that

Her beauty was in itself not altogether incomparable, nor such as to strike those who saw her; but converse with her had an irresistible charm, and her presence, combined with the persuasiveness of her discourse and the character which was somehow diffused about her behaviour towards others, had something stimulating about it. There was sweetness in the tones of her voice; and her tongue, like an instrument of many strings, she could readily turn to whatever language she pleased, so that in her interviews with Barbarians she very seldom had need of an interpreter, but made her replies to most of them herself, unassisted …

PLUTARCH, ON CLEOPATRA VII (*LIFE OF ANTONY*: 27: 2)

Pompey should be welcomed; others that he should be driven away. Theodotos, however, maintained that to avoid future problems, Pompey must be put to death. Thus persuaded, Ptolemy authorized the murder.

A CLIENT QUEEN

Four days later Julius Caesar arrived in Alexandria. Determined to restore stability to Egypt – and to start recovering Rabirius's debt – Caesar summoned Ptolemy and Cleopatra to explain themselves. Leaving his troops at Pelusium under the command of Achillas, Ptolemy travelled to Alexandria. Cleopatra, too, set off for Alexandria but, with Achillas blocking the road through Pelusium and Pothinos guarding the harbour at Alexandria, she travelled inconspicuously by sea. Landing at nightfall, she was smuggled into the palace. Here, in a private meeting with Caesar, Cleopatra was able to convince him that she should not be excluded from the succession. Caesar decreed that brother and sister were to rule Egypt together. This pleased no one, and Pothinos prepared for war.

Cleopatra, Ptolemy and their younger siblings Arsinoë IV and Ptolemy XIV remained trapped in the palace as Alexandria endured four months of bitter land and sea battles. In 48 BC the 14-year-old Arsinoë escaped and was proclaimed queen of Alexandria. Soon after, the Alexandrians requested the release of Ptolemy XIII. Believing, somewhat naïvely, that this might calm the situation, Caesar let him go. He was hurt when Ptolemy immediately joined the opposition. Eventually, troops commanded by Caesar's ally Mithridates of Pergamon marched on Alexandria. There was a short battle, Alexandria surrendered and Ptolemy drowned trying to escape. The Egyptian army surrendered on 15 January 47 BC and Cleopatra VII was restored on her throne alongside her 13-year-old brother Ptolemy XIV.

At some time between 47 and 44 BC Cleopatra gave birth to a son whom she named Ptolemy Caesar. While Cleopatra and Caesar refused to comment on the baby's paternity the people of Alexandria instantly renamed him Caesarion ('Little Caesar') after his putative father. Caesarion's birth was a turning point for Cleopatra. As both dynastic and Ptolemaic tradition allowed mothers to rule on behalf of infant sons, it

Cleopatra VII, shown in the classical rather than Egyptian style. Octavian ordered that all images of Cleopatra be destroyed after her suicide.

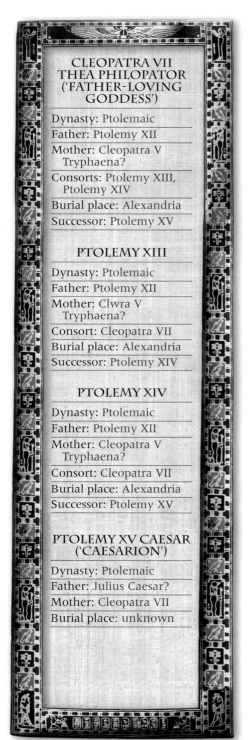

CLEOPATRA VII THEA PHILOPATOR ('FATHER-LOVING GODDESS')

Dynasty: Ptolemaic

Father: Ptolemy XII

Mother: Cleopatra V Tryphaena?

Consorts: Ptolemy XIII, Ptolemy XIV

Burial place: Alexandria

Successor: Ptolemy XV

PTOLEMY XIII

Dynasty: Ptolemaic

Father: Ptolemy XII

Mother: Clwra V Tryphaena?

Consort: Cleopatra VII

Burial place: Alexandria

Successor: Ptolemy XIV

PTOLEMY XIV

Dynasty: Ptolemaic

Father: Ptolemy XII

Mother: Cleopatra V Tryphaena?

Consort: Cleopatra VII

Burial place: Alexandria

Successor: Ptolemy XV

PTOLEMY XV CAESAR ('CAESARION')

Dynasty: Ptolemaic

Father: Julius Caesar?

Mother: Cleopatra VII

Burial place: unknown

freed her from the obligation to remain married to a male co-regent. And, with a son by her side, she could develop a new role as a divine mother. Cleopatra had become a living goddess towards the end of her father's reign. But now she was to be specifically identified with the goddess Isis.

In the summer of 47 BC Caesar left Egypt. He returned to Italy in June or July 46 BC and a few months later Cleopatra and Ptolemy XIV arrived in Rome. They were still there when Caesar was assassinated on the Ides of March (15 March) 44 BC, although we cannot be certain that they spent an unbroken 18 months in Rome; it may be that there were two separate trips. A letter written by Cicero, on 15 April 44 BC, tells us that Cleopatra left Rome within a month of Caesar's death. Four months later Ptolemy XIV conveniently died, and the three-year-old Caesarion became Ptolemy XV Theos Philopator Philometor (the 'Father- and Mother-Loving God').

With her brothers dead and her sister exiled, Cleopatra was at last secure. In Rome, however, things were far from secure. Caesar's friend Antony, his great-nephew and heir Octavian and his supporter Lepidus had resolved to hunt down Caesar's main assassins, Brutus and Cassius and they expected Egypt to help. Meanwhile Brutus and Cassius also looked to Egypt for help. Cleopatra committed herself and, having raised a fleet, set sail to join Octavian and Antony in Greece. But a storm blew up and her ships sustained serious damage. While she waited for a second fleet to be made ready, Brutus and Cassius committed suicide. With Lepidus now sidelined, two men now effectively held power in Rome. Octavian controlled the western empire, while Antony controlled Gaul and the eastern provinces.

BACKING THE WRONG ROMAN HORSE

Antony was busy raising funds. First a letter, then another, then an emissary, arrived to summon Cleopatra to Tarsus (Turkey), where Antony hoped to fine her for perceived disloyalty to Rome. Cleopatra, however, had the measure of Antony. She impressed him by sailing to their meeting in a golden ship with silver oars and a purple sail, reclining beneath a gold spangled canopy, dressed in the robes of Isis. She agreed to part-finance Antony's Parthian campaign. But he, in return, must agree to protect her land. This protection included the murder of her inconvenient younger sister Arsinoë.

Cleopatra and Antony spent the winter of 41–40 BC in Alexandria. Together they formed a society of sybarites, 'The Inimitable Livers' which met to drink, feast and dice. In 40 BC Cleopatra gave birth to twins, Alexander Helios and Cleopatra Selene. Antony had already left Alexandria. The Parthians had launched a dual attack on the Roman territories of Syria and Asia Minor and Antony had rushed to Tyre, where he learned that many of the Roman vassals had defected. Worse was to come. Antony's brother, Lucius Antonius, and his wife, Fulvia, had declared war on Octavian. Lucius now found himself besieged

THE GODDESS ISIS

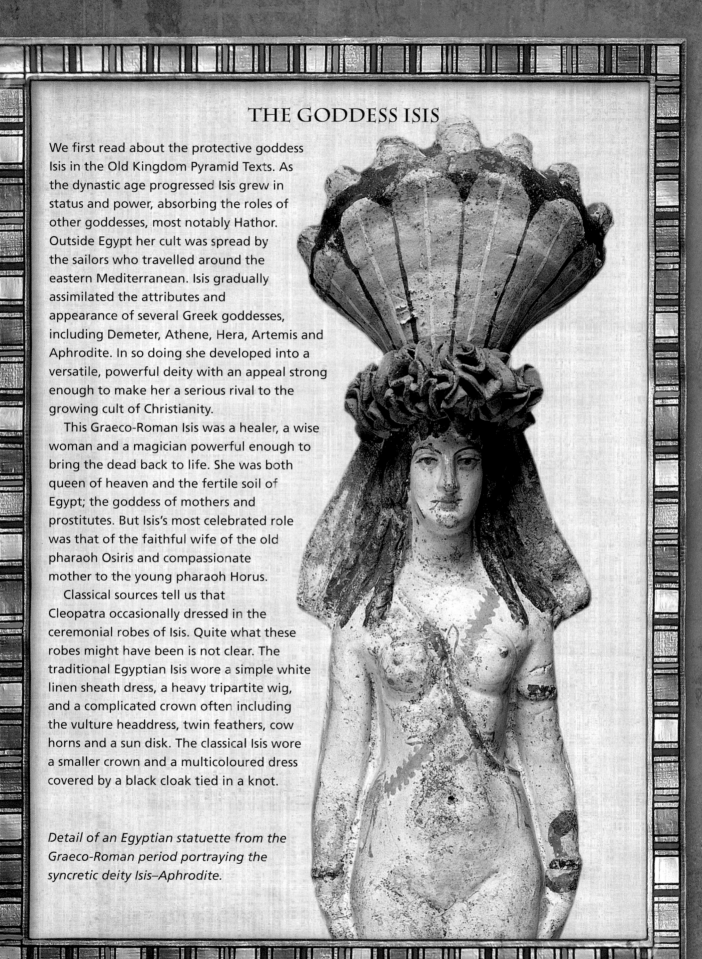

We first read about the protective goddess Isis in the Old Kingdom Pyramid Texts. As the dynastic age progressed Isis grew in status and power, absorbing the roles of other goddesses, most notably Hathor. Outside Egypt her cult was spread by the sailors who travelled around the eastern Mediterranean. Isis gradually assimilated the attributes and appearance of several Greek goddesses, including Demeter, Athene, Hera, Artemis and Aphrodite. In so doing she developed into a versatile, powerful deity with an appeal strong enough to make her a serious rival to the growing cult of Christianity.

This Graeco-Roman Isis was a healer, a wise woman and a magician powerful enough to bring the dead back to life. She was both queen of heaven and the fertile soil of Egypt; the goddess of mothers and prostitutes. But Isis's most celebrated role was that of the faithful wife of the old pharaoh Osiris and compassionate mother to the young pharaoh Horus.

Classical sources tell us that Cleopatra occasionally dressed in the ceremonial robes of Isis. Quite what these robes might have been is not clear. The traditional Egyptian Isis wore a simple white linen sheath dress, a heavy tripartite wig, and a complicated crown often including the vulture headdress, twin feathers, cow horns and a sun disk. The classical Isis wore a smaller crown and a multicoloured dress covered by a black cloak tied in a knot.

Detail of an Egyptian statuette from the Graeco-Roman period portraying the syncretic deity Isis–Aphrodite.

CLEOPATRA EXPERIMENTS WITH POISONS

Cleopatra was getting together collections of all sorts of deadly poisons, and she tested the painless working of each of them by giving them to prisoners under sentence of death. But when she saw that the speedy poisons enhanced the sharpness of death by the pain they caused, while the milder poisons were not quick, she made trial of venomous animals, watching with her own eyes as they were set upon another. She did this daily, tried them almost all; and she found that the bite of the asp alone induced a sleepy torpor and sinking, where there was no spasm or groan, but a gentle perspiration on the face, while the perceptive faculties were easily relaxed and dimmed, and resisted all attempts to rouse and restore them, as is the case with those who are soundly asleep.

Plutarch (*Life of Antony* 71: 4-5)

in Perugia, where conditions were so desperate that the starving slaves were forced to eat grass. In late February 40 BC Lucius surrendered. Fulvia had already fled Italy. Antony met his wife in Athens and they quarrelled bitterly. Fulvia died soon after, leaving Antony free to make a diplomatic marriage to Octavia, half-sister of Octavian.

In the spring and summer of 37 BC Antony, Octavia and Octavian met at Tarentum (Taranto). Antony agreed to supply Octavian with 120 warships, while Octavian would provide Antony with four legions to be used against the Parthians. Antony handed over his ships, but the promised troops never materialized. Cleopatra stepped in to help. She could provide Antony with both fleet and provisions, but in exchange she demanded the return of the eastern empire of Ptolemy II Philadelphos. Almost overnight, Cleopatra gained control of Cyprus, Crete, Cyrenaica, large parts of Coele-Syria, Phoenecia, Cilicia and Nabataea. When, the following year, she bore a son, she named him Ptolemy Philadelphos after the great Ptolemy II.

January 35 BC saw Cleopatra meeting Antony in Phoenicia, bringing much-needed supplies. After a winter in Alexandria, Cleopatra travelled with Antony to the Euphrates then made a lengthy progress home, inspecting her new territories. That autumn came the celebration known as the 'Donations of Alexandria'. Wearing the robes of Isis, Cleopatra sat on a golden throne as Antony gave a lengthy speech outlining ambitious plans. He recognized Cleopatra as the 'queen of kings and her sons who are kings' and Caesarion as the legitimate son of Julius Caesar. The younger children had been dressed in the national clothing of Persia (Alexander), Cyrenaica (Cleopatra) and Macedonia (Ptolemy): these were the lands which, or so Antony believed, they were destined to inherit.

ACTIUM AND AFTER

Cleopatra and Antony spent the winter of 33–32 BC assembling a fleet which they moored in over a dozen different harbours along the Greek coast stretching from Actium in the north to Methone in the south. In late 32 BC Octavian declared war and his admiral, Agrippa, immediately took Methone. Meanwhile Octavian's army set up camp at Actium on the Gulf of Ambracia. Plutarch tells us that Cleopatra and Antony had raised an impressive army: 500 warships, 100,000 legionaries and armed infantry and 12,000 cavalry. In addition, Cleopatra commanded at least 60 Egyptian ships. Octavian, with just 250 ships, 80,000 infantry and 12,000 cavalry, was outnumbered, but his men were fitter and well armed and Agrippa was the better general.

Caesarion's fate was sealed when Antony declared him to be Julius Caesar's rightful son and heir. When Octavian (Augustus) defeated Antony and Cleopatra in the power struggle that followed Caesar's assassination, he had Caesarion summarily put to death, declaring 'Two Caesars is one too many'. Caesarion is pictured on this stela in the company of Egyptian deities.

The sea battle began on 2 September 31 BC. Antony's ships formed three divisions, protecting Cleopatra's fleet which was sheltered by the central division. The right division, commanded by Antony, saw some brisk fighting, but the central and left divisions performed poorly and eventually retreated. Soon after, at a pre-arranged signal, Cleopatra's ships broke through Octavian's line and sailed for Egypt. Antony abandoned his flagship and followed. His fleet fought on, but their situation was hopeless.

Antony made his way to the Greek town of Paraetonium (modern Mersa Matruh) on Egypt's western border. Here he was horrified to find that the garrison had defected to Octavian. Downcast, he spent some time alone on the peninsula of Lochias. His return to Cleopatra saw the disbanding of The Inimitable Livers in favour of the self-explanatory 'Partners in Death'.

In the summer of 30 BC Egypt suffered land and sea assaults from the west while Octavian invaded from the east, passed through the Delta and set up camp outside Alexandria. On 1 August Antony met Octavian in battle. Almost immediately his fleet surrendered and his cavalry deserted. His infantry remained loyal but it was a one-sided battle. Antony withdrew into Alexandria and stabbed himself. Weak from loss of blood, he was carried to Cleopatra. When Octavian entered the city, unopposed, he found Cleopatra barricaded in her partially built tomb with Antony's body. Cleopatra stabbed herself but lived, and was taken to her palace. She committed suicide on 12 August 30 BC. The exact cause of her death remains uncertain.

The death of Cleopatra VII left her son, Ptolemy XV Caesar, as sole pharaoh. His 18-day reign ended when Octavian annexed Egypt on 31 August 30 BC.

As for Antony, he became more than ever a slave to the passion and the witchery of Cleopatra.

CASSIUS DIO (*ROMAN HISTORY* 49: 34)

EPILOGUE
AFTER THE PHARAOHS

OCTAVIAN, NOW THE EMPEROR AUGUSTUS, ADDED EGYPT TO HIS PERSONAL ESTATE. EGYPT'S NEW MASTERS were interested in exploiting Egypt's abundant resources, but few felt the need to visit, and there was no longer a crowned pharaoh to ensure that *maat* triumphed over chaos. Rather than accept this huge gap in their theology – and, presumably, because they had no other means of expressing themselves – Egypt's priests continued to give the Roman emperors royal titles and to depict them on their temple walls as entirely traditional kings.

While Egypt's priests still used the hieroglyphic script, routine documents were now written in Greek or in Egyptian using the demotic script. Then, during the first century AD, Christianity arrived, spreading from Alexandria to co-exist alongside, and take converts from, the old religions. Edicts issued in AD 383, 391 and 435 led to the closure of Egypt's pagan temples, the burning of their libraries and disbanding of their priesthoods. Soon the hieroglyphic script was forgotten and no one could read the beautiful writings decorating the tomb and temple walls. A late form of spoken Egyptian was preserved in the Coptic language, but the Arab invasions of 641 saw the introduction of Arabic, and Coptic quickly became confined to the few remaining churches. Although there were references to Egypt in the Bible and in the works of the classical authors and Moslem scholars, Egypt's history had essentially been lost. So when, in 1817, Percy Bysshe Shelley wrote a sonnet inspired by the sculpture of Ramesses II (whom he knew as 'Ozymandias', a corruption of User-Maat-Re) he had no realistic expectation of ever knowing more about the decayed, once glorious, civilization celebrated in his poem.

There would be no real understanding of Egypt's past until the 19th-century decoding of hieroglyphs made it possible to read the texts. Today we have a good grasp of the basic chronological framework underpinning Egypt's lengthy history. It is, however, important not to overestimate the extent of our knowledge. As this book will have shown, there are many, many gaps; many times when we simply do not know who reigned, or where, or for how long. Meanwhile, new discoveries continue to be made and old data is being continually reinterpreted, so that Egypt's cloudy history is gradually, almost imperceptibly, becoming clearer.

OZYMANDIAS

I met a traveller from an antique land
Who said: Two vast and trunkless legs of stone
Stand in the desert. Near them, on the sand,
Half sunk, a shattered visage lies, whose frown,
And wrinkled lip, and sneer of cold command
Tell that its sculptor well those passions read
Which yet survive, stamped on these lifeless things,
The hand that mocked them, and the heart that fed:
And on the pedestal these words appear:
'My name is Ozymandias, king of kings:
Look on my works, ye mighty, and despair!'
Nothing besides remains. Round the decay
Of that colossal wreck, boundless and bare
The lone and level sands stretch far away.

THE CYCLE OF TIME

The Egyptians themselves respected their long history. They saw it not as we do – as an almost unbroken line of pharaohs stretching over 3000 years – but rather as a pattern of constantly repeating cycles. Each new pharaoh brought a new beginning; each was a renewal of the pharaohs who had gone before. Remembrance of these former pharaohs would benefit both the living and the dead, and kings took care to carve their names on their monuments. Thus, when Khaemwaset, fourth son of 'Ozymandias', set out to restore the decaying Old Kingdom pyramids, he was genuinely shocked to find that 'His [the pyramid owner's] name was not found on the face of his pyramid'. Naturally Khaemwaset added his own name so that he could benefit from the association with ancient, powerful royalty.

Several intricate, conflicting stories explained how this history began. Depending on where and when he or she lived, an ancient Egyptian might believe that time began when a celestial goose laid an egg, or when a lotus bud burst into flower, or when the intellectual god Ptah spoke. We have already read the detailed creation myth developed by the priests of Heliopolis: the emergence of an island from the waters of chaos and the single-handed creation of gods and mortals by the primeval god Atum. Pharaoh would always be closely identified with Atum, Lord of the Two Lands, wearer of the double crown. The Old Kingdom pyramid texts make this clear: 'Your [pharaoh's] arm is Atum's arm; your shoulders are Atum's shoulders; your belly is Atum's belly …'

And how will Egypt's history end? There can be no happy ending; even eternal life is finite. Mortals, pharaohs and gods each have their allotted span, but all can be reborn to restart the cycle of life. After an unimaginable number of years, however, this cycle will fail. The waters of chaos will return and only Atum and Osiris, now taking the form of twin snakes, will survive. Atum's name, which includes the element *tem*, to complete or finish, hints at this eventual apocalypse. Atum has the dangerous ability to truly end all that he has started: he and he alone can complete the cycle of time.

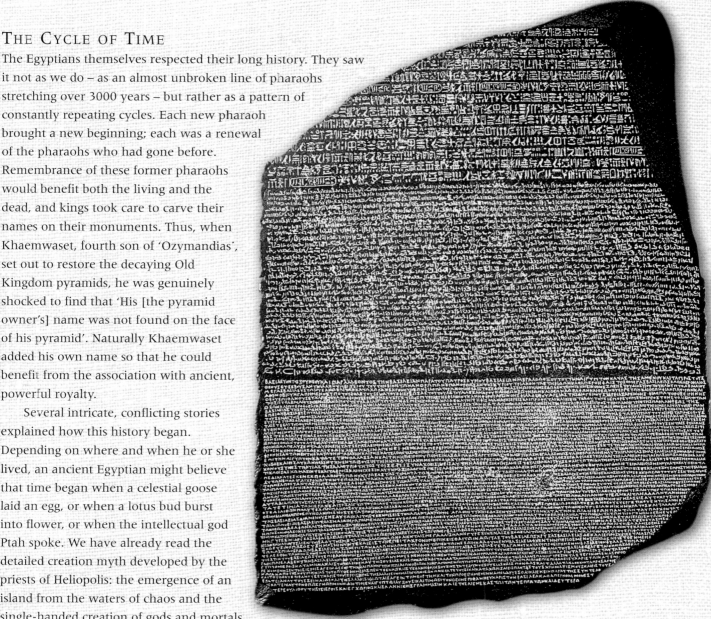

The discovery in 1799 of the Rosetta Stone, on which were inscribed parallel texts in hierogylphs, demotic and classical Greek, greatly advanced the understanding of hieroglyph writing. A key figure in its decipherment was the French scholar Jean-François Champollion.

GLOSSARY

ankh The hieroglyphic sign for life, which resembles a 'T' shape topped by a loop.

canopic jars Vessels used to house the preserved lungs, liver, stomach and intestines removed from the body during the mummification process. The canopic jars were often stored in a canopic box or chest. Not all mummies were provided with canopic jars; some had their linen-wrapped preserved viscera replaced in the body cavity.

cartouche The oval loop that surrounds the names of most kings and queens and some gods.

cataract Shallow regions of the Nile between Khartoum and Aswan, where the water flow is interrupted by boulders and rocky islets, causing problems for shipping. There are six major Nile cataracts.

cuneiform A wedge-shaped writing system that evolved in Mesopotamia during the 4th millennium BC. The wedges were made by pressing reeds into soft clay. The Amarna letters, the diplomatic archive of the Amarna court, were written in cuneiform.

deshret The red crown of Lower or Northern Egypt.

hedjet The white crown of Upper or Southern Egypt.

Horus name One of the traditional names acquired by the pharaoh at his or her coronation.

ka The soul or spirit.

maat A concept of 'rightness' which encompassed truth, order, justice, and status quo. The opposite of *maat* is *isfet*, or chaos. *Maat* was personified in the form of the goddess Maat who may be identified by the prominent ostrich feather of truth worn on her head.

mastaba A tomb in which the superstructure takes the form of a low, rectangular building with a flat roof. The first mastabas were built of mud-brick; later mastabas were built of stone.

nome An administrative district or province, governed by a nomarch.

obelisk A tall, tapering monument. The earliest obelisks were made of mud-brick, but soon they became monoliths, carved from hard stone. Obelisks were often raised, in pairs, in front of temples.

ostracon (plural ostraca) A piece of pottery or a limestone flake used in place of papyrus to record a short text or sketch.

papyrus A form of paper made from the papyrus plant.

saff **tomb** A rock cut tomb. The word '*saff*' – literally 'row'– refers to the lines of square pillars and doors that decorate the façade of the tomb.

scarab A stamp-seal shaped liked a dung beetle. The flat base of the scarab often carried an inscription or design.

sebbakh Decayed ancient mud-brick, which makes a very fertile soil. In the past farmers used to seek out *sebbakh* to spread on their fields, destroying ancient sites in the process. Today, this is illegal.

sed-**jubilee** A festival of renewal celebrated, in theory, after 30 years of continuous rule and then every two or three years thereafter. Many kings celebrated a *sed*-jubilee after less than 30 years on the throne.

serekh The first pharaohs wrote their names within a *serekh*, a ribbed, rectangle representing the gateway to the archaic royal residence, so that the name within the *serekh* symbolized the pharaoh within his palace. Often a falcon, emblem of the god Horus, perched on top of the *serekh*. At the end of the 3rd Dynasty the *serekh* was replaced by the cartouche.

shabti A servant figure included in the tomb to perform work for the deceased.

sistrum A musical rattle, associated with the worship of the goddesses Hathor and Isis.

stela (plural stelae) An upright, inscribed or decorated stone slab, often with a rounded top. Funerary stelae were inscribed with texts relevant to the deceased.

talatat Relatively small stone blocks used to build the solar temples of the Amarna Period. The word derives from the Arabic word for 'three', indicating that the blocks measured three hand-spans.

uraeus The cobra worn on the brow of pharaohs, queens and gods.

vizier The term conventionally used by Egyptologists to denote Egypt's highest-ranking civil servant.

INDEX

FURTHER REFERENCES

GENERAL

The Oxford History of Ancient Egypt, edited by I. Shaw (Oxford, 2000) offers a thorough and very readable introduction to the whole of dynastic history. P. Clayton's *Chronicle of the Pharaohs* (London, 1994) focuses on the individual reigns, while J. Tyldesley's *Chronicle of the Queens of Egypt* (London 2006) offers an alternative, female-based account. Genealogical complexities are explained in A. Dodson and D. Hilton's indispensable *Complete Royal Families of Ancient Egypt* (London 2004). There are many published translations of ancient Egyptian texts, but the most readable remain those given by M. Lichtheim in her three-volume *Ancient Egyptian Literature* (Berkeley and Los Angeles, 1973–80). The Egyptian texts cited in this book are largely based on Lichtheim's translations. Herodotus gives a contemporary Greek view of life in ancient Egypt in his *Histories*; my quotations from Herodotus are based on the translation by A. de Sélincourt (1954, London).

SECTION 1: THE FIRST PHARAOHS

To understand the development of Egypt before the pharaohs consult *The Prehistory of Egypt* by B. Midant-Reynes (2000, London, translated by I. Shaw). T. Wilkinson's *Early Dynastic Egypt* (1999, London) takes up the tale. A first-hand account of the excavation of the Abydos cemeteries are given by W.M.F. Petrie in *The Royal Tombs of the First Dynasty, Volumes I and II (1900, 1901,* London): although the theory has been superseded, these volumes make fascinating reading.

SECTION 2: PHARAOHS AND PYRAMIDS

The classic introduction to pyramid studies is offered by I.E.S. Edwards in *The Pyramids of Egypt* (1961 revised, London). See also M. Lehner's *The Complete Pyramids* (1997, London) and M. Verner's *The Pyramids: their archaeology and history* (2002, London). J. Malek, and W. Forman give an overview of Old Kingdom life in *In the Shadow of the Pyramids: Egypt during the Old Kingdom* (1986, London). Old Kingdom art is presented beautifully in D. Arnold and C. Ziegler, C. (eds.) *Egyptian Art in the Age of the Pyramids* (1999, New York), while S. Quirke discusses the solar religion underpinning the pyramid age in *The Cult of Ra: sun-worship in Ancient Egypt* (2001, London).

SECTION 3: PHARAOHS REINVENTED

The most comprehensive account of the Middle Kingdom is given by W. Grajetzki, in *The Middle Kingdom of Ancient Egypt* (2006, London). For an account of daily life, focusing on an intact tomb group, read R. David's *The Two Brothers: Death and the Afterlife in Middle Kingdom Egypt* (2007, Bolton). Life at Kahun is considered in the same author's *The Pyramid Builders of Ancient Egypt: a modern investigation of pharaoh's workforce* (1986 London, Boston and Henley) and in K. Szpakowska's *Daily Life in Ancient Egypt: Recreating Lahun* (2008, Oxford).

SECTION 4: THE FIGHTING PHARAOHS

J. Tyldesley *Hatchepsut: the Female Pharaoh* (London 1996) offers an introduction to an unusual reign, while *Hatshepsut: From Queen to Pharaoh*, edited by C. Roehrig (New Haven and London, 2005) provides a series of beautiful illustrations. E. Cline and D. O'Connor (eds.) offer a useful range of papers in *Thutmose III: A New Biography* (2006, Michigan). C. Reeves and R. Wilkinson. provide a good introduction to the New Kingdom royal burials in *The Complete Valley of the Kings: tombs and treasures of Egypt's greatest pharaohs* (1996, London).

SECTION 5: PHARAOHS OF THE SUN

Literally hundreds of books of varying degrees of specialization have been published on the Amarna age. G. Martin's *A Bibliography of the Amarna Period and its Aftermath* (1991, London) lists many of these publications. A detailed introduction to the life and times of Amenhotep III, including a review of earlier late 18th Dynasty reigns, is provided by D. O'Connor and E. Cline (eds.) *Amenhotep III: perspectives on his reign* (1998, Ann Arbor). *Pharaohs of the Sun*, edited by R. Freed, Y. Markowitz and S. D'Auria (1999, London) offers a splendid illustrated catalogue of this period. Cyril Aldred's *Akhenaten, King of Egypt* (1988, London) and D. Redford's *Akhenaten: the heretic king* (1984, Princeton) discuss the reign of Akhenaten; J. Tyldesley's *Nefertiti* (1998, London) considers the role of his wife. D. Arnold considers the Amarna period from a female viewpoint in *The Royal Women of Amarna: images of beauty from ancient Egypt* (1996, New York). The best introduction to Tutankhamun is provided by N. Reeves's *The Complete Tutankhamun: the king, the tomb, the royal treasure* (1990, London).

SECTION 6: THE RAMESSIDE PHARAOHS

For the reign of Ramesses II 'The Great' see K. Kitchen's classic, *Pharaoh Triumphant: the life and times of Ramesses II* (1982, Warminster). See also J. Tyldesley's *Ramesses: Egypt's greatest pharaoh* (2000, London). For the background to Egypt's foreign relations read D.B. Redford, *Egypt, Canaan and Israel in ancient times* (1992, Princeton). K. Weeks discussed the tomb of the sons of Ramesses II in *The Lost Tomb: the greatest discovery at the Valley of the Kings since Tutankhamen* (1998, London).

SECTION 7: PHARAOHS AND FOREIGNERS

For a good overview of the 1st millennium BC, see K. Myśliwiec, *The twilight of Ancient Egypt* (2000, New York, translated by D. Lorton). K. Kitchen provides a more specific guide in *The Third Intermediate Period in Egypt* (1986 second edition, Warminster). *The Nubian Pharaohs, Black Kings on the Nile* by C. Bonnet and D Valbelle (2005, Cairo and New York) offers a beautiful photographic record of the 25th Dynasty both in Egypt and Nubia.

SECTION 8: THE FINAL PHARAOHS

R. Lane Fox offers a readable introduction to the Macedonian pharaohs in *Alexander the Great* (2004 updated edition, London). For the background to this most complicated of dynasties see G. Holbl's *A History of the Ptolemaic Empire* (2001, London and New York, translated by T. Saavedra). For a history of Cleopatra VII see J. Tyldesley, *Cleopatra: Last Queen of Egypt* (London, 2008). In *Cleopatras* J Whitehorn (1994, London and New York) focuses on the other queens of this name.

PICTURE CREDITS